December 2000

To Dear Madge —
A little local
Millennium
with love from Mogs
+ Amanda Jane

A PLAN
of the Hamlet of
WEST-HAGBOURN
in the Parish of
EAST-HAGBOURN
and County of
BERKS
Inclosed,
MDCCCXLII.

I certify that this is a true copy of the plan
annexed to the copy award for the Parish of West Hagbourne
deposited in the office of the Clerk of the Peace for the
County of Berks on the 1st day of January 1844
Dated this 11th day of December 1897

J. J. Morland
Clerk of the Peace

Traced by
Howard Goodby, F.R.G.S.
Reading

Windsor Hakeborne:
the Story of West Hagbourne

Windsor Hakeborne:
the Story of West Hagbourne

Published by the West Hagbourne Village History Group
Silva Felix
York Road
West Hagbourne
Oxon OX11 0NH

© West Hagbourne Village History Group, 2000

ISBN 0 9539054 0 3

All rights reserved. No part of this publication may be reproduced, stored in a retrieval system or transmitted in any form by any means electronic, mechanical, photocopying or otherwise without first obtaining written permission of the copyright owner.

All correspondence concerning the content of this volume should be addressed to the West Hagbourne Village History Group

Printed and bound in Great Britain by Biddles Ltd
www.Biddles.co.uk

Front cover:
A painting by Helen Allingham of a house which once stood in the Square, West Hagbourne, circa 1900.
Reproduced by kind permission of Gallery Five Ltd, London

Front endpaper:
A Plan of the Hamlet of West Hagbourn, inclosed, 1843

Back endpaper:
Village map of West Hagbourne, 1990

Frontispiece:
Early steel engraving of a map of Berkshire by J Cary, 1793

Foreword

West Hagbourne is a small village in South Oxfordshire which, like so many others, is facing challenges to its rural character from nearby urban development. This book is a record of the village's evolution over a millennium, and a reminder of the heritage that we need to protect.

Meticulous research over nine years by an enthusiastic group of villagers has revealed how West Hagbourne's past was woven into the history of England. Great national events touched the lives of ordinary people who lived here and worked on the land, and their masters were the confidants of kings.

Nowadays only a minority of the population is involved with agriculture, but there are working farms at the heart of the village and these help to preserve its rural atmosphere. Farming itself is now facing challenges, but the history of the village shows how its essential character has been preserved.

There is no knowing what the next ten years will hold, let alone the next one thousand. We hope that this fascinating book will be an encouragement to all of us to build on the heritage of West Hagbourne and to maintain its unique identity.

We would like to thank all those in the Village History Group who have worked so diligently to produce this excellent book. We would also like to thank the villagers of West Hagbourne for their sustained support in fund-raising. A Village Open Day in 1996 raised a substantial amount of money which the South Oxfordshire District Council matched from its Millennium Fund in 1999.

West Hagbourne Parish Council
September 2000

Preface

The historical information contained within this book has been drawn from a variety of sources, including the British Library, the British Museum, the PRO, the RCHM and many other historical sources. The History Group has also talked to the villagers of West Hagbourne and others who no longer live in the village, in an attempt to retell their stories, and we are grateful to them for their time and generosity in sharing their memories with us.

Every attempt has been made to consult original sources and to verify every fact in this book. During the course of our research we have found some errors of interpretation which have been repeated by successive generations of researchers and hopefully, these have now been corrected once and for all. Some myths have also had to be dispelled and a few apocryphal stories have been put to rest. One of the pleasures in working on this book has been the new discoveries which have come to light during our research. These have given us new insights into the past and we hope they will enrich our story and, for a moment, bring to life the people who lived in this lovely village centuries ago.

This history of West Hagbourne is organised in a chronological fashion, but it is also related as a story, and for that reason, it has been decided not to use footnotes within the text. The sources of information appear at the end of each chapter, where full citations are given in the order in which the material appears within the text. Chapter Two, Ancient Treasures of West Hagbourne, is an exception, as sources there have been cited, as far as possible, according to archaeological methodology. The original spelling of names and places has also been retained.

All the research material and photographs collected for this history will form a village archive for the use of historians in the future. We hope they will enjoy delving into the history of West Hagbourne as much as we have done.

West Hagbourne Village History Group
September 2000

Contents

		page
Foreword		v
Preface		vii
Frontispiece		xi
Poem		xiii
Chapter 1	Introducing West Hagbourne	1
Chapter 2	Ancient Treasures of West Hagbourne	6
Chapter 3	Windsor Hakeborne - A Medieval Village	19
Chapter 4	A Glimpse of Village Life in the Sixteenth, Seventeenth and Eighteenth Centuries	47
Chapter 5	A Changing Landscape	67
Chapter 6	The Hagbourne Charities and the Philanthropic Tyrrells	89
Chapter 7	Church and Chapel	109
Chapter 8	West Hagbourne in the Nineteenth Century	124
Chapter 9	A Farming Village	143
Chapter 10	The Second World War Comes to West Hagbourne	186
Chapter 11	A Village Community	198
Acknowledgements		245
Time Chart		247
Index		255

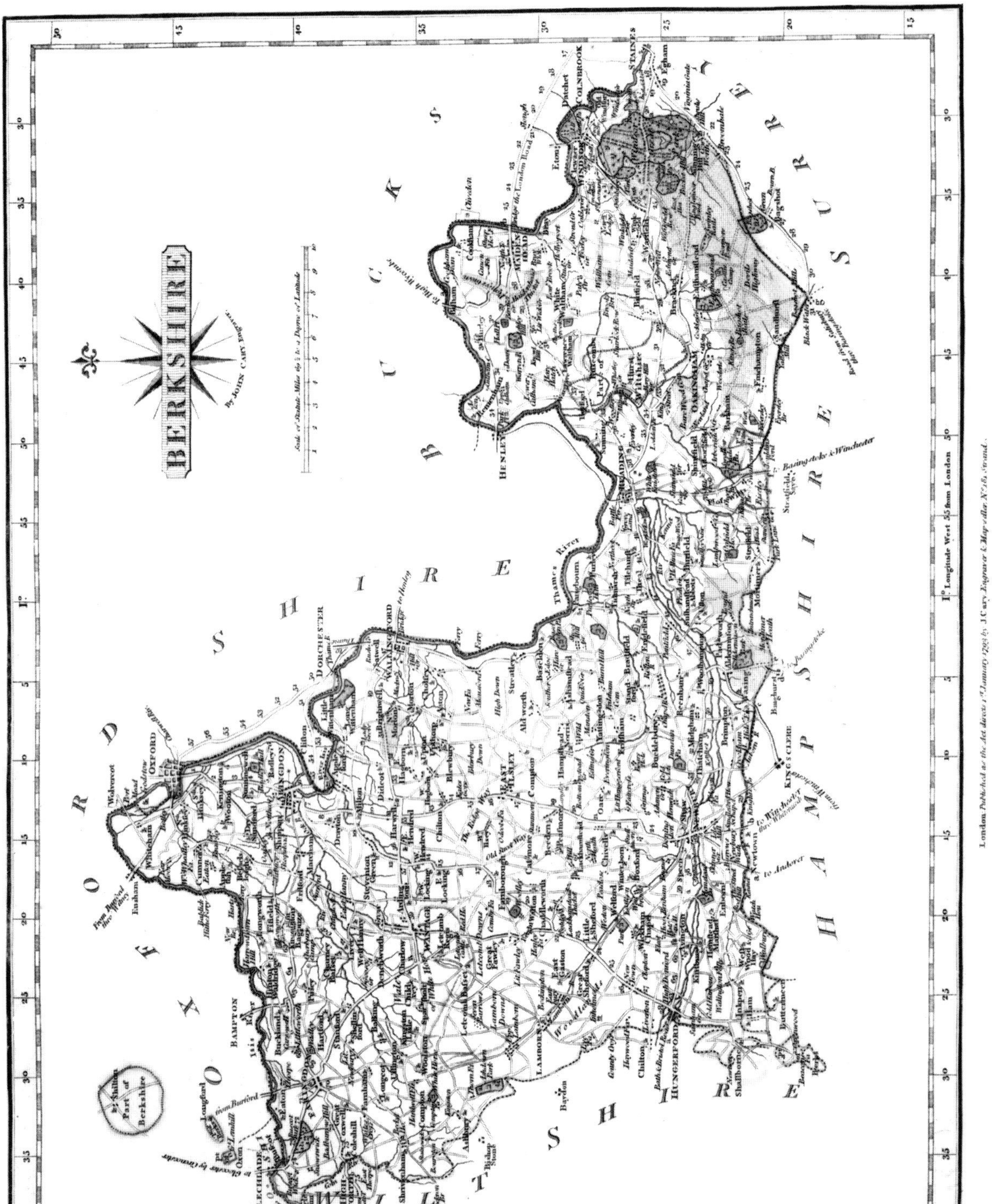
BERKSHIRE
By JOHN CARY Engraver
OXFORD
ABINGDON
READING
HUNGERFORD
WINDSOR
HENLEY
LAMBORN
KINGSCLERE
DORCHESTER
BAMPTON
LECHLADE
COLNBROOK
STAINES

Orchard Twilight

I love to walk down the old orchard
At that special time of day,
When blackbirds sing their late songs,
And noise of traffic's died away,
Just as the sun's low rays are slanting
Over fruit trees summer-bright,
Throwing elongated shadows
Over evening's mellow light.
It's all so calm and peaceful,
But it wasn't always so –
This tiny piece of ground
Has seen its share of joy and woe,
As relics found amongst the soil
Beneath the hedgerows show,
From where, at dusk, appear
My favourite ghosts of long ago.

I see a bare-legged soldier marching
To the beat of mighty Rome,
Yet, with every step he takes,
He's thinking of the folks back home.
And Hakka comes to view his kingdom,
But his wife prefers to look
At children playing in the bushes
Down beside the village brook.
A young monk kneels beneath a window
In the old grey Chapel wall,
Holy Matins all forgotten,
As he hears the cuckoo call.
Then Henry's horsemen gallop up
To rob the Chapel of its wealth,
While an old conniving cleric
Plots to keep some for himself.

An apple picker climbs his ladder,
Reaching out precariously,
Pipe and beer bottle hidden
At the base of his tall tree.

And interspersed with these scenes,
Clouds of conflict vainly strove
To overshadow golden rays
Of hope, self-sacrifice, and love.

And as I watch, the sky grows dark,
With mist the ground is overlaid,
A hooting owl finale ends my twilight cavalcade
Of our forebears, who trod their paths,
Though long and wide life's battle ranges –
Empires all will rise and fall,
But human nature never changes.

Edna Scott
1995

Chapter One

Introducing West Hagbourne

As for West Hagbourne itself, without being in any sense remarkable, it is just one of those tranquil villages making the true country of England the home of placid pleasures

J E Vincent

When J E Vincent wrote these words in 1919, he captured the essence of West Hagbourne and his words still ring true today, nearly a century later. Despite the growth of nearby towns, the building of new roads and the increased volume of traffic through the village, West Hagbourne has managed to retain its essential rural character. Although most of the orchards which once dominated the landscape have disappeared, there are still five farms within a mile of each other and some of the oldest buildings in the village are farmsteads. Whilst agriculture is no longer the main occupation and most people are employed outside West Hagbourne, villagers are determined to retain those elements of the quintessential English village so admired by J E Vincent.

Although there are less thatched cottages in the village today than in 1919, a few remain and a part of one thatched cob wall has survived. West Hagbourne has held on to one of its village pubs, the Horse and Harrow, which dates from at least 1754. The two focal areas of the village: the pond with its ducks and quaint signs reminding motorists to watch out for them, and the chestnut tree in the Square at the centre of the village, which now provides shade for the new seat below, evoke Vincent's "tranquil villages" and "placid pleasures".

One element of Vincent's observations on West Hagbourne, however, is as untrue today as it was in 1919. Whilst the village may appear unremarkable to the casual visitor, particularly as there is no church, school, village hall, shop or post office to define it, West Hagbourne is really quite unique, and steeped in history. Beneath the surface lies a fascinating story which goes back to a Bronze Age settlement; bears close links with William the Conqueror's first constable of Windsor Castle, the manorial lord of Windsor Hakeborne; the rebuilding of the south chapel of St Andrew's Church in East Hagbourne by Clarice de Windsor; intrigue at court on behalf of John York and William de Windsor through the latter's wife, Alice Perrers, mistress of Edward III in the fourteenth century; royal patronage and derring-do by knights and lords of the manor during the reigns of Henry VIII and his daughter Elizabeth and an intriguing brush with Judge Jeffreys of the Bloody Assize in 1687, to name just a few of the stories to be told in the following chapters of this book.

There are also a few enigmas and mysteries yet to be solved, such as the final resting place of West Hagbourne's medieval cross and the true story of Father Antony – was he an ordained priest or a charlatan? There is also a myth to be dispelled. This is the apocryphal story that West and East Hagbourne were once one and the same village, their separate identities only emerging after 10 March 1659 when most of East Hagbourne was destroyed by fire. According to legend, this fire spread to houses between the Hagbournes, thus separating them into two villages. There is, however, plenty of evidence to support the fact that West and East Hagbourne have always been two separate villages. Firstly, the fire started at the east end of East Hagbourne and stopped at the church. Dr J W Walker gave a lecture, reported in the 'Reading Mercury and Oxford Gazette' in 1932, in which he stated:

> *On March 10th, 1659, the greatest calamity that ever befell Hagbourne occurred; on that day a fire broke out at the east end of the village, and, fanned by a strong east wind, spread among the thatched roofs of the houses, causing the destruction of practically the whole village... the flames spread from roof to roof and gutted every house until the church was reached, and that sacred building, being of uninflammable material, was spared, and thus the fire burnt itself out.*

Secondly, historical documents written long before the fire of 1659, treat West and East Hagbourne as two quite distinct villages. In the Domesday Book compiled in 1086, the two villages each have their own separate entries. The villages were certainly tithed and taxed as two separate holdings as far back as the reign of Edward the Confessor (1042-1066). The two Hagbournes paid their taxes to different manorial lords and had their own manors, in fact West Hagbourne had two manors by 1355 and probably earlier. The Lay Subsidy Rolls of 1334 confirm the separate status of the two villages. Lay subsidies – so called because the clergy were exempt – were a form of taxation on certain goods, and they show that the two villages were taxed separately. Furthermore in 1642, seventeen years before the disastrous fire, the two villages each submitted their own Protestation Returns. West Hagbourne's Return was signed by all 36 males of 18 years or over living in the village at the time.

Apart from this documentary evidence of two separate and distinct villages, there are also geographical factors to consider. Centuries ago, villages were nucleated, that is to say, the village buildings were clustered together with their meadows, commons, woodlands and wastelands around them. Given the distance between the two villages, it is most unlikely that West and East Hagbourne could have been one large nucleated village. Furthermore, there are no traces of any foundations of buildings or evidence of any kind of habitation between the two villages and nothing has been revealed by aerial photography. This evidence surely lays to rest the myth which persists to this day that West and East Hagbourne were once one village.

Ancient routes on the Berkshire Downs

West Hagbourne was once a Berkshire village, but a huge reorganisation of county boundaries in 1974 swept the whole of north Berkshire into Oxfordshire. However, these boundary changes cannot sever West Hagbourne's close historical links with the Berkshire Downs. Hagbourne Hill, overlooking West Hagbourne on the southern boundary of the parish, lies on the edge of the Berkshire Downs. Two ancient thoroughfares – the Ridgeway and the Icknield Way – are close by. The Ridgeway stretches across several counties, including Wiltshire, Berkshire and Oxfordshire and was the main route for the warring Danes during their advances on Wessex in the first century AD. Much of it follows the ancient routes of the Wessex Ridgeway and the Icknield Way and it is dotted with archaeological sites.

The Icknield Way, or Ickelton Way as it is called on some early local maps, dates back to between 3000 and 1600 BC. It lies along the edges of the chalk line between East Anglia and Wiltshire and probably originated as a trading route. The Icknield Way crosses Hagbourne Hill close to an area where evidence of a Bronze Age settlement was discovered early in the nineteenth century. Much of the original Icknield Way is still in use today as part of our modern road system, but it is still possible to find many stretches of the old track.

The name Hagbourne has evolved over many centuries. The first part of the word originates from the Saxon word Hacca, whilst bourne comes from the Old English word *burn*, meaning a small stream, thus creating Haccaburn. Local tradition has it that Hacca was the name of a soldier in the Saxon army which came up the Thames and claimed the land near the stream which runs through the Hagbournes and out to the Thames at Wallingford. It is said that Hacca settled there, thus giving his name to the stream and the area which came to be known as the Hagbournes. However, there is no evidence to support this popular myth. The name of the stream has changed over the centuries from such Anglo-Saxon versions as haccaburna, hacceburnam and haccebroc, before finally settling on its modern version, Hakka's Brook. We know this because the stream is mentioned in a very early charter of about 895AD, whereby King Alfred exchanged various pieces of land, including Hagbourne, with the Bishop of Winchester. The words in the charter, *oonon of haccebroce on ealdan lace*, can be roughly translated into modern English as: *then from hacca's brook to the old stream*. This charter refers to Hagbourne as *hacceburnan* and is the earliest written reference to the Hagbournes. Hakka's Brook, on the east side of East Hagbourne village, is linked to West Hagbourne via a whole network of springs, brooks and ditches. The history of West Hagbourne is peppered with stories of local flooding, and various mishaps in overflowing ditches, including at least one fatal accident.

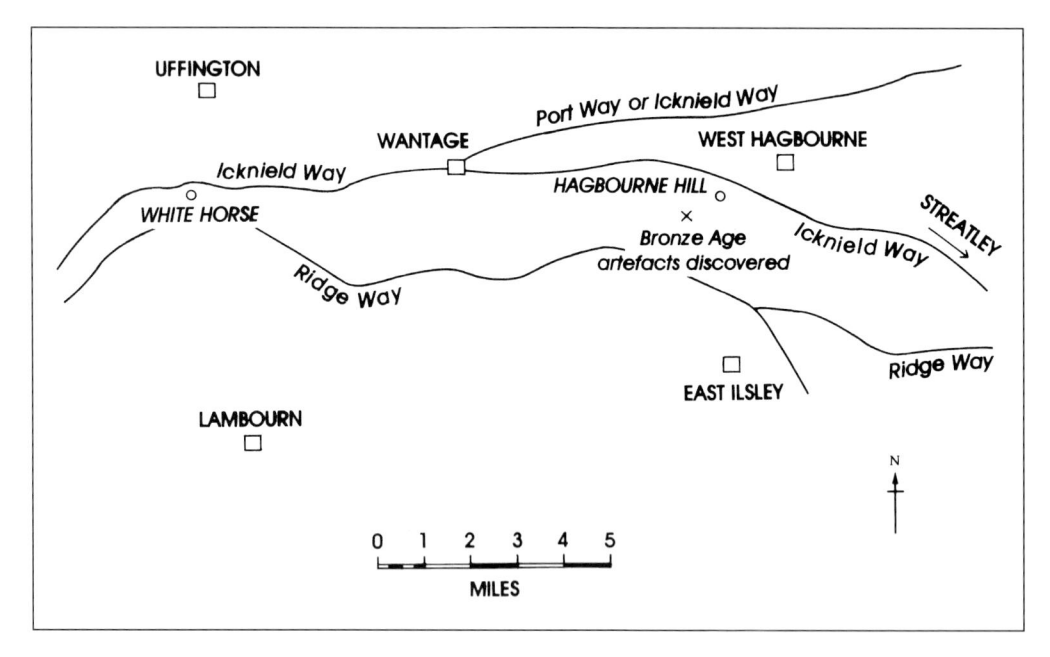

Ancient routes on the Berkshire Downs

Like the name of the stream, the village name, West Hagbourne, has also evolved through numerous variations including Westhacheborne, Westhakeburn, Westhakebourne, West Hagborne and finally, by the nineteenth century, West Hagbourne. Throughout history, places have become strongly associated with the people who have lived in them over a long period of time until they become known by their names. This has applied equally to small cottages and manorial estates. During Medieval times, one of the family names most strongly attached to West Hagbourne was that of the Windsors. According to the Domesday Book, Walter, son of Other (believed to be a Norman knight), held the manor of West Hagbourne in 1068. He was made the first constable of Windsor Castle by William the Conqueror and assumed the surname de Windsor, thus founding the Windsor dynasty. The Windsors held the manorial estate of West Hagbourne for nearly 600 years through various marriages with other dynasties and royal patronage. As a result, West Hagbourne became known as Windsor Hakeborne and hence the title of this book.

Sources:

J E Vincent, *Highways and Byways in Berkshire*, Macmillan & Co., 1919.
Report of Dr J W Walker's Lecture 'The Ancient History of the North Berks. Area', *The Reading Mercury and Oxford Gazette*, 6 February 1932.

Philip Morgan (ed.), *Domesday Book – Berkshire*, Phillimore & Co. Ltd., 1979. Part of general series *History from the Sources*, edited by John Morris.

P H Ditchfield and William Page (eds.), *The Victoria History of the Counties of England – Berkshire,* Vol 1, The St. Catherine Press, 1923, pp354, 366.

Lay Subsidy Rolls, Berkshire, 1334, Public Record Office, Kew. E179 73/9 73/10

Map of 1754 showing Ickelton Way. See page 82.

Bronze Age settlement. See Chapter 2.

Peter Hunter Blair, *An Introduction to Anglo-Saxon England*, Cambridge University Press, 1956. Reprinted as *Anglo-Saxon England* by The Folio Society, 1997.

Fatal accident: the stream which ran alongside the car park at the Horse and Harrow was piped about 1934, after a boy aged 4 years drowned in it.

Origins of the name of Hagbourne: Margaret Gelling, *The Place Names of Berkshire*, Part II, Cambridge University Press, 1973, p519.

King Alfred's charter: Walter de Gray Birch, *Cartularium Saxonicum: A Collection of Charters relating to Anglo-Saxon History*, Whiting and Company, 1887. (NB. According to Gelling the authenticity of this charter has been considered spurious by a Professor Whitelock, but its authenticity has been defended by another historian named Finberg. Gelling, Part III, 1976).

Translation of charter: Margaret Gelling, *The Place Names of Berkshire*, Part III, Cambridge University Press, 1976, p756 and G B Grundy, 'Berkshire Charters', *Berks, Bucks & Oxon Archaeological Journal*, Vol 29, Spring 1925.

Chapter Two

Ancient Treasures of West Hagbourne

The Hagbourne Hoard

Hagbourne Hill rests on a spur of the northern scarp of the Berkshire Downs, rising 400 feet at its highest point. The hill holds a commanding view of the village of West Hagbourne nestling below it. It is intersected by the Icknield Way, an ancient trading route which follows the edges of the chalk line between East Anglia and Wiltshire and dates back to somewhere between 3000 and 1600BC. Over the centuries, Hagbourne Hill has occasionally yielded up its secrets in the form of archaeological finds which tell us something about the people who may have lived there in prehistoric times. These finds, which include both Bronze and Iron Age deposits, have presented something of an enigma for archaeologists as it is most unusual to discover the two periods represented together in the same place.

The first find occurred in the spring of 1803, when several oblong pits were accidentally discovered in a common field on the south slope of Hagbourne Hill by some labourers digging near the parish boundary south of the Icknield Way. The discovery was made within the area of an old chalk pit, suggesting that the workmen may have been extracting chalk at the time. The chalk pit is now completely grassed over. The oblong pits were about four feet below the ground and each one was roughly seven feet long by three feet wide. At the bottom of one of these pits was a hole, or circular excavation, about 18 inches in diameter, containing several items which turned out to be an exciting find of great archaeological significance.

Five years after the discovery, in 1808, Ebenezer King, a Fellow of the Society of Antiquaries, brought the find to the attention of the Society in a letter, accompanied by some of the artefacts. This letter, together with detailed drawings of the Hagbourne Hoard, was published in the Society's journal 'Archaeologia' in 1812. The items King presented to the Society consisted of Bronze Age material and some Early Iron Age artefacts. 'The Victoria History of Berkshire' described the find as "by far the most important discovery of antiquities of the Early Iron Age made in the county…" The find was christened the Hagbourne Hoard and most of the artefacts are now held by the British Museum. King attached a list of the items with his letter but his interpretation of parts of the find was later shown to be mistaken. It is the drawings in 'Archaeologia' which bring the Hoard to life.

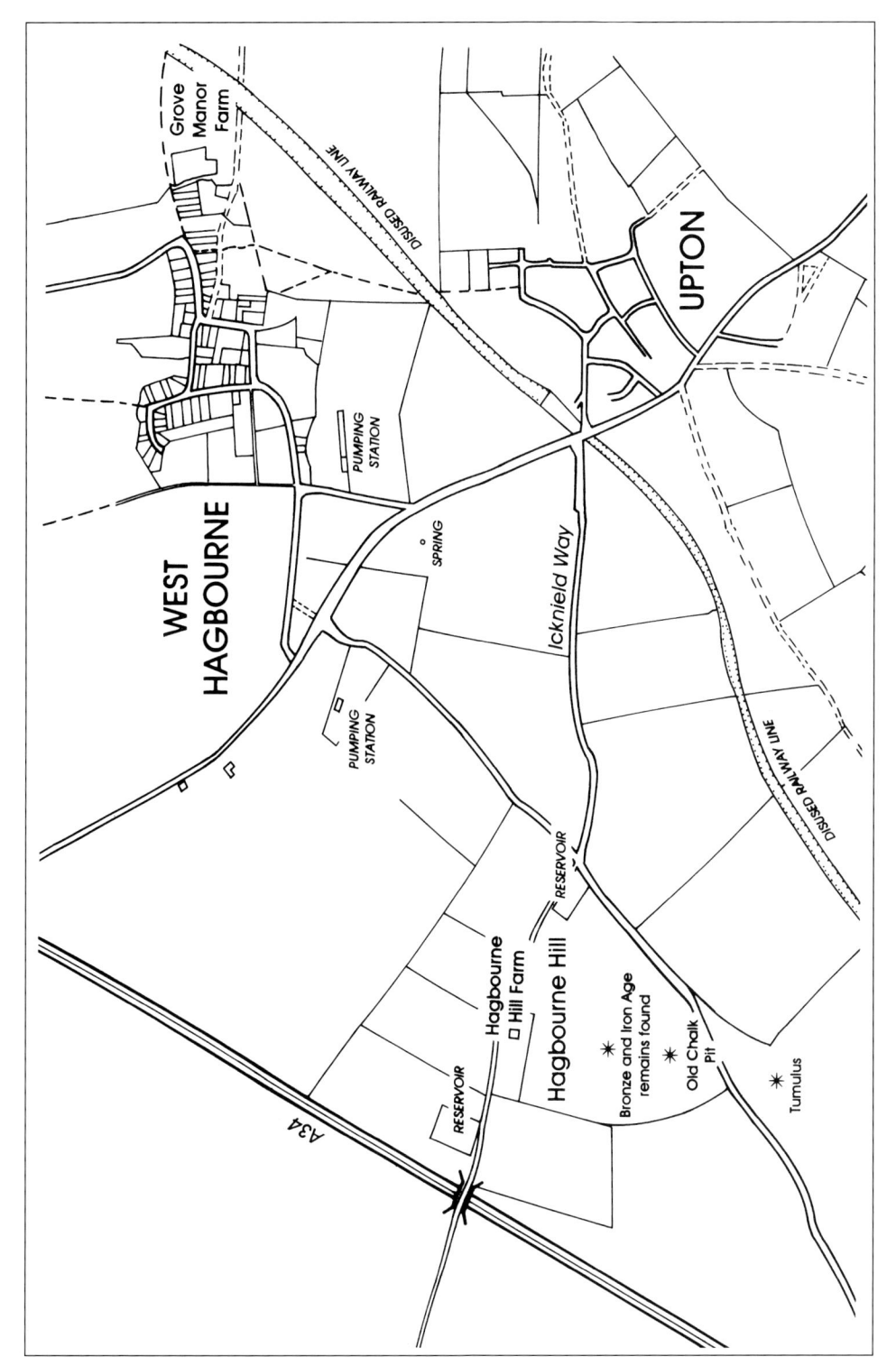

Map showing site of discovery of Hagbourne Hoard on Hagbourne Hill

The illustrations depict ornamentation in the form of two pins, one straight with a solid ring head, the other curved below a perforated head; tools and weapons in the shape of a socketed bronze axe (King used the word celt) with one loop and a socketed bronze spearhead with two loops; and horse tackle which included two terrets (harness rings) and two bridle-bits. King's list implied that there were at least two axes, though only one was illustrated.

Dr Thomas Evans of Gloucester presented all these items, with the notable exception of the socketed bronze axe, to the British Museum in 1861. The whereabouts of this axe have never been discovered. Evans also gave two other artefacts to the Museum, which were included as part of the Hoard, though they were not mentioned by King. These were a fragment of a palstave (type of axe) and part of what is believed to be a Late Bronze Age bracelet.

King's letter also described other items said to have been discovered in the pit on Hagbourne Hill. These were several large rings of brass, likened by King to dog-collars but most likely torcs (neck ornaments of metal) according to the British Museum, and some coins, one said to be of silver and another of gold, which King ascribed to the period of the Lower Roman Empire. Unfortunately he never saw these items himself and was only able to describe them from second-hand reports. In view of King's confused description of the find five years after its discovery, it would be unwise to draw too many conclusions from his interpretation of the objects discovered in the pit, or his account of their discovery.

Further finds on Hagbourne Hill have intensified speculation about the true nature of the discoveries. Fragments of two bronze spearheads found their way to the British Museum in 1862, just one year after the original Hagbourne Hoard was deposited there. These were also said to have been found on Hagbourne Hill. One of these was reported to have been discovered with a skeleton when it was brought to the attention of the British Archaeological Association, together with other artefacts belonging to Jesse King of Appleford – perhaps the son of Ebenezer – in 1845:

> *Mr Smith exhibited drawings of various articles of antiquity, chiefly Roman and Romano-British, found in Berkshire and now in the possession of Mr Jesse King: No 5. Javelin head in bronze, found with a skeleton at Highbourn Hill.*

(Note: the author of this report in the 'Journal of the British Archaeological Association' made an error in referring to Hagbourne Hill as Highbourn Hill).

The date and circumstances of the discovery of this javelin head (spearhead) are not known, though Margaret Ehrenberg, in her study of Bronze Age spearheads, has concluded that it was part of the 1803 find and probably from the same mould as the first spearhead. The British Museum's records also concur with this opinion. The Museum purchased the two damaged spearheads, together with several other items, from the Jesse King collection.

The only reference to a skeleton being found on Hagbourne Hill is this brief mention in the Association's journal, long after its discovery. However, this allusion to a skeleton, together with the discovery of the horse tackle, have led to the

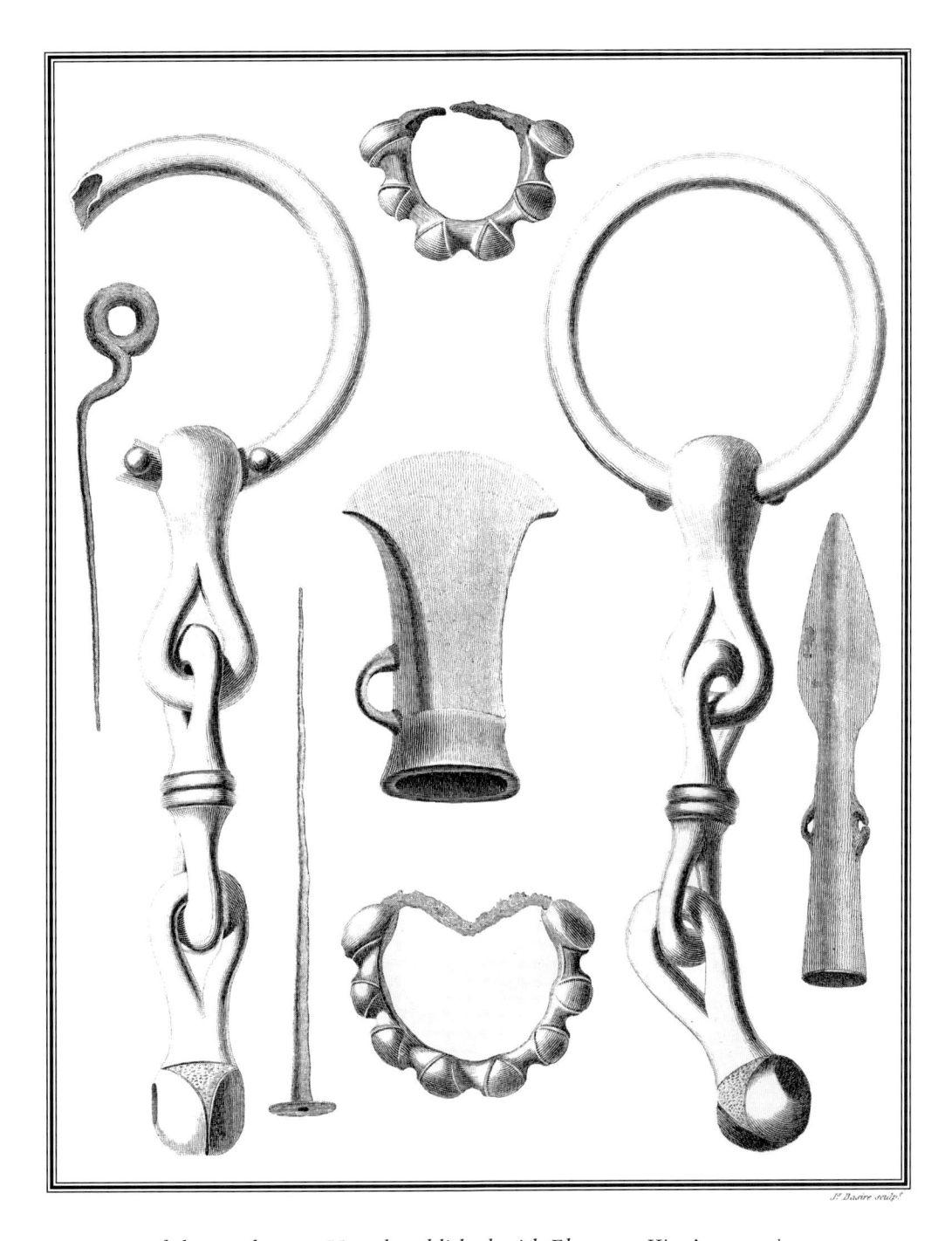

Drawings of the Hagbourne Hoard, published with Ebenezer King's report in 'Archaeologia'. These artefacts were discovered on Hagbourne Hill in 1803 and are now in the care of the British Museum. Bronze Age finds were the axe, spearhead and straight pin. Iron Age finds were the curved pin, two terrets and two horse-bits

hypothesis that the Hagbourne Hoard was evidence of the Iron Age burial of a horseman, along with his horse and possibly his chariot.

D W Harding, in his study of the Iron Age in the basin of the upper Thames, has considered the possible purpose of the pits on Hagbourne Hill, including the idea of a burial site. He finds the evidence inconclusive, especially given the difficulties in dating the Hoard accurately, and the fact that Ebenezer King made no mention, or even hinted that there were indications of a burial. Harding has made

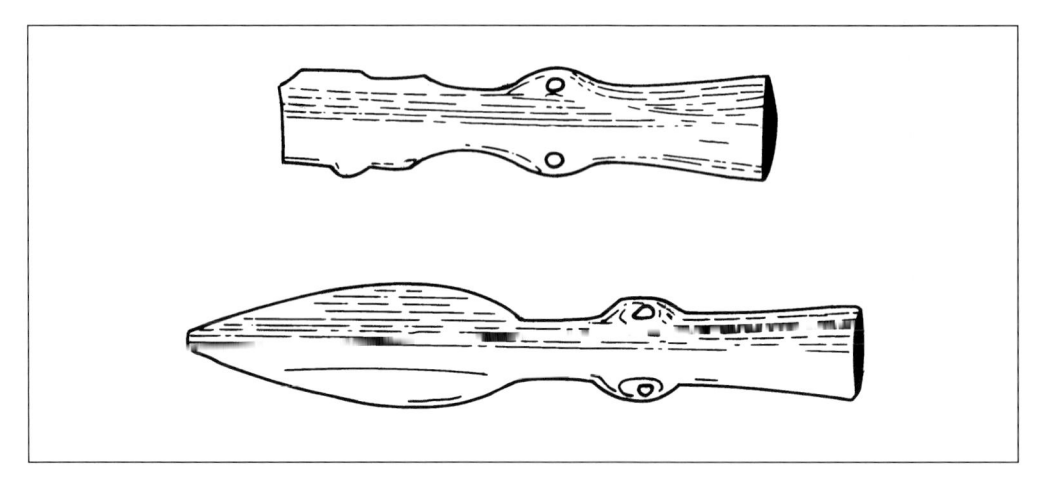

Sketch of two fragments of bronze spearheads also thought to be part of the Hagbourne Hoard

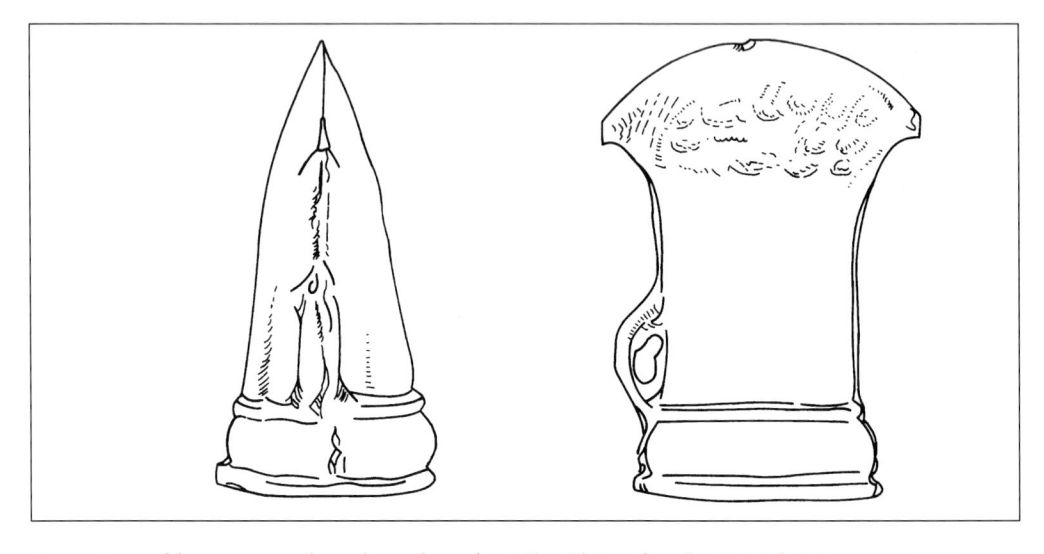

Drawings of bronze axe, based on those by Lily Chitty for the British Museum, 1941

a tentative suggestion regarding the purpose of the excavated pits. He argues that during the Iron Age winters, as in earlier periods of prehistory, it was difficult to feed the livestock and therefore the herds were culled. As a result, pits were needed in Iron Age settlements for the storage of salted meat.

In the summer of 1893, ninety years after the first discovery, yet another socketed bronze axe was discovered by a shepherd while digging a post hole for a sheepfold on Aldworth's farm on Hagbourne Hill. He sold the axe shortly afterwards to Mr Leonard Slade of Manor Farm, Blewbury. Another Fellow of the Society of Antiquaries, Mr W H Richardson, exhibited this bronze axe to the learned Society on the 25th of January 1904. He remarked that the axe was a "small but very perfect specimen", three and one quarter inches by two and a half inches wide and weighing ten and a half ounces. The 'National Bronze Index', published in 1941, describes it as being smooth with oval hammer markings towards the edge on both faces; "a lovely specimen... lustrous black with brown, green and reddish lights. Red-gold metal shows on minor lip."

Not long after it was discovered, the axe was also shown to Dr Stevens, a curator at Reading Museum who suggested that it should be placed in the British Museum alongside the original Hagbourne Hoard. However, this plea was ignored. The axe later came into the hands of Mrs Phyllis Tilley of Kings Sutton, Banbury and was drawn by Lily F Chitty for the British Museum's records in 1941, so its existence is not in doubt. However, there have been no further sightings of it despite many enquiries by interested parties. Miss Chitty OBE was another Fellow of the Society of Antiquaries and lived at Upton vicarage. She contributed a great deal to the study of archaeological finds in Berkshire.

The interest in this axe was fuelled by the previous discovery in 1803 of the Hagbourne Hoard. In his presentation, Richardson complained that because the first axe was not given to the British Museum to be preserved with the rest of the Hoard, it was difficult to make a direct comparison, except through the drawing of it in 'Archaeologia'. He saw differences between the two axes and called for new explorations of the site. Unfortunately his request was never fulfilled, even though he emphasised the importance of the 1893 discovery. He observed that although twenty bronze relics had been found in Berkshire by 1804, socketed axes had been found in only four locations; these being Hagbourne Hill, Yattendon, Wallingford and Windsor.

Interpretation of the Hagbourne Hoard

Since the discovery of the find was first reported, the presence of both Bronze and Iron Age material has caused much speculation among archaeologists as to how material from two different periods came to be together in a single hole at the bottom of one of the pits. Some have accepted King's report at face value, though with reservations. One of these, Dr John Evans, writing a little nearer the time, in 1881, believed that the find represented a transitional stage from the employment of bronze to the use of iron and steel. This view supports the argument that Bronze Age types were still in use after the introduction of iron in Berkshire. Other archaeologists have suggested that there could have been two distinct hoards on the same site, one derived from the Bronze Age and disturbed by another deposit during the Iron Age. More recent scholars take the view that the early reports cannot be trusted and that there were several separate finds, representing various archaeological periods, discovered over a number of years in the vicinity of the old chalk pit and the Romano-British cemetery on Hagbourne Hill. In view of the confusion over the interpretation of the site, the dating of the artefacts has been very important to archaeologists specialising in these periods.

Bronze Age Artefacts

The currently accepted dates for the Bronze Age are 2500-700BC, during which time metalworking was introduced and there was growing contact with Europe. The items found on Hagbourne Hill, which can definitely be attributed to the Bronze Age, are the axes, the spearheads and the straight bronze pin. Of all the bronze implements, the axe is the most common. It was probably one of the earliest instruments to be made of metal. There are several types, including flat, flanged, winged and socketed, the latter evolving from an earlier solid type known as palstave. These axes were cast with a socket to receive the haft, which was actually embedded in the blade. They nearly always had a loop at one side, as in the case of the one found on Hagbourne Hill. The use of socketed axes as cutting tools or weapons became widespread throughout Britain, though the earliest ones were almost certainly of foreign origin. Their use persisted over a long period of time, even to the Late Iron Age, and they must have been among the last of the bronze tools to be superseded by iron.

Bronze spearheads were unlikely to have been introduced before the means of making sockets had been discovered. They closely resembled arrows, darts, lances and javelins and were all used as weapons. There were various types of spearheads. The one found on Hagbourne Hill in 1803 was of the looped variety, with eyes on each side of the socket, on the same plane as the leaf-shaped blade. The loops were used to secure the metallic head to the wooden shaft. Socketed axes were often found together with spearheads, as at Hagbourne Hill. Spearheads have been found throughout the country, but are particularly concentrated around Berkshire, north Wiltshire, Oxfordshire and the Thames Valley.

Pins to fasten the dress or the hair seem to have been in use from very early times when bone was fashioned for the purpose. Bronze pins were used long after the end of the Bronze Age, and the heads were often highly ornamented. The flat disc of the bronze pin found on Hagbourne Hill was decorated with concentric incised circles.

Iron Age Artefacts

The British Iron Age extended from about 800BC to AD43, when the Romans invaded. The Iron Age items of the Hagbourne Hoard are the cast bronze pin with the curve below the perforated head, which the British Museum has dated as second century BC, and the horse tackle consisting of the terrets (rings through which the horse reins passed), and the two horse-bits. Although only two terrets were illustrated in 'Archaeologia', three were deposited with the British Museum as part of the Hagbourne Hoard.

The three-link bridle-bits and terret rings have been linked to the extensive remains of a second or early first century BC bronze foundry, discovered during the excavation of a settlement at Gussage All Saints in Dorset, which according to Professor Cunliffe, has provided archaeologists with "dramatic evidence of bronze-working" (p456). Amongst the remains were thousands of fragments of clay moulds, part of the lost-wax method of casting, whereby objects were modelled in wax to produce clay moulds which were then filled with molten bronze, cooled, and broken open to remove the artefact. The moulds were used for the production of horse gear, including three-link bridle bits and terret rings of a similar type to those found amongst the Hagbourne Hoard, suggesting that there is a strong connection between the moulds found in Dorset and the horse gear found on Hagbourne Hill. Unfortunately this cannot be taken further until more detailed studies have been made.

One of the terrets found on Hagbourne Hill is now on permanent display in the Romano-British galleries in the British Museum (room 50, case 21) and is captioned: *Composite terret of cast bronze with wrought iron cross-bar 250 – 100 BC, Hagbourne Hill, Berkshire.* One of the two horse-bits is also exhibited in case 25 and bears the caption: *three link bridle-bits with iron core in the rein-rings.* The casting process for this type of bridle-bit was current from about 300BC but Harding thought that the ornamentation on the horse-bits would not have been possible before the first century BC. There is strong evidence of the use of horses in the area of Hagbourne Hill, apart from the horse gear found on the hill. A mile or so away, at Blewburton, ten separate horse skeletons have been excavated. Indications are that these horses belonged to a small breed similar to the present day Exmoor pony.

The Iron Age saw a massive increase in activity in the Thames valley. By about 800BC farming was responding to the twin pressures of a growing population, owing to the influx of Belgic Gauls from the Continent, and the deteriorating climate. During the first 2,000 years BC, the weather became wetter and up to two degrees colder, affecting crop yields. Agriculture became increasingly important, providing the mainstay for the economy, with most of the population becoming peasant farmers.

In the Late Iron Age, imports such as amber vessels, glass and ivory ornaments, became available as trade increased between southern Britain and the Continent.

Although those living in the vicinity of Hagbourne Hill may not have enjoyed all these luxuries, they were close enough to the ancient Icknield Way to be in touch with passing traders.

Hagbourne Hill has never been systematically excavated, which makes it difficult for archaeologists to draw any final conclusions regarding the interpretation of the Bronze and Iron Age finds which have been made there over the centuries. The artefacts may simply be evidence of a continuous settlement throughout the two Ages, or Hagbourne Hill could have been a special place, where prehistoric people deposited items of significance. One thing is certain, the Hagbourne Hoard is an unusual and specialised collection which will continue to fascinate and challenge those who seek to unravel the mysteries of Hagbourne Hill.

Romano-British Finds

A Romano-British burial ground lies on the lower south side of Hagbourne Hill and it is understood that there was once a Romano-British settlement on Hagbourne Hill. The Roman occupation of the district was relatively peaceful and the native inhabitants gradually became Romanised. There is evidence for this in the discoveries of pottery and other objects of the Iron Age period associated with items dating from the Romano-British era on Hagbourne Hill.

Pottery

In May 1939, another seven or eight rectangular pits, apparently resembling those recorded by Ebenezer King, were found on Hagbourne Hill when it was occupied by the RAF during the Second World War. A fragment of Early Iron Age pottery was also discovered there about the same time. This fragment, with its incised linear design and dot-filled triangles was observed to have an affinity with similar decorated examples found at Chinnor on the edge of the Chilterns. An Iron Age brooch was also found on the surface in May 1930 but little more is known about its discovery. It was owned by Dr Richard Rice of Harwell and is now part of the Rice collection, which is held in store at Abingdon Museum. Reading Museum records 13 small undecorated sherds picked up on the surface of a field on Hagbourne Hill after ploughing, which it attributes to "Iron Age/Roman".

Coins

Archaeologists have been fairly sceptical about the coins which King said were found with the original Hoard in 1803, particularly as he never saw these coins and was relying on the account given by the workmen. The coins have been described as "intrusive" by Harding, as they were most probably found elsewhere in the vicinity, possibly near the Romano-British cemetery. King attributed the gold coin to the Lower Empire but later commentators have suggested that it could have been British or Gallo-Belgic which would be consistent with the dating of the horse gear.

A further gold coin from the Iron Age was later discovered on Hagbourne Hill. This coin, weighing about four grams, depicts the head of Apollo on one side and the neck of a horse and a sunflower on the reverse. It was formerly in the collection of W R Davies and is now in the British Museum, where it is classified as Corieltauvian B, a common type found in many museums. The Corieltauvi, popularly known as Coritani, were a tribe living in the north-east around Linconshire and Nottingham. The coin is believed to have been brought down by traders using the Icknield Way. Other coins have been discovered in and around West Hagbourne, including Roman coins at Thatch Cottage.

In 1983 a coin was unearthed in a garden in York Road. It shows a head on one side and a full-length image of a soldier on the other. The Museum of Oxford identified the bronze coin as belonging to the brief period when Magnentius was Emperor of part of the Western Empire of Rome between 350 and 353. Magnentius was of barbarian descent and, according to tradition, his father was a Briton. He seized the throne from Constans in 350. The lettering on one side of the coin comprises the name of Emperor Magnentius and his abbreviated titles: *IM CAE MAGNENTIUS AVG*. The other side reads: *FELICITAS REPUBLICE*, meaning 'prosperity to the Republic'.

The Roman garrisons in Britain started to lose their power in the third century, as soldiers were recalled to fight the civil wars in Europe. The death of Magnentius in 353, following a major defeat two years earlier, at the hands of Constantius II at Mursa in Pannonia (a province of the Roman Empire, comprising present-day Hungary, Austria, Slovenia and Croatia), meant further reductions in troops in Britain. By 410 there were no longer enough Roman legions to beat off the attacks of the invading Picts, Scots and the Germanic tribes, resulting in the decline of the Romano-British settlements.

Recent Finds

No further major finds of great archaeological significance have come to light on Hagbourne Hill until recently, when some archaeological studies were made in connection with work carried out in the vicinity of the hill. In 1996 the Cotswold Archaeological Trust was commissioned by Thames Water Utilities to undertake a watching brief during the construction of a pipeline between South Moreton and the service reservoir on Hagbourne Hill.

A sherd (shard) of Roman pottery was recovered south of East Hagbourne, near West Hagbourne Moor, but very little else of archaeological relevance was found along the length of the pipeline. The watching brief's report suggested that this was because the wayleave was not stripped down to a depth adequate enough to address the archaeological potential of the area. The report concluded that "the wayleave stripping on Hagbourne Hill partly revealed the underlying chalk but did not show any evidence of pits or linear features". As the report suggests, this could be because any likely Iron Age activity would be located some distance from the pipeline, given the history of previous discoveries on Hagbourne Hill.

Another much more significant survey took place in 1999, when an archaeological field evaluation was carried out by Thames Valley Archaeological Services on behalf of the owners of the land, in anticipation of the construction of agricultural buildings at Hagbourne Hill Farm. One purpose of the evaluation was to provide information on the archaeological potential of the site, particularly concerning the presence and date of any archaeological deposits within the proposed area of development. Five trenches were dug and excavated under direct archaeological supervision. The evaluation resulted in the recovery of 50 sherds of pottery, mostly from the Early Iron Age. Some of the fragments were very small but amongst the recognisable forms were fineware tripartite bowls of sandy black ware with a burnished finish and a plain slack-sided jar with a roughly wiped finish. One sherd had two parallel incised lines. The bowls were very characteristic of the Early Iron Age. The presence of a significant proportion of fineware to coarseware indicated that this was a relatively high-status site in archaeological terms, according to the survey report.

Photograph taken in the early 1900s on Hagbourne Hill overlooking West Hagbourne. The two men are taking a Berkshire wagon along the Icknield Way

As well as the pottery, there was a small collection of fragmented animal bones, including those of sheep, cattle and possibly pig teeth. An intact struck flake (to initiate fire) of either Neolithic or Bronze Age was recovered from a spoilheap from one of the trenches, whilst two others contained small amounts of burnt flint. A further trench revealed a fragment of a tile. The survey report revealed that the features uncovered during the survey represented settlement deposits, and concluded that the archaeological potential of the site on Hagbourne Hill was good, thus substantiating the opinions of earlier archaeologists.

It may never be possible to determine the true nature of the first archaeological discoveries on Hagbourne Hill nearly 200 years ago. Perhaps the hill will retain its mysteries for future generations to discover. However, the discovery of the Hagbourne Hoard and the subsequent archaeological finds do indicate that there was a settlement on Hagbourne Hill at least 2000 years ago. Perhaps, more than anything else, these discoveries provide tangible links with our past and remind us that we, too, are creating an historical and cultural heritage for the future.

Sources – Finds on Hagbourne Hill

P H Ditchfield and William Page (eds), *The Victoria History of the Counties of England – Berkshire*, Vol 1, The St. Catherine Press, 1923, pp186, 188, 197.

Ebenezer B King, 'A Description of Antiquities Discovered on Hagbourne Hill', *Archaeologia: or Miscellaneous Tracts Relating to Antiquity*, Society of Antiquaries of London, Vol XVI, 1812, pp348–9.

Finds deposited at BM in 1861 and 1862: *Accession Register*, British Museum, unpublished.

Additional artefacts from Dr Thomas Evans: In 1972, D W Harding described one of these as a flat-headed pin but the British Museum has identified it as part of a bracelet (Dr J D Hill, Romano-British Department, British Museum, April, 2000).

Javelin head: 'Proceedings of the Central Committee', *Journal of the British Archaeological Association*, 10 September 1845, Vol I, 1845, p310.

Socketed axe discovered in 1893: W H Richardson, *Proceedings of the Society of Antiquaries*, Vol XX, 1903–1905, pp33–35; *The National Bronze Index*, The British Museum, 1941; and J Stevens, 'Notes and Queries Relating to Berkshire', *Berkshire Archaeological and Architectural Society*, Vol II, 1891-93, pp44–45.

Iron Age Brooch: F M Underhill, 'Notes on Recent Antiquarian Discoveries in Berkshire (II)', *Berkshire Archaeological Journal*, XLII, 1938, p23 and RCHME, No 237595, 1998.

Undecorated sherds: *Oxford City and County Museum Index Cards*, Nos 7822 and 7890, 1973.

Fragment of decorated Iron Age pot: unpublished report by Lily Chitty, quoted by Harding, *The Iron Age in the Upper Thames Basin*, 1972, footnote p91 and Harold Peake, 'Notes on Recent Antiquarian Discoveries in Berkshire', *Berkshire Archaeological Journal*, No 49, 1946, p51.

Iron Age gold coin: Colin Haselgrove, *Iron Age Coinage in South-East England – The Archaeological Context*, Part I, BAR British Series 174 (I), 1987.

Supporting References

Barry Cunliffe, *Iron Age Communities in Britain*, Routledge, 1991.
Margaret R Ehrenberg, *Bronze Age Spearheads from Berkshire, Buckinghamshire and Oxfordshire*, BAR British Series, Vol 34, 1977, pp7, 8, 39, Appendices I and II.
John Evans, *Ancient Bronze Implements, Weapons and Ornaments of Great Britain and Ireland*, Longmans, Green & Co., 1881, pp471, 472.
Sheppard Frere, *Britannia – A History of Roman Britain*, 1967, revised and reprinted, The Folio Society Ltd, 1999, pp343–344.
D W Harding, *The Iron Age in the Upper Thames Basin*, Clarendon Press, 1972, pp41–42, 91–92, 172.
NMR Listings for the Parish of West Hagbourne, RCHM England, 1998. No 233626.
W A Seaby, *Berkshire Archaeological Journal*, No 42, 1938, p86.
Reginald A Smith, *A Guide Catalogue to the Antiquities of the Early Iron Age*, British Museum, 1925, pp88, 97.
Coin discovered by Dr D H Totterdell of York Road, West Hagbourne and identified by a curator at the Museum of Oxford, 1983.

Interpretation of Finds

One single hoard representing transitional period: John Evans, 1881, p471 and D W Harding, 1972, p91.
Bronze Age material used in the Iron Age: Reginald A Smith, *Guide Catalogue*, British Museum, p87.
Iron Age deposits disturbed by Bronze Age artefacts: Colin Haselgrove, BAR, 1987.
Separate finds on a multi-period site: Ehrenberg, BAR, Appendix II, 1977, and Dr J D Hill, Romano-British Department, British Museum, 2000.

Reports

South Moreton to Hagbourne Hill Main, Oxfordshire, Cotswold Archaeological Trust, April 1996.
Joanne Pine, *Hagbourne Hill Farm, Didcot, Oxfordshire, An Archaeological Evaluation*, Thames Valley Archaeological Services, March 1999.

Chapter Three

Windsor Hakeborne – A Medieval Village

Earliest recorded history

The first written reference to the village of West Hagbourne is found in the Domesday Book. In 1086, a year before he died and after nearly twenty years on the English throne, William of Normandy ordered a survey of the land he had conquered in 1066. It was to become the ultimate authoritative register of the rightful possession of land and property throughout the country. The findings were assembled by county and compiled into volumes at Winchester. These became known as the Domesday Book. William's survey registered all arable land, meadows and woodland, the names of the manors, the number of villeins and freemen and the amount of land they held, the mills and the value of the estates. This was done in considerable detail, right down to the number of ploughs and the amount of land held by each freeman.

For the purpose of the survey, villages were grouped by administrative districts called Hundreds, which formed regions within shires or counties. At the time of the Domesday Book, West Hagbourne lay in the Hundred of Blewbury (Blitberie) in the county of Berkshire (Berchescire).

> 7 fracta pax . Val . v . solid . *In Blitberie Hd.*
> Isd . W . ten *Hacheborne* . Aluuin un lib ho te
> nuit . Tc 7 m . x . hidæ ibi . sed p . vi . hid 7 dim se desd.
> Tra . e . vi . car . In dnio sunt . ii . car . 7 xiiii . uilli 7 x .
> cot . cu . v . car . Ibi . iiii . serui . 7 molin de . xii . solid .
> 7 xx.iiii . ac pti . De hac tra ten Robt . i . hid de Walto.
> 7 ibi ht . i . car cu . i . cot . 7 iiii . ac pti.
> Tot T.R.E. 7 post: ualb . xiii . lib . 7 modo: xiii . lib.

West Hagbourne's entry in the Domesday Book, 1086

19

Although the Domesday Book entry for West Hagbourne is brief, it is a rich source of information, indicating the size and value of the manorial estate and providing a glimpse of the feudal structure of the village community. The following entry is from a translation of Abraham Farley's 1783 printed text of the Domesday Book.

> *In BLEWBURY hundred*
> *Walter also holds (West) Hagbourne. Alwin, a free man, held it.*
> *Then and now 10 hides there, but it answers for 6½ hides.*
> *Land for 6 ploughs. In lordship 2 ploughs;*
> *14 villagers and 10 cottagers with 5 ploughs.*
> *4 slaves; a mill at 12s; meadow, 24 acres.*
> *Robert holds 1 hide of this land from Walter; he has*
> *1 plough, with 1 cottager; meadow, 4 acres.*
> *Value of this whole before 1066 and later £13; now £13.*

West Hagbourne appears to have been a typical medieval English village organised around a manorial system based on Anglo-Saxon serfdom. The first manor house of West Hagbourne stood on the site of Manor Farm, slightly apart, at one corner of the village, as was the custom at the time. It is believed that it once had a moat. The villeins and serfs attached to the manor had their dwellings in the village. Typically, in the rural England of the Middle Ages, these were usually small timber-framed cottages or huts, with walls made of wattle and daub and possibly thatched with turfs. Each dwelling would have had a small enclosed plot of land attached, called a close. Until the Reformation, West Hagbourne had its own chapel not far from the manor (see Chapter 7).

In 1086 West Hagbourne boasted ten hides and 24 acres of meadow, some of which would have been common land used by the tenants to graze their livestock. The old Anglo-Saxon word hide – the amount of arable land considered adequate to support one family – could be anything between 60 and 120 acres, depending on the district. In later centuries the word *carucate* (from *caruca* meaning a plough drawn by eight oxen) replaced hide but had the same meaning. The manor had its own *demesne* land which would have included the best arable fields and meadows. This land provided an important part of the lord's income and was for his own personal use. West Hagbourne's open communal fields and downs were situated to the west, whilst the meadows and moors lay to the south and east of the village. Most of the farming land at that time consisted of cornfields. The lord of West Hagbourne had two ploughs for farming the *demesne* land and two slaves (serfs) to work each plough, whilst the villagers had five ploughs between them.

The lord of the manor of West Hagbourne held jurisdiction over 14 villagers (villeins) and their families. The manorial system depended on the servitude of these villeins who were themselves born on manorial land to parents who were also villeins. They were not free to leave the manor but were tied to the land and considered as part of the assets to be bought and sold with it. Freemen, on the other hand, could legally come and go as they pleased, though in reality they often possessed only an acre or two of land and were dependent on getting work from villeins who often had more land than they could cultivate themselves. The villeins were allowed to farm the communal arable land and graze their animals on the commons in return for the payment of rent and labour cultivating the lord's *demesne* lands, tending his animals and performing various other services.

The amount of land held by individual villeins could vary considerably, with those holding the most having to pay the highest rent, as well as owing many and varied services to the lord. In addition to the 14 villagers and four slaves, there were ten cottagers (cottars) attached to the manor. Cottars were considered inferior to villeins and had no share in the common land of the manor and were not part of the ploughing team. They could be serfs or freemen and they eked out a difficult living from what they could grow on their close and by working for others. They paid for their smallholdings by working on the lord's land for a day or two at harvest time. We also know, from a dowry of 1367, that one tenant provided the lord with a hen every year.

West Hagbourne's assets included a mill, which is known to have still been in existence during the reign of Henry VIII, although its exact site is not marked on any surviving maps. The mill would have been driven by one of the many streams or 'bournes' from which Hagbourne derives its name. All manors had one or more mills and the villagers were only allowed to grind their corn at the manorial mill and at a price set by the lord. Mills were therefore an important source of income which is why they were always included as an asset in any evaluation.

Windsor manor

West Hagbourne's first manor was known as Windsor manor after the Windsor family who held it for nearly 600 years following the Norman Conquest. A dowry granted to Clarice de Windsor on the death of her husband Richard, the lord of West Hagbourne in 1367, included property and land as well as income from the tenants of the manor. This dowry gives us a very good idea of what the manor house of West Hagbourne was like when Clarice de Windsor lived there, as it is quite specific about Clarice's share. She had a chamber at the west end of the hall, which in medieval times could be either a large single room, or a whole wing, and was usually of timber-framed construction. We know that the house had more than one storey, because the dowry included a solar (from the French word *solier*) above the chamber. This suggests that the chamber and solar directly above it formed a wing of the manor house. The solar was the principal private apartment of the medieval house where the lord's family could escape from the noise and bustle of the manor's communal hall. A mid-fifteenth century solar, restored by Edwin Lutyens, has survived at Great Dixter, a manor house in Sussex. Interestingly, Dixter (as it was originally known) was also partly owned by the Windsor family in the late fifteenth century. Their coat of arms appears on one of the spandrels of the fireplace installed in the solar when Andrew Windsor held half of Dixter through marriage to the heiress Margaret Blount. Today the house is owned by the Lloyd family.

Adjoining Clarice's chamber was an oratory or private chapel. Oratories had become fashionable in manor houses by the mid-fourteenth century, as reflected in the increase in the issue of oratory licences at that time. Next to the chamber were chimneys, though it is not clear from the dowry whether these belonged to the chamber, the hall or some other room in the manor. A cellar was also included in the dowry. In medieval times, a cellar was a storage room on the ground floor of the house. The manor of West Hagbourne appears to have included all the comforts available to the medieval lord and lady at that time.

Beyond the house itself, Clarice's dowry included all the dwellings between the chamber and the "great gate" towards the north. There was also a little grange to the north which may well have been a granary. Clarice was entitled to a well, a dovecote, the pond by the north gate, the kitchen and bakehouses. Only big houses had kitchens in Clarice's time, and they were built separately from the house. The dowry also granted Clarice a third of the gardens to the rear of her chamber. These were most likely to have been kitchen gardens which would have provided Clarice with fresh seasonal produce. She was granted 91 acres of arable land, as well as 1½ acres, 26 perches and 12 feet of pasture, and a third of the annual income from both the pasture on the downs and the woods. She was also entitled to the rents from the existing tenants, which amounted to 49 shillings, five pence and three farthings. In addition she received one hen per year from one tenant (probably a cottar). For her part, Clarice was to follow the rulings of the manorial courts with regard to the observance of common land, with particular reference to the pasture for the grazing of oxen. This was an important right for the tenants whose livelihoods depended on the ox to drive the plough. Clarice's dowry appears to have been a lawful and fair document, taking into account both the needs of a young widow and the livelihoods of the tenants.

The running of a manorial estate of this size clearly required a whole band of people, including appointed administrators and servants drawn from the village tenants. The whole community would have used one of the bakehouses mentioned in Clarice's dowry, as it was far too dangerous to have ovens in the flimsy dwellings of the villagers. In medieval times it was customary for everyone to use both the manorial mill and oven and there are many records of villagers in some areas being fined for not baking their bread in the lord's oven. The design of the early ovens was fairly consistent; being beehive-shaped domes of brick or stone, built within the masonry of a chimney stack or bakehouse wall. One can imagine the area around the kitchens and bakehouses at the manor house becoming a central focus of village life, particularly for the women.

These details of Clarice's dowry give us a unique glimpse into the kind of life enjoyed by those fortunate enough to live in a medieval manor house. Furthermore it reveals the names of some of the ordinary tenants of Windsor manor who lived in West Hagbourne in the latter half of the fourteenth century. The dowry lists the names of all the tenants who were supposed to pay rent to Clarice, and the amounts payable:

Thomas Modford: 13s 1d
Alice Sweyn: 6s 9d
John Bate: 14s
John Kete: 13s 4d
Richard Robekyn: 3¾d
Thomas Stotland: 2s
Henry Parminter: 1 hen per year

One of these, Richard Robekyn, was a witness to the assignment of the dowry which indicates that the signing of documents took place at the manor itself and that tenants were called to witness the event. The field names mentioned in the dowry were: Estmede, Westmede, Southfeld, Weye Forlong, Brokforlong, Renydiche, Roggerscherd and Nicholasforlong. The name of the area known today as Scotlands Ash, near the Horse and Harrow, is believed to be derived from Clarice's tenant Thomas Stotland and is thought to be the same piece of land he rented from the Windsor manor.

We know that when Clarice died in 1403, the manor house was in ruins because in the account drawn up of her holdings when she died (Inquisition Post Mortem) it stated that she held one "ruinous messuage".

Claricia Yorke uxor Rici Windesore Westhakeborne unum meffuagium ruinofum due carucate terre decem acre prati et quinque folid' redditus...

The income from rent had dropped considerably in the 36 years since Clarice received her dowry. This may have been because the Windsor manor was in ruins and the tenants were renting land and property belonging to West Hagbourne's second manor. The property tax payable by the heirs of the Windsor manor at the time of Clarice's death was 5 marks (£3 6s 8d). A mark was a monetary unit representing the weight of pure silver equal to 13s 4d.

The Windsor family lost its connection with West Hagbourne in the seventeenth century when Richard Windsor sold the manor to Stephen Thompson of London for £600 in 1661. It soon changed hands again until it was acquired by the Pocock family with whom it remained for nearly two centuries, though it was constantly let out to tenants. It may have been the Pococks who rebuilt the manor on the original site in the latter half of the seventeenth century. When it was rented out to William Nelson by Giles Pocock in 1665, the manor consisted of a manor house, a malt house, a foddening house, ox house, dovecote, stables, three barns and gardens. By 1767 when J Bosley was the tenant, the dovecote had been replaced by a pigeon house but otherwise it remained much the same. In 1889 the manor was sold to Eli and Leopold Caudwell of Blewbury and was eventually bought by Dennis Napper in 1909 on the death of Eli Caudwell. Dennis Napper's daughter, Eliza (Tize), inherited Manor Farm and when she married John Lay in 1917, it came to the Lay family who still own and farm it today.

All that is now left of Clarice's dowry is the pond, the possible vestiges of a moat and the land itself which is still mostly farmland to the south and west of the village. The oldest part of Manor Farm, built on the site of the Windsor manor, is late seventeenth century.

Watlingtons manor

It was not unusual for a parish to have more than one manor and West Hagbourne was no exception. The second manor was called Watlingtons and stood on the site of Grove Manor Farm. The origin of Watlingtons is not as well documented as the history of the Windsor manor and the source of the name remains unknown. 'The Victoria History of Berkshire' suggests that Watlingtons could have been the hide of land referred to in West Hagbourne's entry in the Domesday Book:

> *Robert holds 1 hide of this land from Walter; he has 1 plough, with 1 cottager; meadow, 4 acres.*

The hide which Robert rented from Walter was farmed independently of the rest of the manorial land as Robert had his own plough, a cottar to labour for him and a further four acres of meadow for grazing. This land continued to be regarded as a separate holding as subsequent documents relating to land transfers all identified it as distinct from the Windsor manor, even when both were held by the same lord.

The village pond

Robert's hide in 1086 (Domesday Book)
|
Edmund de Chelrey
acquired Watlingtons manor in 1355
d. 1372

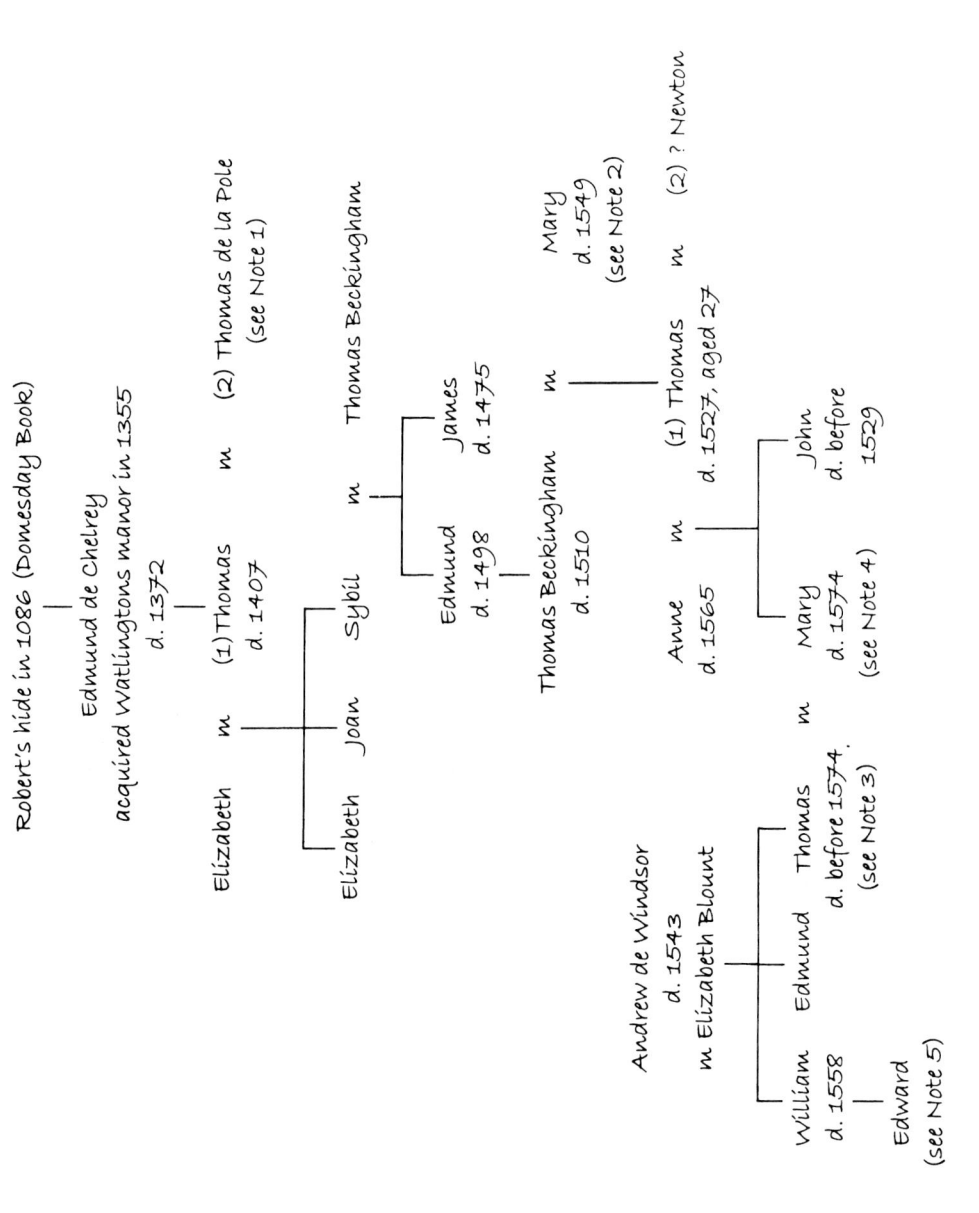

Elizabeth m (1) Thomas   m   (2) Thomas de la Pole
                 d. 1407   (see Note 1)

Elizabeth   Joan   Sybil   m   Thomas Beckingham
                           |
                    Edmund   James
                    d. 1498   d. 1475
                       |
               Thomas Beckingham
                    d. 1510
                       |
            Anne   m   (1) Thomas   Mary   m   (2) ? Newton
            d. 1565   d. 1527, aged 27   d. 1549
                                          (see Note 2)
               |
       Mary   John
       d. 1574   d. before
       (see Note 4)   1529

Andrew de Windsor
d. 1543
m. Elizabeth Blount
        |
William   Edmund   Thomas
d. 1558   d. before 1574.
                       (see Note 3)
Edward
(see Note 5)

NOTES

1 Thomas de la Pole held West Hagbourne in name of his wife, widow of Thomas de Chelrey

2 Mary Beckingham survived her husband, son and grandson. Passed Watlingtons to her granddaughter Mary Beckingham

3 The Windsors regained Watlingtons and Windsor manors through marriage of Thomas de Windsor to Mary Beckingham.

4 Mary Beckingham inherited Watlingtons through marriage of Chelreys and Beckinghams, and inherited Windsor manor from her mother, Anne Newton (widow)

5 Edward de Windsor conveyed Windsor manor to Ann Newton

The descent of Watlingtons manor through the intermarriage of Chelreys, Beckinghams and Windsors

When Sir Edmund de Chelrey acquired Watlingtons in 1355 (not Edmund, earl of Cornwall, as construed by the Lysons), it consisted of a *messuage* and one *carucate*, which was the equivalent of a hide – the same amount of land held by Robert in 1086. Since Walter held the manor of West Hagbourne at the time of the Domesday Book, the hide of land which Robert rented from Walter must have been part of the manorial land in 1086. It is not known when the land acquired the name of Watlingtons or when it became a manor but it was already known as Watlingtons manor when Edmund de Chelrey bought it in 1355. It was never called 'Chelreys' as erroneously stated in 'The Victoria History of Berkshire', though locals may have referred to it by that name when the de Chelrey family owned it.

Edmund de Chelrey was a justice of the king's bench and handled legal affairs for Queen Philippa, wife of Edward III. It is thought that he was well rewarded for his services to the crown as Watlingtons was only the first of many properties he acquired in Berkshire, including Frethornes, one of three manors in Childrey; the other two being Mautravers (Maltravers) and Rampayns (Rampanes). The de Chelreys had held land there for many years and probably took their family name from the parish which was called Chelrey in the fourteenth century. The de Chelreys held Watlingtons until 1411 when it was acquired by the Beckingham family through marriage.

Watlingtons eventually passed back into the Windsor family in 1549 through the marriage of Thomas Windsor, younger son of Sir Andrew, to Mary Beckingham, a descendant of Edmund de Chelrey and heiress of both Watlingtons and Windsor manors. She inherited Watlingtons through the Chelreys and Windsor manor from her mother, Anne Newton, who had been granted the manor by Edward de Windsor following a dispute between his father's widow and his uncle Edmund over the intentions of his grandfather's will. Anne Newton's ancestry is not clear but it is assumed that she was the widow of Mary's father, Thomas Beckingham, and that she married into the Newton family after his relatively early death. She could also have been born into a branch of the Windsor family. By conveying Windsor manor to the mother-in-law of his uncle, Thomas Windsor, Edward ensured that the manor would continue to be held by the Windsor family.

Richard Windsor finally sold the two manors in the 1660s. For the next 250 years Watlingtons was owned by various families, including the Sherwoods, Pollens and Aldworths. It was sold at auction in 1919 by the widow of John Aldworth, a wealthy landowner of West Hagbourne. The land belonging to Grove Manor Farm, as Watlingtons was by then known, had greatly increased from Robert's original hide to 480 acres of land, 15 cottages and extensive homesteads, one of which was York Farm. Dennis Napper bought Grove Manor Farm at the auction and it has remained in the Napper family ever since. There is no sign of the original manor house of Watlingtons, though the present house, built in the late seventeenth century, still retains some of its original features.

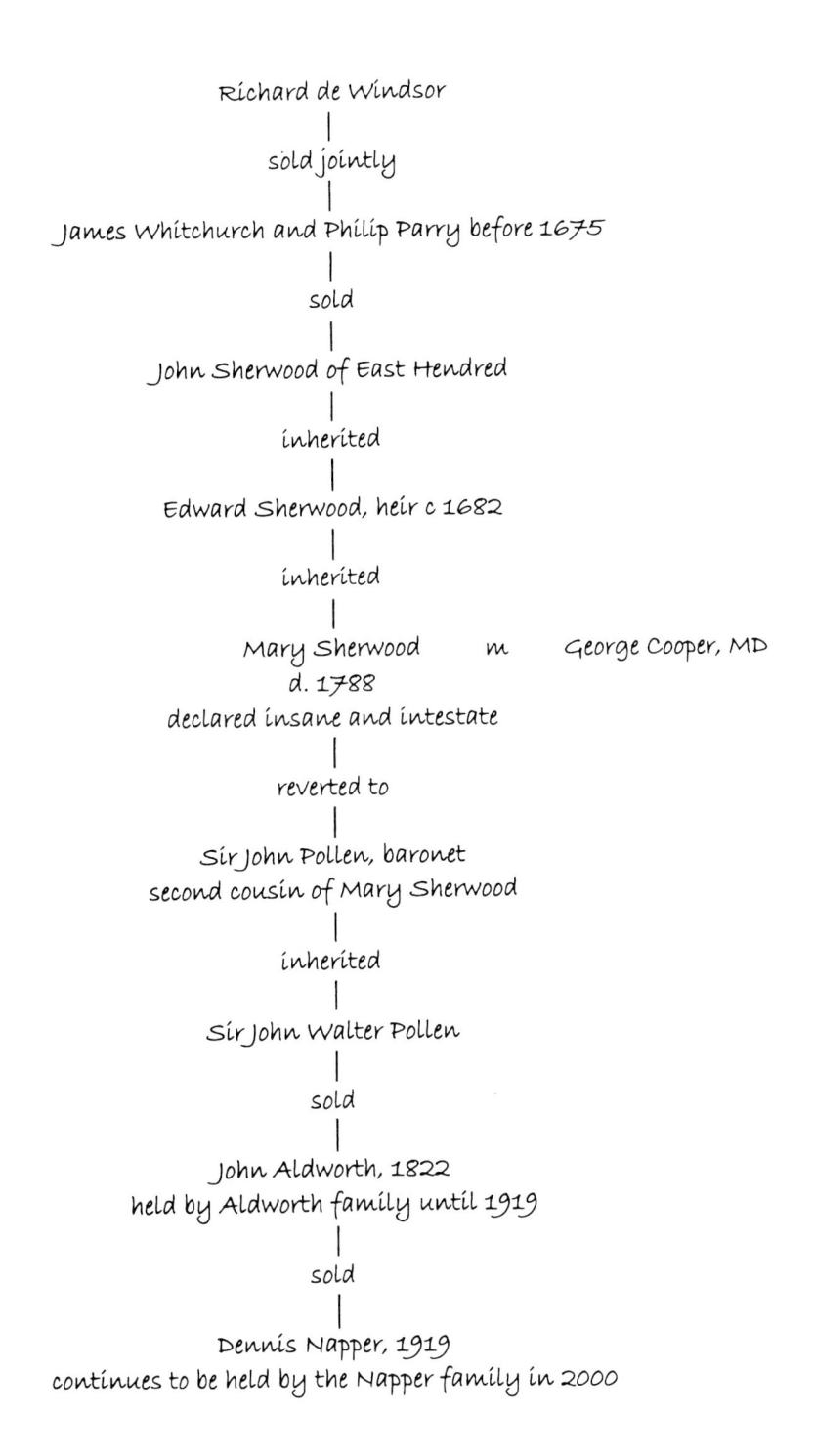

Richard de Windsor
|
sold jointly
|
James Whitchurch and Philip Parry before 1675
|
sold
|
John Sherwood of East Hendred
|
inherited
|
Edward Sherwood, heir c 1682
|
inherited
|
Mary Sherwood   m   George Cooper, MD
d. 1788
declared insane and intestate
|
reverted to
|
Sir John Pollen, baronet
second cousin of Mary Sherwood
|
inherited
|
Sir John Walter Pollen
|
sold
|
John Aldworth, 1822
held by Aldworth family until 1919
|
sold
|
Dennis Napper, 1919
continues to be held by the Napper family in 2000

The descent of Watlingtons manor 1600–2000

Compared with some of the Windsors' other holdings, which included abbeys and church land handed over to them during the Reformation, their manorial estates in West Hagbourne were quite small, but the rights to the land were fiercely guarded by each successive generation, frequently through marriage. Their sale of West Hagbourne's manors, after 600 years of lordship, coincided with the disintegration of the manorial system itself. The system started to crumble with the attainment of free status for serfs. In 1350 half the population of England was made up of serfs but by 1600 there were none. The Black Death of 1348, which killed off at least a third of the population, caused huge labour shortages and the higher wages demanded by the surviving workforce hastened its end.

The Windsor dynasty

As well as indicating the material assets of the village, the Domesday Book introduces us to some of the influential characters of the period. We meet Walter, the son of Other, sometimes referred to as Walter fitz Other. In 1086, Walter held considerable land and property in several counties, including six sites in Berkshire, one of which was West Hagbourne.

Before the Norman Conquest, West Hagbourne's manor and estates were held by the freeman Alwin. Like many others, Alwin had to relinquish his tenancy after 1066 when most Saxon land was handed over to the Norman knights who had accompanied William on the Conquest. During the time of Edward the Confessor (1042–1066), Alwin had held considerable property in the Berkshire area, including land in the Reading, Wantage, Bucklebury, Compton and Thatcham Hundreds, but he lost it all after the Conquest.

Walter was made first constable (*castellane*) of Windsor Castle which William the Conqueror built in Windsor forest as one of a chain of defensive fortresses dominating the Thames Valley. Walter's power was further extended when he became warden of all the Berkshire forests. Walter's seat of power was Stanwell on the north bank of the Thames between Old Windsor and Staines. Old Windsor was an ancient seat of the Saxon kings about two miles from New Windsor. Edward the Confessor had a hall there where he held his court. King William visited Old

The Windsor coat of arms

Windsor in 1077 and it is thought that he may have conferred these honours on Walter at that time. Stanwell was previously held by Azor, one of King Edward's guards. Walter, anticipating the present royal family by several hundred years, assumed the surname de Windsor and founded the Windsor dynasty which held the manorial estate of West Hagbourne for nearly 600 years.

In his rather idealized account of the Windsors, written in 1879, C W Williams claimed that their ancestry went back to the days of King Alfred (871–899). Alfred wrote about a powerful Norse Viking called Othoere whose descendants held considerable power in Saxon England. A P Smyth, in his recent book 'King Alfred the Great', says that among the documented visitors to the court of King Alfred was a Norwegian sailor and trader named Ohthere. It is possible that Walter de Windsor's father Other may have been a descendant of the Viking, though Arthur Collins, writing in 1754, suggested that he might have been a descendant of the dukes of Tuscany who came to England via Normandy from Florence. The Harley pedigree (herald's visitation) of the Windsor family describes Other as a Norman, descended from the noble Florentine family of Fitzgiroldes. Whatever the truth of the matter, the Windsors revived the name, in the form Other, in 1560 and have continued to use it as a Christian name to the present day.

Many Windsors played a prominent role in the affairs of state, being the confidants of kings and queens as well as staunch royalists during the many wars which followed the Conquest. They were proud of their ancestry and their links with William the Conqueror. They were also strongly patriotic, as can be seen in the following quotation from Williams's monograph:

> *The English nobleman who can claim a companion of the Conqueror as his ancestor, and who feels that the honour of a long and unbroken line of illustrious progenitors is in his keeping, inherits a grand patrimony, and has incentives to live a life of noble deeds and patriotic usefulness additional to other men.*

In 1194 William de Windlesore (as the name was then spelled) accompanied Richard I to Normandy on his expedition against the French but did not return, presumably having died in battle. William's eldest son Walter then inherited the Windsor estates and titles but he had no sons. In 1198, therefore, he divided the barony between himself and his younger brother William, who was given the "Lordship of Hakeburn with the appurtenances; Stanwell and the Meres, with the appurtenances; and the advowson of the Church of Stanwell" and much else.

Thus, the manor of West Hagbourne and the family seat at Stanwell were both held by William, now called Lord Stanwell, the title of baron having been lost when the barony was divided between the two brothers. It was not to be revived until the reign of Henry VIII, over 300 years later. The lords of Stanwell continued to flourish in the service of various kings in wars and expeditions both at home and abroad and they maintained their hold on their seat at Stanwell and the manor of West Hagbourne.

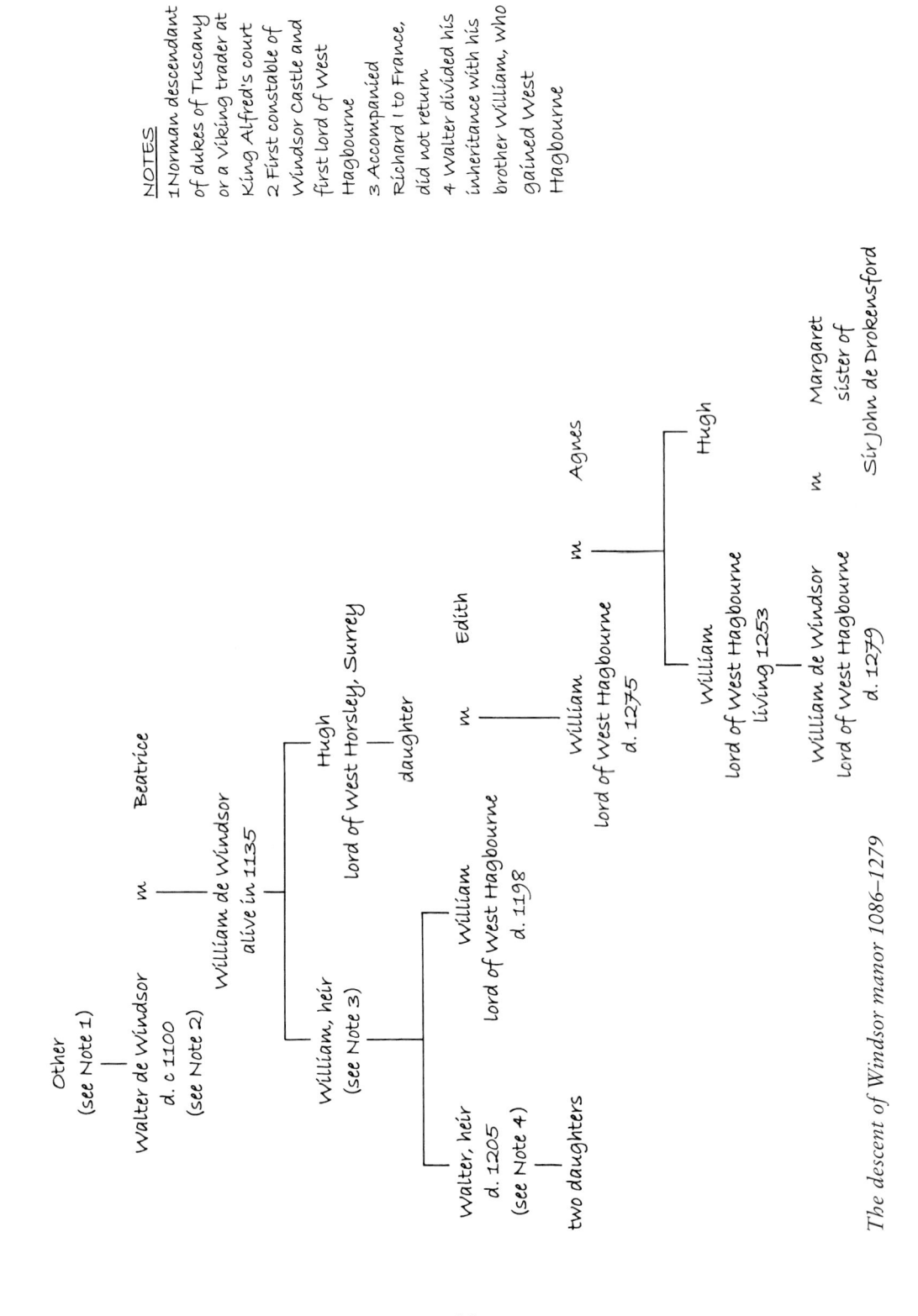

```
Other
(see Note 1)
   │
Walter de Windsor
d. c 1100
(see Note 2)
   │
   ├── m ── Beatrice
   │
William de Windsor
alive in 1135
   │
   ├─────────────────────┐
William, heir            Hugh
(see Note 3)             Lord of West Horsley, Surrey
   │                        │
   │                     daughter ── m ── Edith
William
Lord of West Hagbourne
d. 1198
   │
   ├─────────────────────┐
Walter, heir            William
d. 1205                 Lord of West Hagbourne
(see Note 4)            d. 1275
   │                       │
two daughters              │── m ── Agnes
                           │
                  ┌────────┴────────┐
                William              Hugh
                Lord of West Hagbourne
                Living 1253
                   │
                William de Windsor ── m ── Margaret
                Lord of West Hagbourne      sister of
                d. 1279                     Sir John de Drokensford
```

The descent of Windsor manor 1086–1279

NOTES

1 Norman descendant of dukes of Tuscany or a Viking trader at King Alfred's court
2 First constable of Windsor castle and first Lord of West Hagbourne
3 Accompanied Richard I to France, did not return
4 Walter divided his inheritance with his brother William, who gained West Hagbourne

Thomas Windsor, who was sympathetic to the claims of Henry Tudor to the English throne, died at the Battle of Bosworth in 1485. His son, Andrew Windsor, received several honours from Henry VIII, including Knight of the Bath on the occasion of Henry's coronation in 1509. Sir Andrew was the third knight of 26 of the "most noble persons and of honourable blood, and of ancient houses, to take the order of knighthood". In 1513 Sir Andrew accompanied Henry on an expedition against France and was made a knight banneret for his "valiant behaviour" at the battle of the Spurs – a banneret being a knighthood conferred for valour on the battlefield.

After many other illustrious services to Henry VIII, including being one of the Temporal Lords who signed the celebrated letter to Pope Clement VII demanding a divorce from Queen Catherine, Sir Andrew Windsor was elevated to the peerage. He was created "Baron Windsor of Bradenham, in the county of Buckinghamshire", Bradenham being another holding which Andrew Windsor had purchased in 1505.

The barony was once more restored to the Windsors but they lost their seat at Stanwell in 1541 when Henry VIII forced Sir Andrew to exchange it for Bordesley Manor in Worcestershire. Henry insisted on having Stanwell for himself after being royally entertained there by Sir Andrew, despite the latter's protestations that it had been his family's seat for centuries. However, once Sir Andrew saw that the king was determined to have Stanwell and had already drawn up deeds of exchange, he abandoned Stanwell with a dignity which reflected the old Windsor family spirit and pride. He had already laid in provisions for entertaining guests at Christmas and he left these behind, saying "they should not find it bare at Stanwell".

William, the second Lord Windsor of Bradenham, built a new manor house there around 1545, possibly in response to losing the Windsor seat at Stanwell. Unfortunately much of it was destroyed by fire during the Civil War but the present Badenham manor, now owned by The National Trust, has a room named in memory of the Windsors.

Andrew's grandson Edward found favour with Queen Elizabeth I and he entertained her at Bradenham in 1566 when she stopped there on her way back to London after a visit to Oxford University. His sons Frederick and Henry were also popular with the queen and were known for their deeds of chivalry and their prowess at jousting. Frederick died unmarried and Henry's son Thomas died without male issue in 1605. At this point the barony again fell into abeyance to be revived later when another Thomas Windsor, a royalist who fought bravely at the Battle of Naseby against Cromwell, had the barony of Windsor restored to him by the king. It fell into abeyance yet again in the 1600s through the lack of a male heir. In 1682, Thomas Windsor was made first Earl of Plymouth in recognition of his services in the war with Spain. It was Thomas Windsor who revived the Christian name Other when he gave that name to his son and heir after a lapse of 600 years. The Earls of Plymouth have continued to keep the names Other and Windsor in their titles to this day. The current earl at the time of writing is named Other Robert Ivor Windsor-Clive and he has a sister called Lady Clarissa, perhaps in memory of Clarice de Windsor of West Hagbourne.

The lady of the manor

Following the redistribution of land after the Conquest, landowners sometimes held property in more than one place and these sites were often quite far apart, making them difficult to manage. Many lords, like the Windsors, were knights engaged in foreign wars and had to rely on paid agents to run their manorial estates. Sometimes, however, members of the lord's family did occupy a *messuage* other than the family seat. There is strong evidence to suggest that some members of the Windsor family were living in the manor house of West Hagbourne during the late medieval period.

In 1325, at the age of 27, Richard de Windsor inherited the manor of West Hagbourne, the Windsor seat at Stanwell, and the wardenship of Windsor Castle from his father, also called Richard. He had three wives: Joan who bore him a daughter; Juliana who provided him with two sons called James and William; and finally Clarice Drokensford who was much younger and outlived him. Richard de Windsor died in 1367 at the age of 69 and was buried at Stanwell, but by then his heir, James, had already died. The next heir, Richard's grandson Miles, the son of James, was too young to take up his inheritance.

After Richard's death, an Inquisition Post Mortem was carried out for every county in which he held land. Inquisitions Post Mortem were hearings conducted before a royal executor on the death of anyone who held land directly from the crown. Their main purpose was to ensure that the various property taxes due to the king were levied. The Post Mortem identified the name of the heir, his age and the value of the property in terms of the number of knights the king could claim for his service. Originally a knight's military service amounted to 40 days a year. Rather than sending a knight in person, the lord or holder of the property paid the equivalent of a knight's service which the king then used to hire mercenaries. Some properties were not equal to the value of a whole knight and would be valued at a half, or even a quarter, of a knight's fee.

In cases where land reverted to the king because the heir was a minor, the property was assigned to a ward who held it until the heir came of age. The wardship could be transferred with the king's permission and on payment of a tax. The inheritance always passed through the male line but widows or sisters could hold land until a male came of age or they married, in which case the husband would then hold the land on their behalf. Males could not inherit until the age of 21 but females came of age at fourteen.

The Post Mortem for Richard de Windsor's property in Berkshire was held at Newbury on the 3rd of June 1367. The only property he held in Berkshire was West Hagbourne which was valued at one knight's service. The heir was identified as Richard's grandson Miles, a minor. A writ was then issued to the executor of Berkshire to assign a dowry to Richard de Windsor's widow Clarice (variously spelled Clarica, Clarisa or Clarissa). The dowry consisted of one third of the manors of West Hagbourne and Stanwell. This was done according to provisions on dower laid down in the Magna Carta. In law, dower was a wife's right to life tenancy of one third of her husband's lands after his death. The dower was free and had to be assigned within 40 days of the husband's death. The granting of Clarice's dowry was contingent upon her swearing on oath that she would not remarry without the king's licence. The swearing of the oath was done with considerable speed in the presence of Helmingus Leget (sometimes referred to as Helming or Helmyng Legatt) on the 7th of July 1367.

The assignment of the dowry for her share of Westhakeborne, as it was spelled in the Court Rolls, was made by John de Evesham, the executor for Berkshire, in the presence of Sir John de Flete, attorney for Helmingus Leget. Also present were Gilbert de Hakeborne, Ellis Hereward, John Coke, Richard Robekyn, and others. Clarice's share of Stanmore, the Windsor seat, was assigned three days earlier, on the 23rd of July 1367, by the executor for Middlesex, and witnessed again by Sir John de Flete for Helmingus Leget. The other witnesses were local tenants "and neighbours".

Helmingus Leget, as the king's esquire, was given wardship of the remainder of the manors of West Hagbourne and Stanwell until the heir, Miles de Windsor, should come of age. This explains why his attorney, Sir John de Flete, was present at the assignment of the dowries for both West Hagbourne and Stanwell. In 1369 Helmingus Leget surrendered his wardship of Richard de Windsor's properties to the king who then granted them to Adam de Wymondham, a London textile merchant whose daughter was later to marry the heir, Miles de Windsor. On the death of Clarice in 1403 West Hagbourne reverted back to the king, as the next heir, Richard, son of the late Brian de Windsor and grandson of Miles, was also too young to inherit. This time, all the lands in West Hagbourne (there is no mention of the manor house in this Calendar of Fine Rolls, probably because it was in ruins) were committed into the keeping of Laurence Drue (Drewe), another lawyer in the king's service, until such time as a Windsor heir should come of age. Drue continued to hold the wardship the following year, subject to the payment of an annual property tax of 6 marks (an increase of 13s 4d on the previous year).

When Clarice died she held the whole of the Windsor estate in West Hagbourne. She had previously exchanged her share in the Stanwell manor for the other two thirds of the Windsor manor with Miles de Windsor when he came into his inheritance. It seems that she was prepared to lose her share in the Windsor seat at Stanwell to keep all of the Windsor's West Hagbourne estate.

Helmingus Leget was an attorney who served Edward III in various roles, from collecting debts owed to the king by the merchants the City of London, to "receiver of the king's chamber and keeper of the keys of the coffers of jewels and money". At the time of the swearing of Clarice's oath his title was king's esquire.

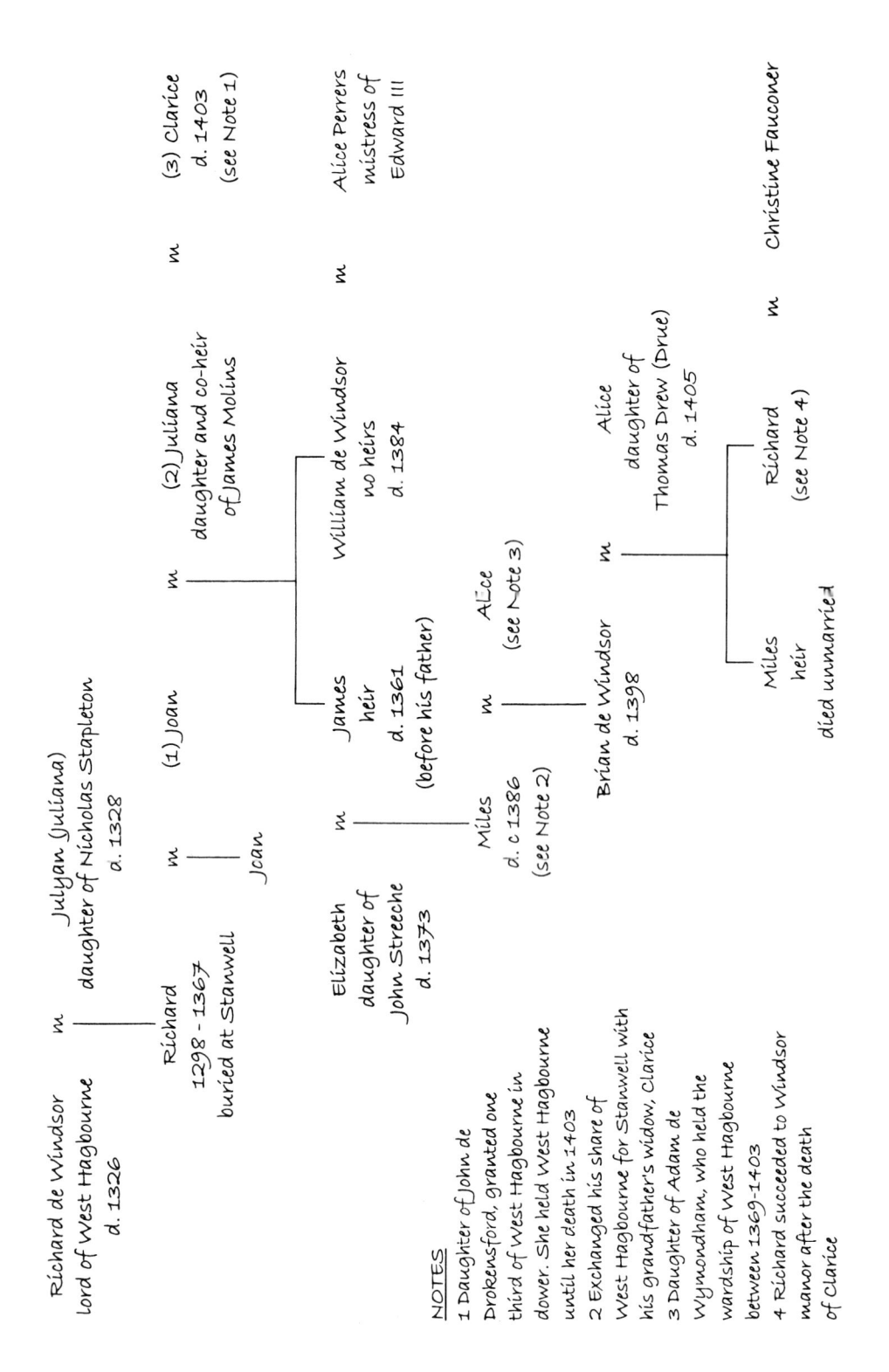

```
Richard de Windsor  m  Julyan (Juliana)
Lord of West Hagbourne    daughter of Nicholas Stapleton
d. 1326                   d. 1328
                    │
                 Richard                m   (1) Joan    (2) Juliana              m   (3) Clarice
                 1298-1367                              daughter and co-heir          d. 1403
                 buried at Stanwell                     of James Molins               (see Note 1)
                    │
        ┌───────────┴─────────────────────┐
        │                                 │
     Elizabeth        m     James       William de Windsor    m    Alice Perrers
     daughter of            heir        no heirs                   mistress of
     John Streeche          d. 1361     d. 1384                    Edward III
     d. 1373                (before his father)
        │
   ┌────┴────┐
   │    Joan  │
  Miles           Alice                Brian de Windsor    m    Alice
  d. c1386        (see Note 3)         d. 1398                  daughter of
  (see Note 2)                                                  Thomas Drew (Drue)
                                                                d. 1405
                                            ┌───────────────────┤
                                         Miles              Richard           m   Christine Fauconer
                                         heir               (see Note 4)
                                         died unmarried
```

NOTES

1 Daughter of John de Drokensford, granted one third of West Hagbourne in dower. She held West Hagbourne until her death in 1403

2 Exchanged his share of West Hagbourne for Stanwell with his grandfather's widow, Clarice

3 Daughter of Adam de Wymondham, who held the wardship of West Hagbourne between 1369-1403

4 Richard succeeded to Windsor manor after the death of Clarice

The Descent of Windsor manor from 1326 until the death of Clarice in 1403

Three hundred years after Richard de Windsor's ancestor Walter had the honour of becoming the first constable of Windsor Castle, Helmingus Leget was also granted this favour in 1369 "for gratuitous service long rendered to the king". Leget came from Essex but his family home, Pondhall, was in Hadleigh, Suffolk. He applied for a licence to crenellate this house in 1371, suggesting that Leget held himself in high regard to want to give his house the appearance of a castle. His daughter and heir, Anne, married into the noble d'Oyley family.

It is not clear why Helmingus Leget surrendered his wardship of Richard Windsor's estates but he was probably an old family friend of the Windsors, given both families' aristocratic connections at court. He was also a distant relative of Clarice through marriage, though he was never married to her himself, as wrongly stated in the 'The Victoria History of Berkshire'. His second wife was Alice Mandeville, the granddaughter of Clarice's brother, Thomas Drokensford. The Drokensford arms are incorporated into one quarter of the Leget family arms.

The Drokensfords were another family with strong links to the court. They took their name from the ancient manor of Drokeireford (later Droxford) in Hampshire. Drokeireford was one of the villages given to the priory of St Swithun at Winchester by the Wessex king, Egbert, in 826, when he conquered Mercia and annexed all the land south of the Thames. Through its links with the See of Winchester and the endowments it received from various kings, Drokeireford grew very wealthy. By 1646, when it was sold as part of the church lands of Winchester during the Civil War, the manor of Droxford was worth over £7,675.

The most distinguished member of the family during the reign of Edward I was Sir John de Drokensford, who rose from Keeper of the King's Wardrobe in 1305, to become the Bishop of Bath and Wells by 1308. On the evidence of several – sometimes contradictory – family histories (known as pedigrees) and various Close and Patent Rolls, the Drokensfords had complicated ties through marriage with the Windsors even before Clarice Drokensford married Richard de Windsor. Two generations previously, William de Windsor, one of the lords of Windsor manor who died in 1279, had married Margaret, sister of Sir John de Drokensford. John was a popular name in the Drokensford family and it has not been possible to ascertain exactly which John de Drokensford was her brother.

The Drokensford coat of arms

Clarice's father, also named John de Drokensford, is believed to be the son of Michael, one of the brothers of the Bishop of Bath and Wells. He was a clerk in the service of the king, an elevated position in late medieval times. He had two sons, Thomas and Michael. His heir, Thomas, was a knight who spent a lot of time abroad in the king's service. In 1305, the knight Richard de Windsor, son of Margaret Drokensford and William Windsor and father of Clarice's husband, received a licence to *enfeoff* his manors of West Hagbourne and Stanwell to John de Drokensford, Clarice's father. 'Enfeoffment to use' was a device whereby an individual conveyed legal tenure of land to someone else, often a tenant, whilst still retaining *de facto* control of the property. This suggests that John de Drokensford could have been a tenant of either West Hagbourne manor or the Windsor seat at Stanwell, though the former is more likely as the Windsor lords tended to live at Stanwell themselves. Richard de Windsor may have given this right of *enfeoff* to a relative because he was constantly away on the king's service and wanted John de Drokensford, a king's clerk, to have responsibility for his properties in his absence. He may also have been trying to avoid death duties or even forfeiture of land which could often be avoided through *enfeoff*. Richard de Windsor continued to *enfeoff* the Windsor manor to John Drokensford for more than 20 years which suggests that the Drokensfords had links with West Hagbourne long before Clarice married Richard de Windsor's son.

When John Drokensford died in 1341 he left a considerable amount of land in several counties including Somerset, Hampshire and Middlesex. Some of the property had been passed to him by his father Michael, the rector of Drokensford and some was held for life from his uncle John, the Bishop of Bath and Wells. His Inquisition Post Mortem also mentions valuable property he inherited for life from the estates of his late wife Margaret in Hertford and Essex.

Not only was Clarice born into the wealthy Drokensford family but she was also well-connected on her mother's side. Her mother, Margaret, became the heiress to the Tany (originally de Thany) family property when her brother Lawrence died in 1317 at the age of nineteen. Margaret de Tany was 16 at the time. The Tany's ancient family seat was Stapleford Tawney in Essex (named after the Tany family to differentiate it from Stapleford Abbots). The Tanys held land from the time of the Conquests. Henry III granted them hunting rights in the king's own forest of Essex, whilst Richard de Tany was made keeper of the Essex coast in 1295. They also owned the wealthy manor of Eastwick in Hertfordshire which was valued at three knights' service.

Clarice's brother Thomas died in 1361, leaving an only daughter Anne, who was four when her father died. She grew up to marry Thomas Mandeville and their son, also Thomas, inherited both the Drokensford and Tany properties but he died in 1400 without any heirs. His two sisters, Alice and Joan then shared the inheritance and Alice, the second wife of Helmingus Leget inherited the land which had been passed down from John and Margaret Drokensford, the parents of Clarice.

Drokensfords of Droxford, Hampshire

```
                    Philip de Drokensford        John de Drokensford
                           |
         ┌─────────────────┼──────────────────┐
    John                Michael            Philip
    Bishop of          Rector of         heir of John
    Bath and Wells     Droxford          the Bishop
    d. 1329            d. before 1332    d. 1356
                           |
                  John de Drokensford
                       d. 1341
                           |
                           m
                           |
                        Clarice        m    (1) Richard de Windsor
                        d. 1403                  d. 1367
                        (see Note 2)
         ┌──────────────────┼──────────────────┐
      Thomas             Anne                Joan         m    Helmingus Leget
      heir                                  Alice              held wardship of West
      d. 1362            m                  (see Note 5)       Hagbourne 1367-1369
                      Thomas Mandeville
                           |
                        Thomas
                        d. 1400
                        without heirs
                        (see Note 4)
```

Tanys of Stapleford Tawney, Essex

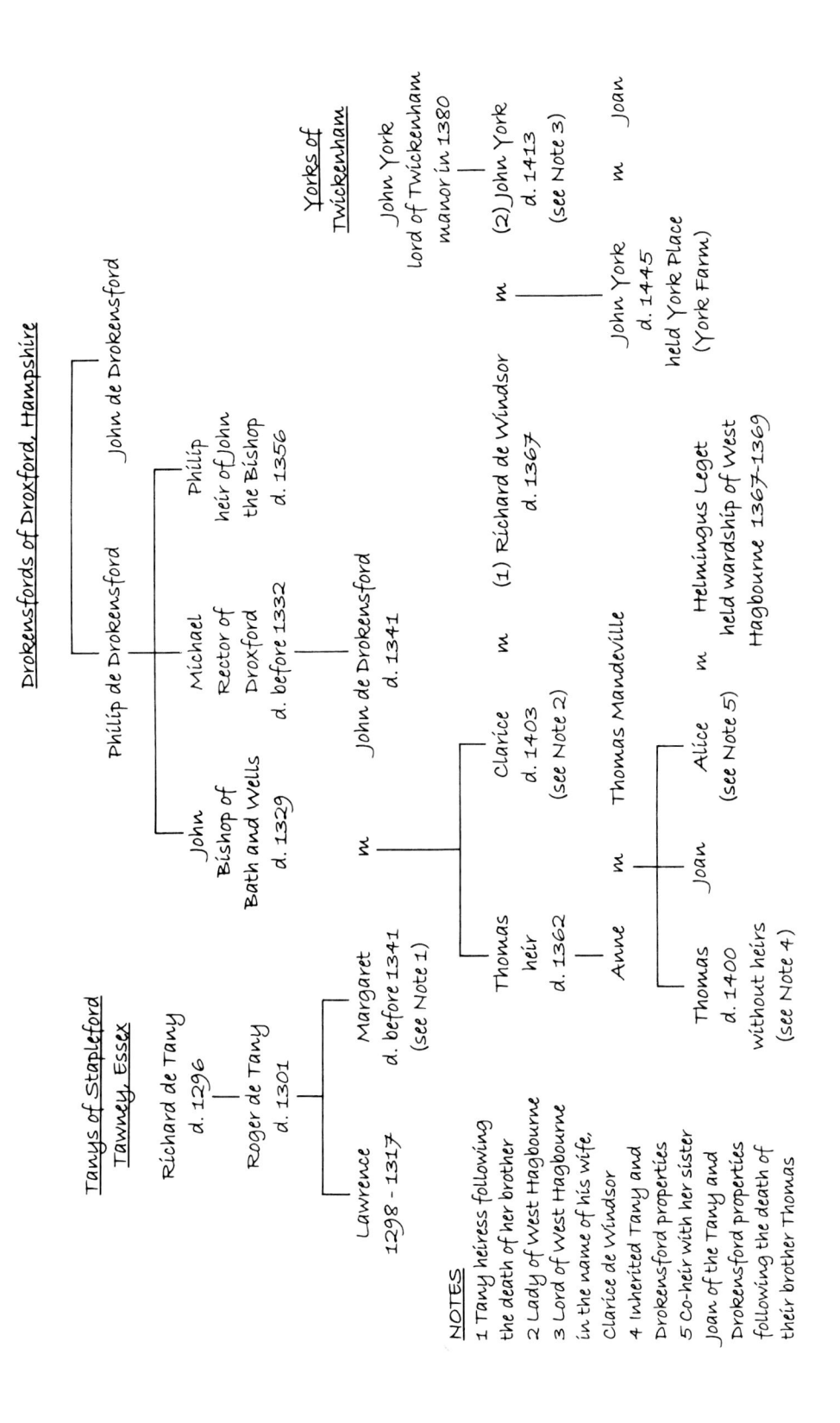

```
    Richard de Tany
    d. 1296
    Roger de Tany
    d. 1301
         |
    ┌────┴────┐
  Lawrence   Margaret
  1298-1317  d. before 1341
             (see Note 1)
```

Yorks of Twickenham

```
    John York
    Lord of Twickenham
    manor in 1380
         |
    (2) John York        m    Joan
    d. 1413
    (see Note 3)
         |
         m
         |
    John York
    d. 1445
    held York Place
    (York Farm)
```

NOTES

1 Tany heiress following the death of her brother
2 Lady of West Hagbourne
3 Lord of West Hagbourne in the name of his wife, Clarice de Windsor
4 Inherited Tany and Drokensford properties
5 Co-heir with her sister Joan of the Tany and Drokensford properties following the death of their brother Thomas

The pedigree of Clarice de Drokensford

Clarice's link with West Hagbourne did not end with the death of Richard de Windsor. Within less than six years of his death, Clarice had taken a second husband, John de Yorke (later York). His family came from Twickenham where John York's father acquired part of the manor of Isleworth in 1381. This vast estate had become known as Twickenham manor and York's Hold by the fifteenth century. Clarice's second husband, John York, inherited this land from his father in 1410, a few years before he died. The York line descended through John, the son of Clarice and her second husband. The Yorks continued to hold the Twickenham property through several generations. They also acquired manors in Chilton, West Lockinge and Wantage in the latter half of the fifteenth century. The Twickenham estates were finally lost to the Yorks in 1538 when Thomas York of Hilldrop manor, Ramsbury, in Wiltshire, sold them to the Earl of Hertford. Thomas York was the sheriff of Wiltshire and the great grandson of Clarice and John. He died in 1542 without any heirs.

John York was the first member of the York family to be associated with West Hagbourne and it is thought that he acquired rights to the land which later became known as York Place, now called York Farm, some time after marrying Clarice. It is conceivable that Clarice moved to York Place when she married John York and this could explain why the Windsor manor had fallen into ruin by the time of Clarice's death. The early history of York Place is speculative but it was a freehold of the Windsor manor for several centuries and was probably part of the holding of Walter, son of Other, in 1086.

When Clarice married John York she broke her oath and married without the king's permission. Clarice and John York were fined ten marks (nearly £7) for this crime but in 1373 they were pardoned by the king. This was not the first time that John York had received a pardon for committing some quite serious offences. He was a great friend of William de Windsor, the second son of Richard and the stepson of Clarice and the two had served the king together in Ireland. John York was indicted in 1360 for having "ravished Isabel late the wife of Thomas de Haryngton and carried her away... with her goods to the value of 5s". William de Windsor used his influence with the king to plead for a pardon for his friend on the grounds of John York's "good service in Ireland" with William. The pardon was

The York coat of arms

granted in 1364 and renewed the following year. There is no mention in the records of what became of poor Isabel de Haryngton.

William de Windsor himself was not without notoriety. As Lieutenant-Governor of Ireland from 1369 he imposed heavy taxes on the Irish people which were found to be unlawful as well as unpopular. He was recalled in 1372 whilst an enquiry into these taxes took place. He returned to Ireland as Governor in 1374 but was soon recalled again in 1376 to answer 36 charges against himself and others. These charges included the imposition of unlawful taxes, tyrannical misconduct and embezzlement in every department of government. He was briefly imprisoned in the Tower of London for taking bribes whilst in Ireland.

If William de Windsor seemed to be acting with impunity in Ireland, it may have been because he held an ace up his sleeve in the form of his wife, the celebrated Alice Perrers, mistress of Edward III. Alice Perrers held considerable sway at court which may explain how William was able to obtain a pardon for the misdemeanours of his friend John York. Shortly after William's return from Ireland, King Edward died and Alice Perrers was impeached for wasting the king's goods, bribery in the courts and illegal profiteering. The accusations were later squashed but her influence at court was over, though William de Windsor was later able to recover some of his wife's property.

Later, John and Clarice received yet another pardon, this time from Richard II. When Miles, the Windsor heir, exchanged his two thirds of the West Hagbourne estates for Clarice's share of the Windsor's main seat at Stanwell, the Yorks were fined 20s for completing this exchange without a licence. Once again their influence at court brought them a pardon from the king sometime between 1391 and 1396.

By the time of Clarice's death in 1403, the Windsor manor house of West Hagbourne was in ruins and the income from rents much reduced. Clarice also held other property in West Hagbourne in joint ownership with her son John who was 24 when she died. She left five houses, 80 acres of arable land and four acres of meadow in the York name.

The marriage of the young Clarice de Drokensford to the elderly Richard de Windsor, his heir having predeceased him, is a good example of the medieval attitude to marriage. The purpose of marriage amongst the landowning classes was to provide heirs, thus keeping the property within the family. This explains why female heirs could inherit at a much younger age than male heirs. The property could then be held in their names until a male heir came of age, or a suitable husband could be found. Women were often married to men much older than themselves, often outliving several husbands. They could not inherit titles (the Windsor barony died out for a time in 1198 for the lack of a male heir). When they did marry, their property was automatically held by their husband, as happened when Clarice married John York. He held the Windsor manor in his name until Clarice's death in 1403, when it reverted back to the Windsors.

Clarice was a member of the aristocracy, born into the well-connected Drokensford and Tany families and married into the noble line of Windsors. Her second husband John York held vast estates and became one of the most important and influential landowners in West Hagbourne. In medieval times women shared the social status of their husbands even though they were subject to them. They were also accorded superior status to any males of a lower order than that of their husbands. Thus, despite being a woman, Clarice de Windsor would have held an important position in the social structure of West Hagbourne in the late fourteenth century. Apart from the surviving written records, there are few tangible reminders of the Windsors in West Hagbourne today, though the Yorks gave their name to a farm and a road. However, the memory of Clarice and John York is very much alive in St Andrew's Church in East Hagbourne where they were buried and where they are commemorated through their brasses. The brass commemorating Clarice reflects her status as lady of the manor and is strong evidence that Clarice lived in West Hagbourne.

> *Here lies Claricia Wyndesore one time Lady of Westhakburn and wife of John York who caused this chapel to be built and died on the 22nd day of March in the year of our Lord 1403 on whose soul God have mercy, Amen*

The medieval cross of West Hagbourne

Although nothing remains of it today, enough documents and anecdotal evidence exist to indicate that there was once a cross in West Hagbourne. The earliest written record referring to this medieval cross is a rental survey of land and property in West Hagbourne held by the knight Thomas de la Pole and his wife Elizabeth. Thomas de la Pole held the land through his wife who inherited it after the death of her first husband Thomas de Chelrey, the lord of Watlingtons manor. The survey took place some time in 1410 or 1411 and identifies the successive tenants of land and property held by Thomas and Elizabeth de la Pole from the heirs of Richard de Windsor. The survey names the tenants and identifies their holdings and the amount of rent paid to the de la Poles. The total value of the rental was 100 shillings per year.

Part of the original rental survey is torn, badly damaged by damp and illegible but at least 15 *messuages* (houses), three cottages and a croft can all be identified in the manuscript. West Hagbourne's cross is mentioned in relation to the holding of Richard Wyndeford who "holds one messuage with curtilage formerly of Elias Skynner at the High Cross in the Vill of Westhakeborne". This is the first piece of written evidence that West Hagbourne did once have its own cross. It must have been situated within the village as the survey mentions a house nearby. It may have stood near the pond, not far from the original chapel and manor, or it could equally have stood at the crossroads now called the Square and once occupied by the village stocks, or even at the approach to West Hagbourne near Grove Manor Farm. Some commentators have assumed that this "High Cross" was at Coscote where the stump of a cross remains today. However, the document clearly states that the cross was in the "Vill of Westhakeborne". Coscote was much larger in the Middle Ages than it is today, having then at least six houses. It has always been part of the parish of East Hagbourne and its tithes were always included with those paid by East Hagbourne. The rental survey tells us that the house and land which Richard Wyndeford, and before him, Elias Skynner, rented near the cross belonged to the manor of West Hagbourne which never owned Coscote.

Several people have recorded their own memories of the existence of various medieval crosses in the Hagbournes and many myths and legends have grown out of these sometimes contradictory reports. In a paper read to the Berkshire Archaeological Society in 1912, Charles Keyser, Fellow of the Society, identified three crosses in Hagbourne (he did not differentiate between East and West): "a large Village Cross near the Church, a second in the hamlet of Crosscot, and a third in the hedge between the main village and hamlet", that is, between East Hagbourne and Coscote. Strangely, he makes no mention of the remains of the medieval cross which today shares a raised mound with the War Memorial in East Hagbourne and is now referred to as Lower Cross.

Keyser suggests that the presence of the three crosses, together with the ancient knocker on the fourteenth century north door of the church, have given rise to the tradition that the area between the crosses was a place of sanctuary for those fleeing pursuit, whether as common criminals or political fugitives. This suggestion has taken hold in the imagination of many subsequent commentators but there is no evidence to support Keyser's theory. There is no documentation of anyone ever seeking sanctuary in St Andrew's Church, nor indeed that the knocker on the church door was a symbol of sanctuary. Furthermore there is no history of crosses being used to mark areas of sanctuary. Crosses were often erected at crossroads,

The Lower Cross, East Hagbourne

many being market crosses providing a focus for people to gather and to sell local produce, giving rise to 'butter crosses' which are still in existence today in some market towns.

In a letter to John Richards, Job Lousley, farmer and bibliophile of West Hagbourne manor, writes in 1836:

> *A stone cross remains in Hagbourne Street, and there was one formerly about half a mile lower down called the lower cross, but that is not now in existence. About half way between Hagbourne and Croscott (which is another Hamlet of East Hagbourne) is another cross; one other at Crosscott and between that place and Harwell there was formerly another (if not two) and one still remains in Harwell Church yard.*

This account by Lousley, a reliable, contemporary eyewitness to the location of these Hagbourne crosses accords with Keyser's observations 76 years later of a cross near the church, a cross at Coscote and another between Coscote and East Hagbourne. It seems unlikely that a cross would have been erected in a hedge where Keyser observed it, suggesting that it had been moved there from its original site.

A parish map of 1876 shows three Hagbourne crosses: one cross near the church, Lower Cross in pretty much the same place as it is today and the remains of a cross at Coscote. This implies that 50 years after Lousley wrote to John Richards, lower cross had been reinstated. An article published in the journal of the Berkshire Archaeological and Architectural Society in 1892 also describes the same three crosses which appear on the 1876 map. This report is quite detailed in its description of Upper Cross and includes this sad tale of vandalism: "On the top of this sundial there used to be a large ball which was thrown down by a drunken grocer of West Hagbourne a few years ago".

In the 'Notes and Queries' section of another learned journal published in 1907 is an intriguing story behind the move of one of the crosses.

> *... there is also a broken cross, just a base and portion of a pillar, standing on a mound at the cross roads, as you enter the village from the direction of Didcot. I believe it is well-nigh forgotten that this cross is not in its original position. My father who was born in the ancient moated Manor house of East Hagbourne (since pulled down) in 1818, told me that it formerly stood on a hedgerow bank by the way-side, at the little hamlet of Crosscutt, now called Cosscut, near Hagbourne, and that the field on the edge of which it stood was called Broken Cross Piece. I believe he could perfectly well remember it there. A relative of his, an uncle I think, but am not clear on this point, removed it to the place where it now stands.*

We know that Lower Cross was in its present location at the turn of the century from a photograph taken at the time. In a later photograph, taken in the early 1920s when the War Memorial was erected next to it, Lower Cross was surrounded by railings, perhaps to protect it from further interference. The railings have since disappeared, possibly taken down during the War when iron was a scarce resource.

To complicate matters even further, a report of a meeting of the East and West Hagbourne Society, published in a local newspaper in 1963, recounted a story of how the Lower Cross came to be there. This was prompted by proposals to move the stump of the lower cross near the Old Travellers Rest because of traffic congestion. The author, Mr Spinks, produced no written evidence but based his story on what he had been told by other villagers of long standing:

> *In its original position in West Hagbourne it formed a point in a triangle, the other points being Upper Cross at East Hagbourne and that other old stump which is near Coscote Farm House. But at the turn of the century, high-spirited young men of East Hagbourne went with a horse and cart to West Hagbourne, uprooted the stone, and deposited it in East Hagbourne.*

This apocryphal story appears to have evolved from several elements contained in many of the reported sightings of the Hagbourne crosses, including echoes of Keyser's triangle of sanctuary, the knowledge that there was once a cross in West Hagbourne and the report of the cross in the hedge being moved. In the light of all these accounts, it is not unreasonable to surmise that the cross seen in the hedge between Coscote and East Hagbourne by so many local villagers, as well as learned historians and archaeologists, could have been the original "High Cross in the Vill of Westhakeborne" mentioned in the 1411 rent survey. It may have been uprooted and cast into the hedge by the same Parliamentary troops who badly damaged Upper Cross when they were quartered in East Hagbourne during the Civil War. The fact that a nearby field was named Broken Cross Piece because of its proximity to the cross implies that the cross had been in the hedge for a long time.

What is clear from all these reports, going as far back as Job Lousley's letter of 1836, is that market crosses were quite prolific in the Hagbournes in past centuries and an easy target for youthful high jinks, drunks and vandals who have their counterparts in modern life. Furthermore, the Lower Cross in East Hagbourne was not always in the place where it stands today and could well be the same cross which had languished in the hedge after being removed from West Hagbourne. Whether this stump of a cross, now in East Hagbourne, was the original West Hagbourne cross we shall probably never know for certain but taken together, these observations do suggest that it was a possibility.

Sources – Earliest recorded history

M T Clanchy, *Early Medieval England*, The Folio Society, 1997, p38.
Philip Morgan (ed.), *Domesday Book – Berkshire*, Phillimore & Co. Ltd, 1979. Part of general series History from the Sources, edited by John Morris.

Medieval houses: Eric Overton, *A Guide to the Medieval Manor*, Local History Publications, 1994.

Manor houses and moat: C R J Currie, 'Larger Medieval Houses in the Vale of White Horse', *Oxoniensia Journal*, Vol LVII, 1992, p87.

West Hagbourne wood: B F Lingham, *The Long Years of Obscurity – A History of Didcot, Volume One to 1841*, Didcot Press, 1978, p43.

P H Ditchfield and William Page (eds.), *The Victoria History of the Counties of England – Berkshire*, Vol 3, The St. Catherine Press, 1923, p475.

Sources – Windsor manor

Dowry of Clarice de Windsor: *Calendar of Close Rolls*, 1364–1368, 41 Edward III, p394, Public Record Office, Kew.

Christopher Lloyd and Charles Hind, *A Guide to Great Dixter*, Angel Design, 1997.

Great Dixter: L F Salzman (ed.), *The Victoria History of the Counties of England – Sussex*, Vol IX, Oxford University Press, 1937, p273.

Oratories: C R J Currie, 'Larger Medieval Houses in the Vale of White Horse', 1992, p94.

Mill and ovens: Eric Overton, *A Guide to the Medieval Manor*, 1994, p26.

Manor in ruins: *Calendar of Inquisition Post Mortem*, 5 Henry IV (1404), Public Record Office, Kew. C137/42 No 20.

Sale of Windsor manor: *Lessees of the Manor of West Hagbourne*, 29 November, 1661, Berkshire Record Office, Reading. D/EM/T63.

Sources – Watlingtons manor

Daniel and Samuel Lysons, *Magna Britannia Berkshire*, with a new introduction by Jack Simmons, E P Publishing, 1978, p284.

The Victoria History – Berkshire, Vol 3, p272.

P J Jefferies, 'Social Mobility in the Fourteenth Century: The Example of the Chelreys of Berkshire', reprinted from *Oxoniensia Journal*, Vol XL1, 1976.

Sale notice for Grove Manor Farm Estate, 1919.

Sources – The Windsor dynasty

Susan Reynolds (ed.), *The Victoria History of the Counties of England – Middlesex*, Vol 3, Oxford University Press, 1962, pp36, 37.

C W Williams, *A Monograph of the Windsor Family*, W.P., 1879.

Alfred P Smyth, *King Alfred the Great*, Oxford University Press, 1995.

Arthur Collins, *Historical Collections of the Noble Family of Windsor*, 1754. Bodleian Library.

Harley, *Pedigrees and Arms*, 1530–1686, British Museum. Harl. MS 1154.

Kenneth Glass, *The History of Bradenham Manor*, Grant Thornton International, 1990s.

Charles Mosley (ed.), *Burke's Peerage and Baronetage*, 106th edition, Vol 2, Burke's Peerage (Genealogical Books) Ltd, 1999.

Sources – Lady of the manor

Richard Windsor: *Calendar of Inquisition Post Mortem*, 41 Edward III (1367), Vol XII, p153.
Dowry: *Calendar of Close Rolls, 1364–1368*, 41 Edward III, p394.
Peter Coss, *The Lady in Medieval England 1000-1500*, Sutton Publishing Ltd, 1998, p143.
Wardship to Leget: *Calendar of Fine Rolls*, 41 Edward III, Vol 567, p352.
Wardship to Wymondham: *Calendar of Fine Rolls*, 39 Edward III, Vol VIII, p2.
Wardship to Drue: *Calendar of Fine Rolls*, 5 Henry IV, Vol XII (1404, p244), (1405, p296).
Helmingus Leget: *Calendar of Patent Rolls*, 27 March 1368, 19 February 1369 and 1 March 1371.
The Victoria History – Berkshire, Vol 3, p478.
William Dugdale, 'Winchester Cathedral and Monastery of St Swithin', *Monasticon Anglicanum*, Vol I, 1655. Translation from Latin published 1846.
William Page (ed.), *The Victoria History of the Counties of England – Hertfordshire*, Vol 3, Constable and Company Ltd, 1912, pp317, 318.
Pedigree of Clarice: P S Spokes, *Berks, Bucks and Oxon Archaeological Journal*, Vol XXXIX, 1933, pp157–159.
Enfeoff of manor: *Calendar of Patent Rolls*, 4 November 1305 and 26 April 1328.
John de Drokensford: *Calendar of Inquisition Post Mortem*, 24 February 1341 and 7 March 1341.
The Victoria History – Hertfordshire, Vol 3, p318.
The Victoria History – Middlesex, Vol 3, pp147, 148.
John York's pardons: *Calendar of Patent Rolls*, 10 May 1373 and 9 January 1364.
Maude Violet Clarke, 'William of Windsor in Ireland 1369–76', paper read before the Royal Irish Academy, 11 April 1932. Printed in *Proceedings of the Academy*, Clarendon Press, August 1932.
James Bothwell, 'The management of position: Alice Perrers, Edward III, and the creation of a landed estates, 1362–1377', *Journal of Medieval History*, Vol 24, No 1, 1998, pp 31–51.
Pardon: *Calendar of Patent Rolls*, 1391–1396, Vol V, p280.
Clarice and John York: *Calendar of Inquisition Post Mortem*, 12 April 1404, Public Record Office. E152/395, No 2.
Clarice de Windsor's commemorative brass in St Andrew's Church, East Hagbourne. See Chapter Seven, 'Church and Chapel'.

Sources – The medieval cross of West Hagbourne

Rent survey of the manor of West Hagbourne, Public Record Office, Kew. SC 12.1.1(4)
Elizabeth de la Pole: *Calendar of Inquisition Post Mortem*, 11 February 1412, Public Record Office, Kew. C 137/87, No 34.

Charles E Keyser, 'Notes on the Churches of Steventon, Harwell, Didcot and Hagbourne', read before Berks. Archaeological Society, 28 March 1912, printed in *Berks, Bucks and Oxon Archaeological Journal*, Vol 18, No 4, January 1913.

Job Lousley's letter: John Richards, *Berkshire Collections, Parochial Memorials*, Vol ii, G to Y, 1837, British Museum. Additional Manuscript 28.664.

Ordnance Survey of England, Parish of East Hagbourne, County of Berks., 1876, British Library.

John Denis de Vitre, 'Some Berkshire Crosses', *Quarterly Journal of Berkshire Archaeological and Architectural Society*, Vol II, No 5, April 1892.

Mary L Stevenson, 'Notes and Queries Relating to Berks, Bucks and Oxon', *Berks, Bucks & Oxon Archaeological Journal*, Vol XIII, 1907–1908, pp59, 60.

The Didcot Advertiser, 26 September 1963.

A Visit to the Hagbournes, CPRE, Wallingford Branch, 1980s.

Chapter Four

A Glimpse of Village Life in the Sixteenth, Seventeenth and Eighteenth Centuries

Two centuries of turmoil

The dawn of the seventeenth century brought with it the reign of the Stuarts. Queen Elizabeth I died in 1603 to be succeeded by her cousin James I, the King of Scotland. The upheavals of the previous century, such as the dissolution of the monasteries, the gradual enclosure of land and the rise of the merchant classes to become the new landowners were all factors which contributed to great distress and discontent amongst England's agricultural communities, including the villagers of West Hagbourne. The conflicts between Catholic and Protestant and between King Charles I and Parliament eventually resulted in the Civil War in 1642. Some of the fiercest fighting of the six-year war took place in Berkshire and Oxfordshire, not far from the Hagbournes. There were two battles at Newbury, the first at Wash Common in September 1643, the second a year later. There were also skirmishes even closer to home at neighbouring Harwell.

Following the beheading of Charles I, Oliver Cromwell governed the country as Protector of the Commonwealth between 1649 and 1660. This was followed by the Restoration of Charles II whose reign was relatively peaceful, but the religious conflicts continued to rumble on, coming to a head during the reign of his successor, James II, a Catholic. An uprising, led by the Duke of Monmouth, came within the first year of his reign and, though it failed, the Bloody Assize of Judge Jeffreys which dealt with the rebels has long been remembered for its ferocity. England was at war with France almost continuously throughout the eighteenth century and these wars, together with the cost of protecting England's American colonies, depleted the nation's coffers and placed further burdens on the population.

Life in rural West Hagbourne was not untouched by these momentous events. Whilst there is a sparseness of written material, enough documents exist to be able to build up a picture of the social, political and domestic life of the villagers during these two centuries. The Protestation Return of 1642; the proceedings of the manorial courts, including a curious link to Judge Jeffreys; and the wills and inventories made by the new land-owning classes, all help to build up a picture of life in West Hagbourne during the seventeenth and eighteenth centuries.

West Hagbourne's Protestation Return

The religious struggles leading up to the Civil War and the battles which raged not far from West Hagbourne all had an effect on the life of the villagers. Trouble had been brewing for some time between Charles I and Parliament over the future of the King's chief advisor, Thomas Wentworth, the Earl of Strafford. His tyrannical rule in the north of England and Ireland had made him very unpopular and he had turned against Parliament in favour of the King. The Commons brought in a special Act of Parliament to charge Strafford with high treason and, though the King fought hard to defend Strafford, Parliament finally forced him to sign his death warrant. Strafford was executed in 1641.

Following this struggle between King and Parliament, the Commons felt the need to build a united front by ensuring that the King had "good counsellors about him" and that he understood that he was "bound to maintain the laws and... the Word of God". Part of the reasoning behind these declarations was that Charles I had a Catholic wife, Henrietta Maria, and there was fear that the Catholic faith would once more gain strength and overturn the Protestant religion, as it had done before during the reign of Mary I.

Parliament remembered the Oath of Association taken in the reign of Elizabeth I and decided that something similar was required to show the world that the Commons was united and supported by the will of the people. On the 3rd of May 1641, a committee of ten members was chosen to draw up a form of Protestation and all the members were ordered to sign it that same day. The Protestation was agreed by the House of Lords the following day and all Protestant peers signed it. Those who took the Oath of Protestation agreed to:

– Maintain and defend the reformed Protestant religion against popery
– Defend the king
– Support parliament
– Take lawful means to oppose all plots, conspiracies or otherwise against the Protestation
– Preserve the unity and peace between the three kingdoms of England, Scotland and Ireland

On the 6th of May a bill was introduced by the Commons which effectively obliged every Englishman of 18 years and over to sign the Protestation. The Oath of Protestation was finally printed eight months later and sent to the high sheriff and justices of the peace of every county in the land for their signatures. They were ordered to call together the ministers, constables, churchwardens and overseers in their divisions to take the Oath in their presence. Finally, the Protestation was read to the local parishioners who were also required to sign it. Lists of signatories, called Protestation Returns, were drawn up and sent to Westminster. Those Protestation Returns which have survived are housed in the Record Office of the House of Lords in the Palace of Westminster.

The Protestation Return for West Hagbourne was collected under the Hundred of Morton, within the division of Abingdon, in the County of Berkshire. The ministers, constables, churchwardens and overseers of the poor of Abingdon took the Oath of Protestation there on the 28th of February 1642 before Charles Tooker, a justice of the peace for Berkshire. They, in turn, supervised the signing of the Protestation within the parishes.

Fortunately West Hagbourne's Protestation Return has survived in its entirety. It provides a complete list of the names of all 36 males of 18 years or over living in the village in the middle of the seventeenth century, just before the outbreak of the Civil War. Many of the young men on the list were, no doubt, about to become embroiled in one of the most momentous wars in English history, whilst some of the families named in the Return continued to live in West Hagbourne for generations, their names continually appearing in wills, censuses and deeds throughout the intervening centuries.

The Return for West Hagbourne appears exactly as follows, including variations in the spelling of some family names:

A Bill of all the names and surnames of those p'sons in ...
West Hagborne w'ch have taken their protestacon.

Henry Cressell	Robert Winter
Robert Walter	William Louch
Robert Townesend	Thomas Goode
Stephen Silence	Thomas Asheridge
James Perker	Mathew Dearlove
William Tirold senior	William Dearlove
William Burrough	Peter Buttler
Thomas Field	John Rose
Gyles Hasley	Thomas Hutchens
William Ling	John Fray
Avery Dearlove	Thomas Bosley
Robert Tirold	Stephen Clift
William Tirrold jun	Richard Coxhead
Richard Thatcher	Fraunces Coxhead
Gregory Coxhead	John Stacy
William Wellman senior	Avery Reinolds
William Welman jun	Richard Cressell
Richard Sayer	Henry Fluddier

All these sev'all p'sons above written respectively have taken their
p'testacon accordingly
Richard Bristow, Vicar
Richard Simmes, Henry Fludier his mark, Constables
John Dandredge, John Stacy, Churchwardens
Henry Bunce by his mark, Overseers [sic]

Those responsible for drawing up the Protestation Returns were also ordered to send lists of those who refused (recusants) to sign the Protestation to Westminster. The existence of the lists of recusants indicates that one of the objectives of the Oath of Protestation was to find out the names of those still faithful to the Roman Catholic Church. Those who refused to sign were considered incapable of holding office in the church or parliament. Most parishes, including West Hagbourne, were totally in favour "and none of all those persons did refuse but all very willingly take it at the sayd time". Whatever action was planned against the recusants never came to pass as the country was soon to be plunged into war.

In spite of everything, the situation between the King and Parliament worsened, particularly after King Charles personally attempted to arrest his most outspoken opponents in the House of Commons in January 1642. After this, both sides began to prepare for war, with Oliver Cromwell in charge of the Parliamentary army. Since Parliament sat in London, the King moved to Oxford where his royalist supporters were concentrated. Thus the villagers of West Hagbourne would have been aware of troop movements between Newbury, Oxford, Wallingford and Abingdon where skirmishes often took place. Two indecisive battles were fought at Newbury in 1643 and 1644.

Records of the day refer to the villages of Hagbourne, Chilton, Harwell and Blewbury quartering, in turn, royalist and Parliamentary armies. Indeed, on the 24th of May 1644 the Earl of Essex, having routed the King from Reading the day before, quartered his troops in East Hagbourne for the night before moving on to Abingdon, from where the royalist army had retreated to Oxford. Although their stay in East Hagbourne was brief, Cromwell's troops did enough damage to leave their mark on the village, seriously damaging the upper cross. The smallest window in East Hagbourne, in the upper storey of a house called The Gables in Main Road, is said to have been used to spy on Cromwell's troops as they approached from lower cross. There are also rumours of ghostly sightings of cavaliers in the village street of East Hagbourne by local inhabitants.

West Hagbourne probably suffered similar plundering until 1645 when the King moved north after the surrender of Oxford and Wallingford. Villagers had no option but to accommodate these moving armies as the soldiers lived off the land through which they passed and food and shelter were commandeered. Recruitment of local able-bodied men would also have taken place. There must have been relief, as well as apprehension, when peace finally came with the beheading of Charles I in January 1649.

Wills and household inventories

The wills and inventories of people's possessions provide a fascinating glimpse into the life and times of earlier centuries. The wills of several of the inhabitants of West Hagbourne have survived as witnesses to life in the village hundreds of years ago.

One of these early wills was written by Alice Aldworth on the 7th of September 1545. The will was written at a time when the plague had its grip on the parish. Her brother had died two years earlier and her husband, John Aldworth, had only been dead two months when Alice, "fearying the feerce and cruell plage of the pestelence being sicke of my body", and being close to death, wrote her will. The first part is dominated by thoughts of the afterlife, the arrangements for her funeral, and provision for an annual memorial service. These were the first considerations of most wills written at that time.

It is when Alice turns to her bequests that we are given a remarkable insight into what life was like in West Hagbourne for women from well-off families. Alice herself was born into a wealthy family and her ancestors were buried in the churchyard near the south aisle of St Andrew's Church; she herself hoped to join them there. Both her husband and brother were buried in the south aisle, together with other families of West Hagbourne. Alice's brother, Edward Clark, left the Aldworths all his land and the farm he leased in West Hagbourne from William Windsor, lord of the manor. The Aldworths had a close relationship with the Windsors and in her will Alice requested that Lord Windsor should make sure that her last wishes were carried out.

At least two of Alice's children were of school age and she took pains to make arrangements for the education of her sons Edward and William in her will. Alice appears to have been a pious woman and an intimate friend of the clergy, including Robert Pounde, the vicar of Hagbourne, Sir Henry, the chantry priest at Fyfield and Sir John Parker, the local curate, to whom she bequeathed her late brother's best gown and velvet jerkin. Judging by her will, Alice could afford to be generous as she left a considerable amount of money to the clergy for various offices in connection with her funeral and memorial services at which bread, cheese, ale and money were to be distributed to the poor.

Alice also left money to her godchildren and asked that her many servants should receive a few extra pence on top of their regular wages. It seems from the clothing that she left to her friends and family that Alice probably enjoyed quite a rich social life as she owned an extensive wardrobe with dresses and petticoats for "best" as well as smocks for ordinary everyday wear. She also bequeathed jewellery, "silver gaudies" (pieces of finery) and kerchiefs to her women friends and cousins.

Alice Aldworth's will not only gives us an inkling into the lives of those fortunate enough to hold land in West Hagbourne in the mid sixteenth century, but it also reflects on how precarious and uncertain life could be for everyone, regardless of personal wealth or social background.

In the seventeenth and eighteenth centuries wills were sometimes accompanied by detailed inventories of the contents of people's houses, including both livestock and produce, and though their houses disappeared long ago, these documents help us to understand what life was like for the people who lived in West Hagbourne during those centuries.

Two such wills and inventories, such as the one made by Henry Fluddier dated 1643, and one made almost a century later in 1738 by John Harwood, document some of the improvements in living standards which had been taking place since the Middle Ages. In earlier centuries money was scarce and rarely mentioned, but by the seventeenth century, money had become the most valuable bequest a person could make. Inventories mostly concentrated on agricultural produce such as corn, as well as farm animals and implements, household goods and clothes; these latter items often being the only thing of value the less well-off had to leave their children and other relatives.

Will of Henry Fluddier

Henry Fluddier was a relative of the Tyrrells and constable of West Hagbourne in 1641 at the time of the signing of the Oath of Protestation, just before the start of the Civil War. We know that he was unable to write because, as constable, one of his duties was to witness the signatures (or marks in the case of those who could not write) on the Protestation Return and he did this with his mark rather than a signature. His will was drawn up on his deathbed on the 9th of August 1643. It reads:

> *These were the words which Henry Fluddier late of West Hagborne in the county of Berks, yoman deceased did declare a little before his death by his will nuncupative on the 9th Day of August, 1643, as followeth.*
>
> *Imprimes I do give and bequeath unto my two children the some of fortie pounds apiece*
>
> *And I do appoint my cousin William Tirrold the Elder and Robert Tirrill of West Hagborne aforesaid yoman to be my overseers, these being Witnesses.*

The witnesses referred to were John Fluddier of East Hagbourne and Richard Coxhead of West Hagbourne, who both made their marks on the will in lieu of signatures.

Fluddier's will was nuncupative, which means that it was made verbally on his death bed, written down and sworn by witnesses but not signed by him. As no executor was appointed, his widow Dorothy Fluddier had to obtain letters of administration from an Ecclesiastical Court to carry out the terms of the will. She also paid a bond and agreed to pay any outstanding debts and honour any legacies contained in the will. Finally she signed a written undertaking to make an inventory of all her late husband's goods and chattels. Having done all this she was given permission to administer the will according to its "tenor and purpose, intent and meaning". Her inventory was drawn up and signed by three appraisers and exhibited in Abingdon on the 16th of September 1643, just 23 days after the death of her husband:

A True and perfect Inventarie of all the goods, cattells chattels and credits of Henry Fluddier late of West Hagborne in the County of Berks yoman deceased made, taken and apprized by Richard Pomfrey, Peter Brooker and John Fludier yoman, the Thirtieth day of August in the Nyneteenth yeare of the raigne of our soveraigne Lord Charles etc Anno Domini 1643 as followeth

	Li	s	d
Inprimis in redie monie	v	00	00
Item his wareing Apparrell	iii	iii	iiii
Item in his Bedchamber one Standing bed and Tester with the Furniture thereunto belonging	v	00	00
Item one Table and forme, Joyned stooles and one Chest with other things there	i	00	00
Item Eight paire of sheets, one duzen and a halfe of Napkines, Two table clothes with other linnen	iii	00	00
Item in the Chamber at the Staire head one Bedstede one Trundle bed with their furniture and other household stuffe there and the bedding in the servants roome	ii	x	00
Item owing upon desperate debt	v	00	00
Item in the Milkehouse, trayes Buttercharnies with other vessells	x	00	00
Item three Flitches of Bacon	i	x	00
Item one furnace three brasse Potts, three kettles one warming Panne, with other small brazen vessells and one still	iii	00	00
Item the Pewter	i	00	00
Item one Iron Pott, three spitts, one dripping pan, one paire of Andirons and other thinges belonging to the Fire	xiii	iiii	00
Item one table and forme in the Hall	v	00	00
Item the Drinke Barrells and other Tubbs one Salting Trough, a stand and other lumber in the kitchen	i	x	00
Item Old Corne in the house	xx	00	00
Item Eight Tods of Wooll	vi	00	00
Item all the sacks, one Bushell and a screene	i	00	00
Item Five Horses and Geldings with their harness and all thinges thereunto belonging	xiii	vi	viii
Item Six Rother beaste, Five Bullocks, three Heifers and one weaninge calf	xx	00	00
Item Six hogges and Tenne Stoores	v	xviii	00
Item seven score and [?] sheepe	xxiii	00	00
Item three long carts three dung carts with their Tacle thereunto belonging	v	00	00

(one line indecipherable at bottom of first page)

Item Parcel of old hay	(Value indecipherable)				
Item Sheepe rackes, Cowracks hurdles and Blocks	i	-	oo	-	oo
Item a fan to winnow Corne with seives and a Cartlyne	oo	-	x	-	oo
Item horse locks, fetter, prongs, shovells spades, hatchetts, rakes and other such like things	x	-	oo	-	oo
Item the ladders	i	-	oo	-	oo
Item Ducks hennes and Turkies	xv	-	oo	-	oo
Item the whole Cropp of Corne and other Grayne uppon the ground	Cxx	-	oo	-	oo
Item the Tilth and other things	v	-	oo	-	oo
Sum Totall	CCxLv		vi		(£265 6s)

Inprimis: in the first place
Standing bed and tester: a four poster bed
Trundle bed: bed on wheels which could be pushed under another bed
Flock mattress: a mattress filled with wool
Desperate debt: money owed to Henry Fluddier (and now unlikely to be paid)
Rother beaste: a cow
Turkeys: eaten for the first time at the English Court in 1524
Cartlyne: probably a rope for tying up hay
Stoore: an animal between weaning and productive life
Horse lock: type of fetter for tethering a horse by the leg
Tilth: the whole crop of tilled ground

The marks of the three appraisers: Richard Pomfrey, Peter Brooker and John Fluddier appear at the bottom of the inventory.

The inventory mentions at least five rooms in the Fluddier house, namely Henry's bedchamber, a chamber at the top of the stairs, the servants' room, a hall and the kitchen. The "milkehouse" (possibly a local name for dairy) could either be a room within the house or a separate building.

The overall furnishing and apparent use of the rooms is a little outdated, suggesting that fashionable trends had not quite reached West Hagbourne by 1643. For example, no chairs are mentioned. Whilst more than one chair was not usual in houses before 1600, the number of chairs gradually increased during the seventeenth century. Also, the kitchen contains storage items and equipment for preserving food but does not appear to have been used for cooking. This was typical of inventories in other parts of Berkshire before 1600, but from then onwards the term 'kitchen' gradually attached itself to the room where food was actually cooked.

Traditionally the hall had always been the main room of the house, serving as a living room, communal dining area and kitchen. It was usually open to the roof timbers with high unglazed windows, at least until the seventeenth century when glazed windows started to become commonplace. By today's standards the hall was a dark, draughty, smoky room, particularly when fires were in the centre of the room, the smoke escaping through a hole in the roof. Bacon and other meats were hung from the roof beams to cure in the smoke from the open fire. There is only one fire in the Fluddier house which also serves for cooking and appears to have been in the hall. A pair of andirons (appliance for use on a hearth to support logs) is inventoried, suggesting that this was not an open hearth since the andiron replaced the double-ended fire dog when the wall hearth replaced the open central fire. Thus the house must have had a chimney.

The note about the chamber at the "staire head" tells us that the house had two storeys, the upper being reached by a staircase rather than a ladder, and suggests that the servants' room and possibly any other rooms on the first floor were entered through that chamber. Both brick chimneys and staircases were improvements introduced in the latter half of the sixteenth century. The hall and kitchen were both on the ground floor of the Fluddier house but Henry's own bedchamber might have been on either floor. However, the inclusion of the table, stools and other furniture in that room suggests that it was more likely to have been on the ground floor and to take the position of a multi-purpose room, sometimes called the parlour. The mention of "old corne in the house" may not refer to the house in which the people lived, but to a separate building known as a granary. It is possible, though, that the roof space of the house was used for this purpose, but the sequence in which the items are listed suggests that the place where corn was housed was approached from the kitchen.

The long list of livestock, including sheep, cattle and poultry, as well as corn and hay, give the impression of a busy and productive mixed holding. Fluddier must have held a considerable amount of land since his corn crop was his most valuable asset. He would have also needed quite a bit of grazing land to feed his sheep, cattle and horses. The fact that he was able to leave his two children £40 each suggests that his holdings were profitable.

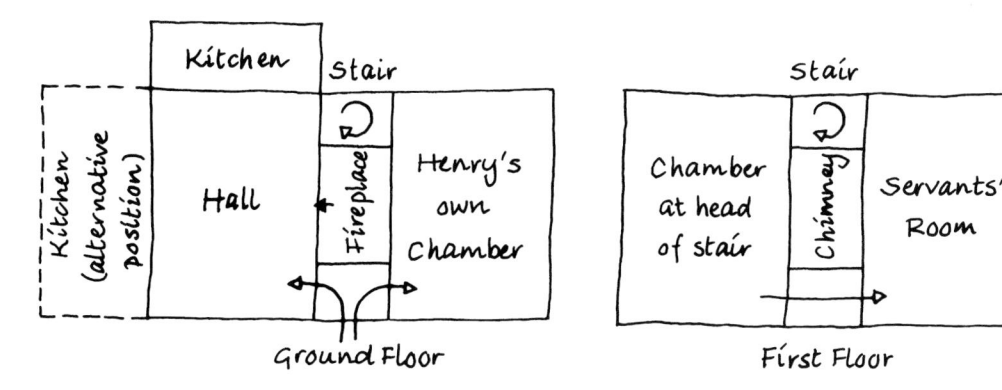

Possible layout for the house of Henry Fluddier

Will of John Harwood

The second will of interest is that of John Harwood, yeoman of West Hagbourne. The name Harwood first appears in the parish registers in 1617 with the birth of Margaret Harwood. The last Harwood entry records the death of Mary Harwood in 1790. The Harwoods were an influential land-owning family in the Hagbournes during the seventeenth and eighteenth centuries and left a generous bequest to the poor of both West and East Hagbourne in 1734. Several Harwoods from West Hagbourne are buried under memorial slabs in the floor of St Andrew's Church.

The yeoman John Harwood died on the 14th of October 1738, in the twelfth year of the reign of George II. It is not known how old he was, but looking at the birth dates of his children he was possibly born about 1686. Yeomen began to emerge as a separate class towards the end of the sixteenth century. They were freeholders farming their own land, with the right to serve on juries and vote for shire representatives if their land was valued at 40 shillings a year. By the time of Harwood's death most farmers, regardless of the value of their land, were calling themselves yeomen in their wills, though some, like Fluddier, were really husbandmen or tenant farmers. However, they were still the more prosperous members of the rural community and their wills and household inventories reflect this. John Harwood's will commences as follows:

> *In the name of God Amen. I John Harwood of West Hagborne in the county of Berks yeoman being of sound and perfect memory and understanding praised be to God for the same. Do make my last will and Testament in writing in manner following. And first I commend my soul to God that gave it and my Body I commit to the earth to be therein decently Interred at the discretion of my Executrix herein after named and for my worldly Goods and Estate, I give and Devise and dispose of the same as follows...*

Harwood's wife was called Jane and they had three children named John, Jonathan and Mary, all born between 1707 and 1716. To Jane he left the following: ten acres of arable land in West Hagbourne Fields with the appurtenances (usually farm buildings), rented by Timothy Tirrold at the time of Harwood's death; his house, called Baker's Close, and garden; one acre of land in Ditchfurlong and one acre in Rodger's Shade; plus his household implements, goods and furniture. On Jane's death the eldest son, John, was to inherit the ten acres. He was also to share £12 equally between Harwood's four grandchildren when they each reached 21 years of age. Harwood also left John four and a half acres of grass land on Hagbourne Hill above Eccleton Way (Icknield Way), in the possession of Thomas Parsons at the time of the will.

To Jonathan, his younger son, he left a house named Chaulks in West Hagbourne and the two butts of arable land adjoining the house. He left his daughter Mary an orchard and garden in West Hagbourne held by copyhold from the late Edward Sherwood, accused of evicting the widow Martha Tyrrell from her widow's estate. After her mother's death, Mary was to inherit all the land and property left to her mother. Jane, his wife, was appointed executrix and his signature to the will was witnessed on the 15th of September 1738 by John Reynolds and his son John of West Hagbourne and Edward Dandridge of East Hagbourne.

In this will of 1738 we can see the emergence of the land-owning classes. John Harwood's main bequest was valuable land and property amounting to two houses and gardens in West Hagbourne, 13 acres of arable land and four and a half acres of grass land, all of which he owned outright, and an orchard and garden (this would have been a productive market garden) for which he held the copyhold. There is no trace of either Baker's Close or Chaulks in the village today but it is believed that Chaulks may have been situated close to the stone pit on Hagbourne Hill.

Harwood's will was proved on the 21st of May 1739 but the inventory was dated the 15th of March 1738, suggesting that it had been drawn up before his death. This was unusual as inventories were usually written after the testator had died. However, the footnote to the inventory suggests that it was altered and brought up to date before being lodged with the Ecclesiastical Court at Abingdon:

> *This Inventory was Exhibited at Abingdon the twenty first day of May one thousand seven hundred thirty nine by Jane Harwood Widow and Executrix of the said deceased for a true and perfect Inventory of all and singular the Goods and Chattels of the said deceased She being first sworn of the Truth of the Same and of adding thereto and so forth.*

It is possible that John Harwood had been ill for some time and had been expected to die when the inventory was first drawn up 14 months before his death. The inventory reads as follows:

> *A True and perfect Inventory of all & Singular the goods chattels and personal Estate of John Harwood of West Hagborne in the county of Berks. yeoman late Hereby taken valued and Appraised on or about the 15th day of March 1738 by Thomas Parsons and Zach Keate.*

	Li	-	s	-	d
In the chamber over the hall where he died					
Inprimis his wearing apparel & ready money	1		10		0
one feather bed, one rug, two blankets, one bolster and pillow, one bedstead and curtains one chest one box one desk and other things	2	-	10	-	0
In the chamber over the buttery					
item one flock bed, one blanket, one rug one bedstead, one coffer and odd things -	0	-	15	-	0
five pair of sheets, six napkins, one tablecloth and odd linnen	1	-	0	-	0

In the hall
item one table, one dresser, seven chairs
five brass ketles, one brass pott, one
skillett, eight pewter dishes, six plates
two spitts fire shovel tongs & other things   1   -   1   -   0
In the drink house
item four tubbs, three barrels one kiver and
lumber   0   - 10   -   0
In the barn
item a parsol of wheat valued at 12 bushel   1   - 16   -   0
three tubbs and one barrel   0   - 10   -   6
In the orchard
item a parsol of hay   0   - 10   -   0
a parsol of wood   0   -   5   -   0
a parsol of aples   0   - 12   -   0

The benefitt of the Executors Year   5   -   0   -   0

                                            Total   15   -   9   -   6

Kiver: a trough
Coffer: a chest
Parsol: a portion of no standard size
Bushel: a dry measure equivalent to about eight gallons

 This inventory describes a simple house, two storeys high with two rooms on each floor. The ground floor comprises the hall and the buttery, though the buttery is only mentioned in relation to the chamber over it. Presumably there was nothing of consequence in that room at the time of appraisal.

 Again, there is only one fire in the house, and this was in the hall, which also appears to have been used as the cooking room. Like Fluddier's, the house is quite old fashioned for the time, as the hall still seems to have been used for everything apart from sleeping. The "drink house" could be a separate building or a lean-to adjoining the main house. It was sometimes called a malt house because it was used for brewing beer which was the most widely available drink in those days. Tea was not generally drunk until the late eighteenth century, and water was considered unsafe. Beer was brewed in every home, barley being the most common ingredient. It was usually made by the women of the household who took great pride in their own particular brew.

 Although the Harwood house was a fairly basic two-storey structure, the inventory lists several 'luxury' items amongst its contents which do not appear in

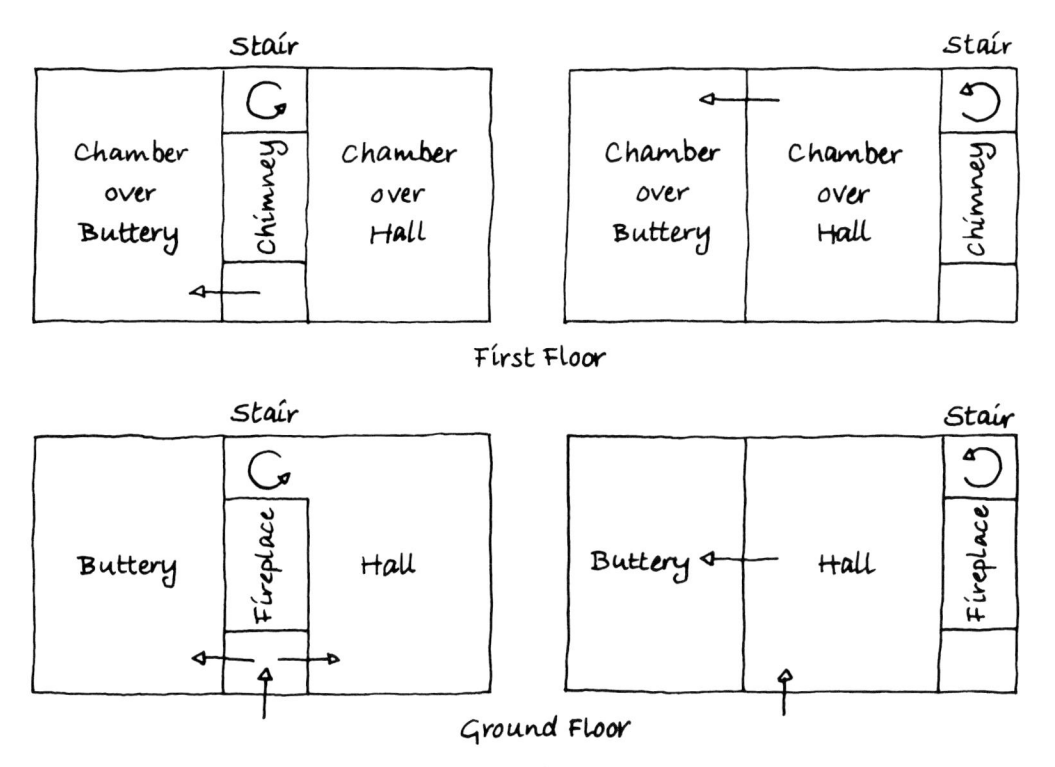

Possible layout for the house of John Harwood

the Fluddier inventory, indicating a better standard of living, at least for the better-off inhabitants of West Hagbourne in Harwood's time. Items such as a feather bed, a desk, seven chairs and eight pewter dishes suggest that the Harwoods enjoyed a few more home comforts than the Fluddiers.

The wills and inventories discussed in this chapter reveal the difference between the lives of those who owned land and those who made their living through farming other people's land. The total value of the contents of Henry Fluddier's inventory is much higher than that of John Harwood, but it represents Fluddier's total assets. Harwood was a landowner whose wealth was accumulated through the rents on his land and property which is not reflected in his inventory. However, his true worth is revealed in his will which lists the land and property to be passed on to subsequent generations of Harwoods.

The manorial courts of West Hagbourne

For several centuries West Hagbourne had two manors: Windsor and Watlingtons and courts were held for both of them at various times. One of the earliest known records of a manorial court in West Hagbourne is that of a Court Baron held for

Watlingtons in 1375. Later documents refer to several courts which Richard de Windsor held between 1638 and 1656 when he owned both manors. Unfortunately, few written records of court proceedings – known as Court Rolls – held for West Hagbourne are known to have survived from later centuries. There is no reason to believe, however, that the West Hagbourne courts were any different from those held for other manors in the parish.

One such court, held in 1760 for Lord Craven, lord of the manor of East Hagbourne and holder of tithing rights for West Hagbourne, gives a very clear picture of the way the courts maintained order and stability within village communities. The proceedings for this court highlight the main concerns of the villagers whose lives were inextricably linked to the farming of the land and to the welfare and husbandry of their animals. The 1760 manorial court laid down rules to protect the crops and to ensure that the animals only grazed in designated areas. Individual freedom, so important at the close of the twentieth century, was unheard of 300 years ago. Everyone worked for the common good of the community and the villagers themselves were responsible for the upkeep of the village, including the maintenance of fences and the clearing and drainage of ditches. The Court Roll also reflects the power of the lord of the manor over the village and his rights to all the penalties and fines levied by the court. By 1760 there were no longer any serfs remaining in England but the tenants of the manor were still under the authority and jurisdiction of the manorial lord.

Manorial courts not only dealt with the management of the land but they also controlled rents, freeholds, copyholds (tenure of land held according to the custom of the manor) and leases. A rare document entitled 'Precedents from the Court Rolls of 1660' lists some of the men who held freehold and leasehold land from the two West Hagbourne manors. William and Richard Tyrrell were freeholders (they held tenure which was not subject to the custom of the manor or the will of the lord) whilst Thomas Bosley, William Woolman and Avery Reynolds were leaseholders of the manor of Watlingtons. Gregory Coxhead paid rent to the Windsor manor for Pighays and also a malt house in the village. Richard Sawyer and Richard Cresswell of the Cresswell Charity are also mentioned in the Roll.

The importance of the transcripts of the proceedings of the manorial courts cannot be underestimated. The Court Baron enforced the customs of the manor. Through continued usage over time these customs acquired the force of law. Copyhold tenure was dependent on custom and the tenant was protected by the title written into a copy of the Court Rolls – hence the term copyholder. Tenants could refer to the Court Rolls for support in cases of dispute between the lord and copyholder over rights enjoyed according to the customs of the manor. The lord, for his part, could try to avoid fulfilling his obligations by failing to hold a court at all. In 1687 Martha Tyrrell, a widow of West Hagbourne, brought such a case against Edward Sherwood, the lord of the manor of Watlingtons, in a Bill of Complaint. This document, together with Sherwood's defence, sheds some light on the way the customs of the manor were enforced by the manorial courts.

The case of Tyrrell versus Sherwood

The story behind this case begins with the Windsor family who owned West Hagbourne manor from 1086. Watlingtons, the second manor, came into the Windsor family by marriage and eventually descended to Richard Windsor, the younger son of Andrew Windsor. In 1661 Richard sold the Windsor manor to Stephen Thompson and a few years later he sold Watlingtons jointly to Philip Parry, a London haberdasher, and James Whitchurch, a gentleman, who eventually sold it on to John Sherwood of East Hendred.

Edward Sherwood inherited the manor of Watlingtons from his father in 1682. At that time William Tyrrell held titles to four copyhold estates, worth about eighty pounds per year, belonging to the three manors of Watlingtons, West Hagbourne (Windsor) and Upton Russell. When he died in 1685, his widow Martha Tyrrell laid claim to her husband's copyholds "during the time of her widowhood", paying four heriots (payment to a lord on the death of a tenant), as was the established custom of the manor. However, in 1687 she brought a Bill of Complaint against Edward Sherwood claiming that he had ignored the customs of the manor and had denied her rights to her widow's estate. She presented her plea to none other than the Lord High Chancellor of England, George Jeffreys, the same Judge Jeffreys who, as Lord Chief Justice, had presided over the infamous Bloody Assize and sentenced hundreds of men to death or transportation to the colonies for their part in the Duke of Monmouth's rebellion against the Catholic King, James II, in 1685.

Martha Tyrrell accused Sherwood of letting out part of her estate to another tenant "for a considerable sum of money", regardless of the fact that it was contrary to the law and custom of the manor. She believed that this person's name had not been presented at any court because he would have known that she had a legal right to her widow's estate. Sherwood had also rented her land for forty pounds a year to a man called Robert Sayer who then took possession by force,

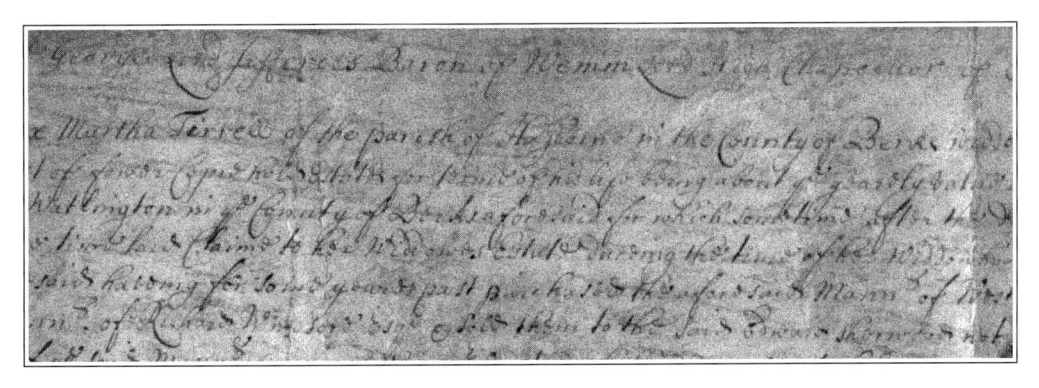

Martha Tyrrell's Bill of Complaint, 1687

ploughed up the land and sowed corn on it, "contrary to all equity and justice" in Martha's view. She claimed that Sherwood then called a Court Baron on the 29th of September 1686 during which he and his steward, a stranger to Martha, connived together to turn her out of her widow's estate, regardless of the fact that she was left to bring up ten children.

In addition she believed that Sherwood had tried to persuade two young men, who were also copyholders on the estate, to let her rooms to some other tenants, and furthermore to testify to the court that she had no right to her widow's estate, even threatening them with violence when they refused to do so. In her Complaint she said Sherwood used bullying tactics on Martha's son, William, who also held a copyhold valued at twenty five pounds a year, and threatened that he would forfeit his copyhold after his mother's death if he did not pay eleven shillings and six pence to secure it.

Martha argued that since Richard Windsor sold the manor no manorial courts had been held for about 36 years. She believed that this had been done on purpose because a copyholder's tenure was maintained through the Court Rolls and if no manorial courts were held, there would be no records regarding tenure of property. She placed great emphasis throughout her Complaint on the words "according to the customs of the manor", rightly regarding this as legal sanction of her rights. She went on to compare her situation with that of two other widows who had claimed their widows' estates from Richard Windsor's properties in West Hagbourne, Upton Russell and Watlingtons. Forty years before, Widow Heeres had enjoyed her widow's estate for eight years even though she had remarried. Thirty years previously Widow Day had also been allowed to continue enjoying her widow's estate despite being married.

According to Martha, Sherwood consistently refused to produce any deeds or Court Rolls which would have confirmed the customs of the manor so that she felt helpless, being unable to force him to acknowledge the manorial customs or produce anything in writing. Furthermore, any likely witnesses were either dead, had moved far away or their whereabouts were unknown.

At the end of her Complaint she requested that Edward Sherwood be subpoenaed to appear before the court of the Lord High Chancellor, Judge Jeffreys, to swear on oath whether or not he knew about the ancient customs of the manors of West Hagbourne regarding a widow's rights to claim her widow's estate. She also asked him to produce all the deeds, Court Rolls and presentments in his keeping concerning a widow's estate which he acquired when he bought the manor. Martha pleaded that all her rights should be restored to her "according to justice and equity".

On the 9th of May 1688, Edward Sherwood presented a robust defence to the court. His legal advisers had meticulously prepared supporting evidence, citing every Court Baron at which the copyholds to Watlingtons had been granted to the Tyrrells. The first court mentioned by the defence was held on the 4th of July 1638 when a considerable amount of land and property was granted to William Tyrrell the elder, father of Martha's husband and a distant cousin of William Tyrrell, founder of the Tyrrell Charity. Richard Windsor granted him titles to:

> *One yardlands of arable land and halfe an acre of meadow ground and fifteen acres of arable land and one acre of meadow ground and Comon of pasture for sheep with the appurtenances in West Hagborne aforesaid the part of Customary Lands and Tenements of the Mannour aforesaid.*

The Court Baron decreed that this tenancy also extended to Tyrrell's two sons: William, the husband of Martha, and Brook who lived in East Hagbourne. The two brothers would hold the land for "their lives and the life of the longest liver" and they would pay the yearly rent and the customary heriots at the appropriate time.

Sherwood also cites two other courts which Richard Windsor held, one on the 8th of May 1649 and the other on the 27th of October 1651. As well as arable land, meadows and farm buildings, Richard Windsor granted the Tyrrells two houses, plus two acres of land and outbuildings at the stone pit in West Hagbourne, probably on Hagbourne Hill. Brook had died sometime between the court held in 1638 and that of 1649, so that his brother William became "the longest liver". The Rolls of a further court held on the 13th of May 1656, the last to be summoned by Richard Windsor, do not mention William Tyrrell the elder who had presumably died by this time. The copyhold titles of the manor of Watlingtons were granted to Martha's husband and their son William "for the terms of their lives and the life of the longer liver... according to the customs of the Mannour aforesaid... as by the said grant remaining upon the Roll of the said Court or the copy thereof" on payment of the usual rents, services and heriots.

A court was held for Watlingtons on the 15th of April 1675, some years after Richard Windsor sold the manor to Parry and Whitchurch. At this court William Tyrrell the elder and his son William themselves requested that their rights to the copyholds should be entered in the Court Rolls. At this point in his defence, Edward Sherwood confirmed that he held these Rolls and was ready to present them to the court. He also denied that he had ever withheld them from Martha Tyrrell.

A few years later Watlingtons manor was sold to John Sherwood who held it for about four years before he died, passing it on to his son about 1682. Sherwood claimed to have held two courts since becoming lord of the manor, one being held the previous October, but he does not mention the court held on the 29th of September 1686 at which Martha accuses him and his steward of plotting to have her evicted. Edward Sherwood tells the court that by the time he inherited Watlingtons, William Tyrrell the elder, his wife Elizabeth and their son Brook had all been dead for some time. On the death of Martha's husband, William, four heriots were due for the four best cattle, which Sherwood estimated were worth twenty pounds. However, he maintained that "in kindness to the said Complainant" he accepted fourteen pounds from Martha Tyrrell.

Edward Sherwood then reaches the heart of his defence which is to argue that according to the custom of Watlington manor, the widow of any copyholder could only hold on to the copyhold estate during the executor's year and no longer. In the Tyrrell case, William the elder and his son William were now both dead, and in Sherwood's opinion Martha was only entitled to retain the land for one year. He made no mention of any rights to a widow's estate, implying that this was not a custom of the manor. On the basis of this interpretation of the law, Sherwood felt justified in instructing his steward Charles Holloway, Esq. to let some land and property to John Herbert and also to Robert Sayer of Coscote. Furthermore, he claimed that Martha was well aware that she was not entitled to a widow's estate and that she had never claimed it but had in fact tried to negotiate a lease on the estate at the end of the executor's year.

Sherwood discounted Martha's accusation of threats made against other tenants of the manor and said that both her son William and the late Brook Tyrrell's son had been admitted to their copyholds according to the custom of the manor. William had not been threatened but merely warned that if he did not attend the Court Baron to hear his presentment, he could forfeit his copyhold. Sherwood dismissed the idea that other widows had set a precedent by enjoying their widow's estate, saying that Widow Day was a tenant of Upton Russell, not Watlingtons, and that he knew of no custom at the other manors whereby a widow could hold copyhold for life. In summing up his defence, Edward Sherwood denied all the accusations contained in Martha Tyrrell's Bill of Complaint and requested that his case be dismissed with "reasonable costs by him most wrongfully sustained".

There are no rulings regarding the outcome of this case, suggesting that it may have been settled out of court. Although we will never know the truth behind the struggle between Edward Sherwood and Martha Tyrrell, the case does portray the precarious situation in which widows found themselves, particularly if Sherwood's defence was upheld. It also illustrates the workings of the manorial courts, not only in West Hagbourne, but throughout the country. The upholding of the customs of the manor, as witnessed by the Court Rolls, was part of a land owning system which had been in place for centuries. However, it would probably be wrong to assume that it was common for tenants to take their lords to court.

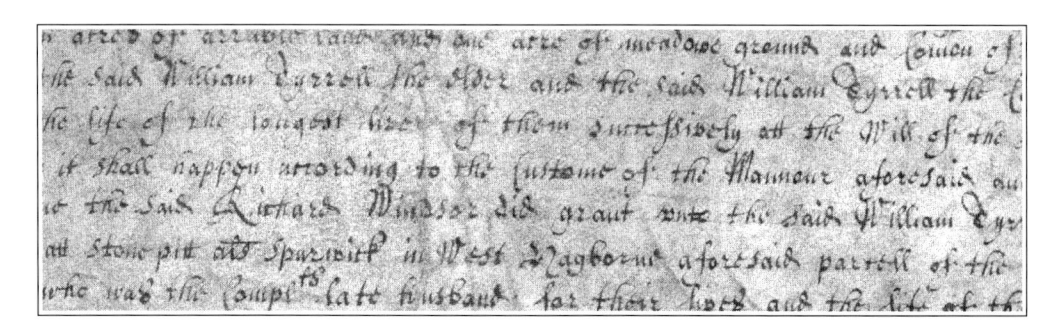

Excerpt from Edward Sherwood's defence document, 1688

Martha Tyrrell was no ordinary widow, but came from a family of some substance and influence in the local community and could afford to engage the best lawyers. At least three generations of Tyrrells had been granted copyholds for substantial amounts of land and property by the Windsors and had accumulated considerable wealth from the income of arable land. We have seen the results of their philanthropy through their bequests to West Hagbourne. They had their own coat of arms and a family pew in St Andrew's Church where several Tyrrells are buried. No doubt the arrogant Edward Sherwood underestimated his widowed tenant who took her case to the highest court in the land.

The case also reflects the changes taking place in society in the late seventeenth century. The Windsors were first granted their land in West Hagbourne by William the Conqueror and we have seen in the chapter on the medieval period how it was held at all costs by the Windsor dynasty through inheritance, marriage and various alliances with kings and other noble families. No doubt Richard Windsor's ancestors would have been turning in their graves to see him sell off both the manors of Windsor and Watlingtons within a few years of each other.

By 1687, when Martha Tyrrell brought her Bill of Complaint, manorial estates could be bought by anyone who could afford them, regardless of class or social status. Many of those buying land were successful businessmen from London, such as the haberdasher Philip Parry, and they saw these investments in land as commercial ventures. In a sense, this new breed of landowners could be seen as the *nouveau riche* of the seventeenth century. Land was no longer held by generations of one family but changed hands quickly. Men like Edward Sherwood were not interested in the niceties of manorial customs but in getting the best out of their investment. It was, perhaps, this attitude which Martha Tyrrell was really struggling against. Richard Windsor came from a long line of titled knights ennobled by kings and probably took a more paternalistic attitude towards his tenants, as in the examples Martha Tyrrell gave of the two widows, Heeres and Day. He had also shown particular favour to the Tyrrells and, had he been alive, things may have been different for Martha. Ultimately, the case of Tyrrell versus Sherwood can be seen as the final death rattle of the medieval manorial system in West Hagbourne.

Sources – Two centuries of turmoil

G M Trevelyan, *England Under the Stuarts*, The Folio Society, reprinted 1996, pp 226, 234.
Judith Hunter, *A History of Berkshire*, Phillimore & Co. Ltd, 1995, p74.

Sources – West Hagbourne's Protestation Return

Jeremy Gibson, ed., *Oxfordshire and North Berkshire Protestation Returns and Tax Assessments 1641–42*, The Oxfordshire Record Society, Vol 59, 1994.

Report of Dr J W Walker's Lecture 'The Ancient History of the North Berks. Area', *The Reading Mercury and Oxford Gazette*, 6 February 1932.

Sources – Wills and household inventories

Will of Alice Aldworth of West Hagbourne, 7 September 1545, Public Record Office, Family Records Centre, London.
Will of Henry Fluddier, 9 August 1643, Berkshire Record Office, Reading. D/A1/68/59.
Admonition of will of Henry Fluddier, 4 September 1643, Berkshire Record Office, Reading. D/A1/68/59a.
Inventory of Henry Fluddier, 16 September 1643, Berkshire Record Office, Reading. D/A1/68/59c.
Will of John Harwood, 15 September 1738, Berkshire Record Office, Reading. D/A1/84/161.
Inventory of John Harwood, 21 May 1739, Berkshire Record Office, Reading. D/A1/84/161a.
Clive D Edwards, *John Gloag's Dictionary of Furniture*, Unwin Hyman, Ltd, revised 1990.
B F Lingham, *The Long Years of Obscurity – A History of Didcot, Vol One – to 1841*, Didcot Press, 1978.

Sources – The Manorial Courts of West Hagbourne

Precedents from the Court Rolls of 1660, Berkshire Record Office, Reading. D/EAH E10.
Manor of Hagbourne Court Books, 1720–1841, Berkshire Record Office, Reading. D/EM M 6-10.
'Hamilton Bundle', *Chancery Bills and Answers*, Public Record Office, Kew. C7 337/59.

Chapter Five

A Changing Landscape

West Hagbourne Inclosure Award of 1843

Changes to the old land divisions which began in Tudor times continued throughout the succeeding centuries. During times of upheaval the changes were very gradual. For example, in the seventeenth century, when the country was occupied with the Civil War, the Commonwealth, the Restoration and the ravages of the plague, there was very little change to the way land was farmed. However, after 1700 the enclosure movement gathered momentum, culminating in various private and public parliamentary enclosure acts in the first half of the nineteenth century. By 1845, four thousand acts, mostly carried out at local level, had been passed and 5,000,000 acres of common land had been enclosed. This resulted in a major redistribution of land and the modernisation of farming methods throughout the country.

Enclosure took many forms, including the consolidation of strips of land so that common fields could be cultivated communally and thus more productively than under the old strip system. Wastelands and woods were enclosed to create fields, whilst meadows and arable land were converted to pasture for sheep grazing at a time when the wool trade was flourishing. Sheep could be looked after more easily on enclosed land, sheep rearing required fewer workers than for the growing of crops and landowners could make a good living by selling wool.

Whilst the enclosure acts did improve agricultural practices, thus making the land more productive, the poorer farmers lost out to the wealthy landowners who were able to consolidate large areas of the best land. Not only were the open fields enclosed, but large areas of common pasture, where peasants had previously had rights to graze their livestock for generations, were also absorbed by the manorial estates. Large scale enclosures brought prosperity to some but they also brought misery to others who lost their livelihoods and sometimes their homes. Eventually an act of 1876 stopped any further enclosures of land but by then it was too late as most land worth cultivating had already been enclosed.

West Hagbourne did not escape these fundamental changes to the old feudal system of farming. Land had gradually been enclosed over a number of years, including the enclosure of 20 acres of arable land in 1517 which resulted in three people losing their homes. A telling postscript to a Court Roll of 1660 for West Hagbourne noted that "the Inclosure of Common will improve the two manors

Detail from the Rocque map of Berkshire, 1761

and the copyholders very much". By the early 1840s as much as 114 acres had been enclosed in West Hagbourne but 903 acres still remained untouched.

The Rocque map, a very early map of Berkshire, was published in 1761. John Rocque was a French-born topographer by appointment to His Majesty, George III and his map of Berkshire, consisting of over 18 sheets, was drawn up over a period of nine years. Although the boundaries are not well marked and West Hagbourne's fields are not named, the Rocque map illustrates the open field system around all the villages in the area before the Inclosure Award. It shows West Hagbourne's meadow and commons, including some common land which had already been enclosed around Down Farm by 1761.

Under the impetus of the 1836 Enclosure Act, which was designed to encourage the enclosure of any remaining open fields, a public meeting was called by landowners with an interest in enclosing land in West Hagbourne. Daniel Lousley of Blewbury was appointed as the sole commissioner for dividing and allotting the land and for drawing up the Award. The first public meeting was held on the 4th of July 1842 at the offices of solicitors Graham & Son in Abingdon, to discuss "the expediency" of enclosing land in West Hagbourne. The meeting was advertised in the Berkshire Chronicle on the 18th of June and a notice was placed on the door of St Andrew's Church in accordance with the rules laid down in the enclosure acts. Shortly after the meeting, the majority of the interested parties consented in writing to enclose the "open and Common Arable Meadow and Pasture Lands and Fields and to extinguish the right of intercommonage as well … in respect of such Land". This was carried out according to the terms of the Inclosure Act which stated that "such inclosure might, after such meeting, be proceeded with by and with the consent in writing of two third parts in number and value of the Proprietors and Persons interested in the Lands intended to be enclosed…"

On a 1754 map of West Hagbourne, a handwritten note makes it very clear where this common land was and that it was shared by the tenants of both manors:

> *The Commoners of both Manors in West Hagbourne, stock together and alike in the Moor Common, Down Common, Oxlease and Ashmead and all other commonable places in the said Manors. The Commoners of either of the said Manors reserving no common or commonable places to themselves.*

This common land was owned by the lords of the two manors but was subject to rights of common enjoyed by the commoners. However, the Inclosure Award was to change all that.

Following the usual notices, a further public meeting was held on the 11th of August at the "House of George Napper called or known by the name or sign of the Horse and Harrow Inn at Scotlands Ash in the Parish of East Hagbourne" (West Hagbourne was included in the ecclesiastical parish of East Hagbourne). At this meeting Lousley considered the various claims to the land, bearing in mind both the rights of the supplicants and the laws governing the parliamentary enclosure acts. The Award, written on parchment, was finally executed, signed and sealed before witnesses on the 27th of July 1843, almost exactly a year after the first public meeting was held to discuss the possibility of enclosing the land. Although the word 'enclosure' was widely used, the West Hagbourne Award was entitled the 'West Hagbourn Inclosure Award'.

The following landowners witnessed the Award and their names, together with their seals, all appear on the 1843 Inclosure Award for West Hagbourne (spelled Hagbourn throughout) and they all benefitted from the Award:

John Blagrave Pococke, esquire of Twickenham Common, Middlesex, lord of West Hagbourne manor (the Pocockes bought the manor in the late 1600s)
William Aldworth, lord of the manor of Watlingtons and his son John Aldworth, gentlemen of Frilford
Nathan Thomas, baker of Harwell and John Keates, yeoman of Harwell (both divisees of John Austin of Harwell)
Thomas Bosley of East Hagbourn
John Childs of East Hagbourn
Joseph Humphrey Fuller of East Hagbourn
Robert Hopkins, gentleman of Rowstock
James Holliday, gentleman of East Hagbourn
James Hyde, yeoman of Drayton
William Lanham, gentleman of Abingdon
William Morland, gentleman of West Ilsley
John Shawe Phillips, esquire of Culham
Jane Woodley, widow of West Hagbourn

The churchwardens and overseers of the poor of the parish of East Hagbourne and "the proprietors of Lands, Grounds and Common Rights in the Hamlet of West Hagbourne" were also included as beneficiaries. The Vicar of East Hagbourne (and his clerical successors), Elizabeth Elderfield and James Norris were also awarded land but they were not witnesses to the document. None of these landowners, with the exception of Jane Woodley, actually lived in the village.

The Award is extremely detailed and identifies the amount of land assigned, and to whom, and its exact location in respect of adjoining properties. The following extract is a typical example:

Unto and for Jane Woodley... One plot or allotment of land or ground containing by admeasurement Two acres and one rood bounded on the North East by the said Wantage Turnpike Road on the South East and South West by the first allotment hereinbefore awarded to the said James Hyde and on the North West by the allotment hereinbefore awarded to the said William Lanham...

The Inclosure Award is accompanied by a plan or map which shows the new enclosure boundaries and the names of the new landowners. Not surprisingly,

John Pococke, the lord of the manor of West Hagbourne (previously Windsor manor) and William Aldworth, the lord of Watlingtons manor (now Grove Manor Farm), were the main beneficiaries. Pococke also gained vast tracks of land in the area at the time of the Didcot enclosure in 1841. His name is spelled Pococke throughout the Award but Pocock on the plan.

Inserted at the foot of the plan is a table entitled 'Reference to Old Inclosures', which gives details of the land and property already enclosed before 1843. Most of this land, apart from Down Farm, is confined to the central part of the village, in the most populated area (see map on page 73). Down Farm had acquired over 70 acres of land during an earlier enclosure of common land. The rest of the Down, namely, the Cow Down and the Sheep Down was finally enclosed in 1843, together with the remainder of West Hagbourne's open fields.

This table of old enclosures lists each piece of land, who owned it and its exact measurement – right down to the last perch. This table is particularly valuable because it provides a snapshot of how West Hagbourne appeared when the Inclosure Award was drawn up and who lived in the village in 1843. It also informs us that the total size of the village of West Hagbourne was 1039 acres and 20 perches in 1843. This measurement included over 21 acres of roads and paths and over 114 acres of land which had previously been enclosed.

The village consisted of orchards, six farms, numerous cottages and gardens, as well as two public houses (the Horse and Harrow and another near Down House on the Wantage Road which later became the Wheatsheaf Inn), a malt house next to Woodleys and several houses which also served as shops (all referred to as "premises"). The table provides evidence of barns and buildings, including a chapel attached to a cottage in Moor Lane, none of which still exist and for which there is little other proof, apart from memories passed down the generations in the oral tradition. This chapel, belonging to a Mr Robinson, was not the only chapel ever to appear in Moor Lane (for further details see Chapter Seven).

In West Hagbourne and the surrounding villages fruit growing had begun to play an important part in the life of the area by the time the Inclosure Award was drawn up. Apart from the fruit trees grown in most kitchen gardens, the plan lists more than 20 orchards and names several, including York's, Fowler's, Rose's, Hogg's, Old Boy's, Reynolds's, Moggs and Lower Moggs. As fruit growing became less profitable, the land became more valuable for housing and several orchards disappeared under bricks and mortar.

The West Hagbourne Inclosure Award and the accompanying plan also provide written evidence that the spirit of the will of William Tyrrell, who left land for the benefit of the poor of West Hagbourne, was to be honoured. The land which William Tyrrell left in 1662 existed as strips of land distributed over a wide area. When the Inclosure Award was drawn up, these strips were exchanged for a single plot assigned on the plan as an "Allotment to the Poor" at the bottom of Hagbourne Hill.

The Award does not mention Tyrrell by name but refers to the common land

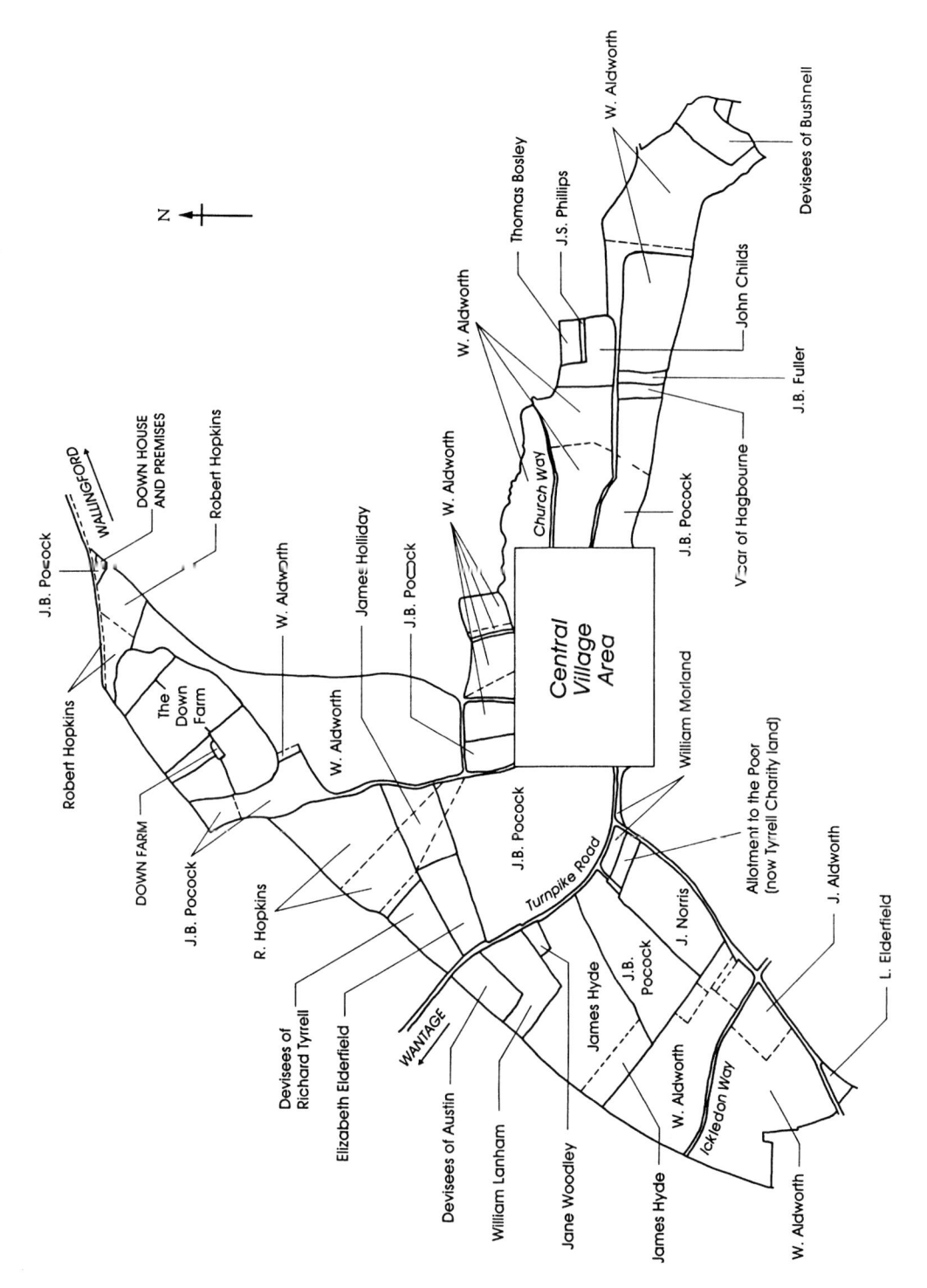

Part of the Inclosure Award of West Hagbourne, 1843 (redrawn)

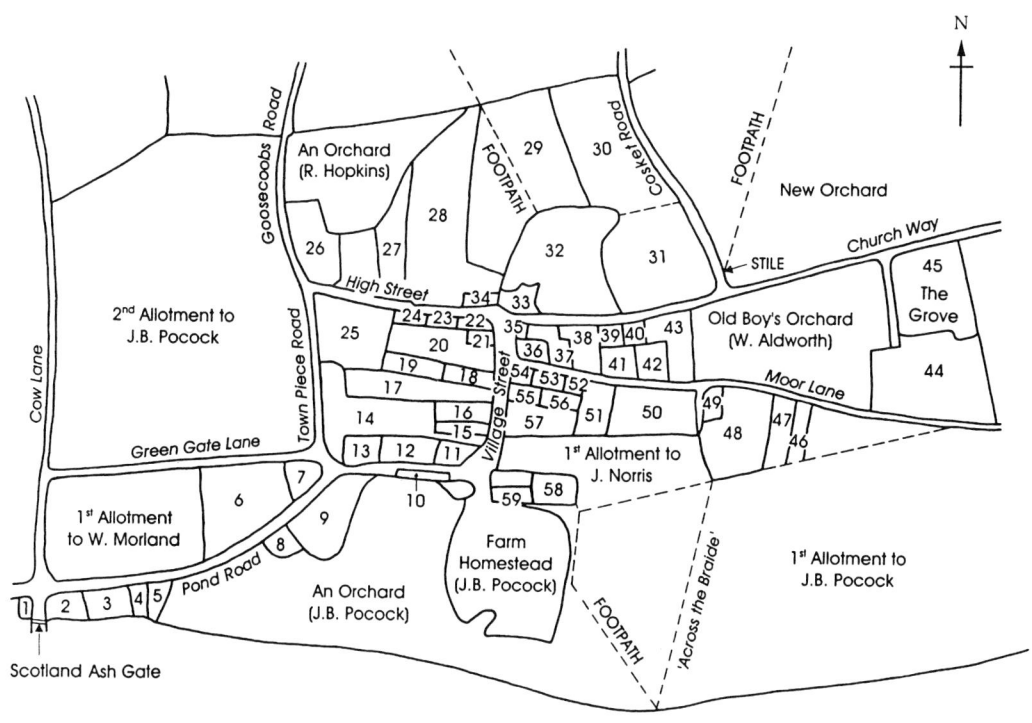

#	Description	Owner
1	Toll House and Garden	Commissioners
2	Houses and Premises	W. Morland
3	An Orchard	W. Morland
4	A Garden	W. Morland
5	Cottage and Garden	A. Roberts
6	An Orchard	W. Morland
7	Farm Homestead	W. Morland
8	Cottage and Garden	Loder
9	An Orchard	Loder
10	Cottage and Garden	F. Redwood
11	Houses and Premises	Late E. Britton
12	An Orchard	W. Hall
13	Cottage and Garden	W. Hall
14	Grass Close	W. Aldworth
15	Cottage and Garden	R. Fidler
16	A Garden	W. Aldworth
17	An Orchard	T. Dearlove
18	House and Premises	Jane Woodley
19	An Orchard	Jane Woodley
20	Orchard and Malthouse	J. Holliday
21	Cottage and Garden	J. Holliday
22	House and Premises	T. Dearlove
23	An Orchard	T. Dearlove
24	A Garden	T. Dearlove
25	Fourth Allotment	W. Aldworth
26	Farm and Homestead	R. Hopkins
27	An Orchard	R. Hopkins
28	Farm Homestead	R. Hopkins
29	York's Orchard	W. Aldworth
30	Fowler's Orchard	W. Aldworth
31	Rose's Orchard	W. Aldworth
32	An Orchard	J. Holliday
33	House and Premises	J. Holliday
34	Cottage and Garden	W. Aldworth
35	Two Cottages	W. Aldworth
36	Two Cottages and Gardens	W. Aldworth
37	House and Premises	Allen
38	An Orchard	Allen
39	Two Cottages and Gardens	T. Higgs
40	Three Cottages and Gardens	Late T. Loder
41	One Cottage and Garden	R. Dawler
42	One Cottage and Chapel	Robinson
43	Hogg's Orchard	W. Aldworth
44	Farm Homestead	W. Aldworth
45	The Grove	W. Aldworth
46	A Garden	Late T. Loder
47	A Garden	F. Loder
48	Reynolds's Orchard	W. Herbert
49	Cottage and Garden	W. Herbert
50	Lower Moggs Orchard	W. Aldworth
51	A Garden	S. Taylor
52	Three Cottages and gardens	T. Norris and Others
53	An Orchard	J. Norris
54	Home and Premises	J. Norris
55	Four Cottages and Gardens	T. Higgs
56	An Orchard	T. Higgs
57	Moggs Orchard	W. Aldworth
58	An Orchard	T. Norris
59	House and Premises	J. Norris

Reference to Old Inclosures from the redrawn Inclosure Plan, 1843 (opposite) held by the churchwardens and overseers of the poor who were responsible for distributing charity to the needy within the parish:

> *Unto and for the Churchwardens and Overseers for the time being of the Parish of East Hagbourn aforesaid and their Successors for and in lieu of their Common Lands in West Hagbourn aforesaid. One plot or allotment of land or ground containing by admeasurement three acres three roods and six perches bounded on the south east by Chilton Road on the South West by the Second allotment hereinafter awarded to James Norris on the North West by the fifth allotment hereinafter awarded to the said John Blagrave Pococke and on the North East by the third allotment hereinafter awarded to William Morland.*

This "Allotment to the Poor" was over one acre less than that in the original Tyrrell bequest, the details of which are explained in Chapter 6, and has been managed by the trustees of the William Tyrrell Charity ever since the Award was drawn up in 1843.

The West Hagbourne Inclosure Award and the plan were deposited in the office of the clerk of the peace for Berkshire on the 1st of January 1844. After the establishment of parish meetings, it was agreed on the 25th of March 1897 to investigate the purchase of a copy of the Award for the village. A handwritten copy, duly signed by J Morland, Clerk of the Peace, was obtained by Mr Slade for the sum of £10 10s. The following April a case was purchased for the Award and plan at a cost of 3s 3d. The Award and the plan have been the responsibility of the West Hagbourne Parish Council ever since.

Roads, Railways and Rivers

West Hagbourne is criss-crossed with footpaths to neighbouring villages. The history of the development of these paths begins at a time when the only form of transport was on foot. Wherever there were settlements, tracks emerged for the movement of people and livestock. There was once an Iron Age settlement, even before the Romans arrived, on Hagbourne Hill not far from the Icknield Way. As trading developed, the need for routes between settlements became more urgent and the footpaths and tracks became more heavily used, even crossing rivers and streams. When packhorses, and later, carts were used to transport goods, the route had to follow the firmer ground required by the horses and the vehicles they pulled. Some of the oldest West Hagbourne paths followed the baulks and headlands created for the medieval ploughing system. South Vearns Mere and Langland's Mere on the north west boundary with Harwell are good examples of this development of paths along headlands.

Some tracks eventually developed into roads, whilst others, such as Cow Lane, became driftways for driving cattle to market. Many have remained bridle-paths or public footpaths to this day. The oldest of these is Moor Lane which was once a well-used track leading to the village commons, moors and meadows. It was also the only direct route to the mill at East Hagbourne. Moor Lane used to be classified as a "carriage road used as a bridleway" but is now a "byway open to all traffic". The total length of the path is one and a half miles but the last 200 yards is in the parish of East Hagbourne. Moor Lane is believed to have originally joined one of the many branches of the nearby Icknield Way.

Village roads and footpaths were once cared for by the parish. In fact, one of the first civil powers given to the parishes was enshrined in the Highways Act of 1555 which formally made the parish liable for the repair of all highways within its jurisdiction. This was enforced until the Municipal Reform Acts of 1835. The minute book of the Annual Assembly of the parish meeting (later to become the Parish Council) of West Hagbourne, is a litany of care and anxiety over the maintenance of the footpaths and roads which were such vital links to neighbouring villages before the advent of motorised transport. The footpaths in the Braid, Moor Lane and the path to Upton were in constant states of repair, usually with ashes, whilst Church Path was treated with granite chippings. Stiles in Brook Lane, the Braid and the path to Upton were repaired many times. An intricate network of ditches and streams threads its way through West Hagbourne, requiring footbridges called 'archways' at many points. These required constant upkeep because of recurring damage from flooding; most notably, the archways over the Braid ditch, Brook Lane stream and Coscote Path.

The routes beyond the village boundaries were nobody's particular responsibility and there was no money, nor incentive, to maintain roads in poorly populated areas. In 1707 there was a suit between Didcot and West Hagbourne over responsibility for the repair of the main highway between the two parishes (now Wantage Road). West Hagbourne lost the case when it was proved that the road lay within its parish as the boundary ran along the northern edge of the road.

One answer to the problems of road maintenance was to set up trust companies which would keep a section of road in good repair and charge for its use at toll gates, or bars, set up at strategic points along its route for collection of the appropriate toll. These toll roads were known as turnpikes, a term still used in the United States of America today. The trustees of these companies were usually local landowners who, no doubt, hoped to make a little profit out of their efforts through increased trade. The first act of parliament empowering a local trust company to charge travellers a toll was passed in 1663. The following century saw a great expansion in the number of turnpike roads all over the country, with individual acts being passed for each road.

West Hagbourne was bordered on two sides by turnpike roads. One, the Wallingford – Didcot – Faringdon turnpike, set up in 1752, ran along what is now the Broadway and the Wantage Road, passing the Wheatsheaf Inn which once stood on the northern boundary of the village. The other was the Harwell – Streatley turnpike which followed the ancient Icknield Way and is now part of the A417. The milestone, which now stands opposite the grain store on the A417 road towards Harwell, provides a reminder that this was once the Harwell – Streatley turnpike. The milestone reads "Reading 17" on one side and "Wantage 7" on the other. A trust was set up for this turnpike by an act of parliament in 1803. The road ran from Harwell to Streatley, a distance of eight miles, five furlongs and three perches. By law, new turnpikes had to be linked to existing ones so it joined the Wallingford – Faringdon turnpike at Harwell and another turnpike near the village of Streatley.

Two subsequent acts, passed in 1836 and 1845, relating to the Harwell – Streatley turnpike, were concerned with widening and improving the road and keeping it in good repair. The gravel for road repairs came from East Ilsley and Streatley and was paid for out of income from the tolls. The 1845 Act also laid down the toll rates and appointed the justice of the peace for Berkshire and 46 local men, including some from West Hagbourne, to be trustees of the trust for the Harwell – Streatley turnpike. These are some examples of the tolls levied in 1845:

8d for each beast drawing a coach
3d for animals not drawing a vehicle
1s 3d for each score of bulls, cows or calves
7d for each score of pigs, lambs or goats
6d for a dog or goat cart
2s 6d for a steam or mechanical vehicle

Wagons were charged according to the number of animals pulling them, the size of their wheels and even the season. The trustees could reduce the toll for lime, manure or chalk and toll gates and bars could be removed or set up at will. The income from the tolls had to pay off the loans incurred from setting up the turnpikes, the interest on the loans, and the cost of administering the act, as well as keeping the road in good repair. It was not a very profitable road.

The Harwell – Streatley turnpike passed the Horse and Harrow Inn on the southern boundary of West Hagbourne at Scotland's Ash and a toll gate was set up there. The Inclosure Award indicates that the Inn was then owned by William Morland who owned a brewery in West Ilsley. Thomas and William Morland were two of the local men named as trustees of the Harwell – Streatley turnpike in 1845. The toll gate, conveniently positioned at the Horse and Harrow, would have brought prosperity to the inn owners and trade and commerce to the village. All those who passed through the toll gate, including travellers, horses, carts and coaches would have needed rest, food, possibly accommodation, and the attention of a blacksmith or other services. George Napper, publican of the Horse and Harrow in 1841, and owner of nearby Rose Cottage, also earned a living as a wheelwright. His nephew, William Napper, who had followed in his uncle's footsteps as publican by 1861, was also a skilled blacksmith.

The toll house stood on the other side of the road, opposite the Horse and Harrow. It projected into the road so that approaching traffic could be easily seen from either direction. The toll keeper lived there with his family in cramped conditions. In 1870 it was sold by the trustees to E H Morland for £35. The late Alice Powell remembered that in 1900 the occupants of the cottage were the Brown family and that Mrs Brown used to look after Arch Napper, the future landlord of the Horse and Harrow, as a small boy. They were probably the last family to live there as the county councils took over the responsibility of the roads following the municipal reforms of 1835 and the turnpikes gradually disappeared. The tiny toll house was used as an apple store for a while and some of the village men would play cards there whilst waiting for the pub to open. It was tumbled down by 1908 and finally disappeared altogether.

At the same time that the turnpike trusts were being set up, the railways were also expanding their networks and services. Didcot became an important junction on the Great Western Railway's London to Bristol line when a railway link was built to Oxford from Didcot. The Oxford line and Didcot station were both opened on the 12th of June 1844.

The railways had an important impact on trade as heavy goods could be more easily and quickly transported by rail, much to the detriment of the river, canal and road transport companies. As goods started to be moved by rail, the long-distance stage wagons and carriers quickly ceased operating, directly affecting the turnpike trusts which had all been wound up by 1870.

The Didcot to Newbury section of the Didcot, Newbury and Southampton Railway opened in 1882. One of the stations on its route was Upton, which was within easy walking distance of West Hagbourne and much closer than the station at Didcot. This must have made a great difference to West Hagbourne, as it increased opportunities for trade in local agricultural produce and the possibility of travel. The Newbury line opened up the wool-producing countryside of the nearby Berkshire Downs. Records show that, in 1889, the Junction Hotel in Didcot kept as many as 16 post horses to carry wool buyers to the sheep sales in East Ilsley. It is likely that they rode through West Hagbourne on their way to the sales. During the Second World War, the Americans increased the Didcot to Newbury line from one track to two in order to transport war supplies from Didcot where there was an army ordnance depot. One local farmer remembers sugar beet being transported from his farm to the station at Upton during the War. The line was never economic and consequently was closed to passengers in 1962, and then to freight two years later.

Rivers also played an important role in the story of the Hagbournes. They were once used much like roads for trade and travel as well as by warlords or conquering armies to overpower the local communities along the way. The Saxon chief, Hacca, is believed to have come up the Thames in the fifth century to settle by a local stream and give his name to the Hagbournes. The Thames was studded with castles built for defence and abbeys which became seats of power. Most of these are now in ruins but the settlements which were established beside the Thames expanded into the towns which thrive today.

West Hagbourne is no longer a small rural community connected to the land but a 'commuter' village where people are dependent on motor cars for transport and tend to work in towns and cities as far away as London. It is not the wool buyers who now pour out of Didcot Railway Station to hire their pack horses at the Junction Hotel, but the commuters who get into their cars to return home to the surrounding Oxfordshire villages. The station hosts a museum dedicated to preserving the history of the Great Western Railway Company which had so much influence on the development of West Hagbourne in the nineteenth and twentieth centuries.

West Hagbourne Place Names

Some of the names used in West Hagbourne today can be traced back to Anglo-Saxon times. One of the reasons that names were first given to individual pieces of land was so that farm labourers could be directed to their daily tasks. As the teams of workers went to and from the fields, paths and lanes emerged and they too acquired names. When farming methods changed and machinery took over the work of the labourers, many place names went out of daily use and have been forgotten in the mists of time. Also, with the gradual enclosure of land, many strips, and even whole fields, disappeared along with their names. In the twentieth century, hedges were taken out to make larger fields, losing the names of the small plots of land along the way. Many more traditional names may have disappeared from official maps but they are still used locally, having been passed on from one generation to the next. In fact the early cartographers based their maps on local knowledge and wrote down the names repeated to them by the villagers, many of which had already been in use for several centuries. These ancient names have evolved and changed but their origins are still recognisable, and a few can be traced back to our Saxon ancestors.

Various documents and maps have survived which help us to follow the development of West Hagbourne place names. The very earliest extant document to mention Hagbourne land is the Saxon survey attached to the charter of about 895 AD, whereby the Bishop of Winchester exchanged various pieces of land, including Hagbourne, with King Alfred. The survey refers to a wide gate: "Thonon to Widan Geate", thought to be on the north west boundary of Hagbourne near Down Farm. A field called Gate Piece, north east of Down Farm, is marked on an early Ordnance Survey map and is also mentioned on the Tithe Award for 1841. Whether Gate Piece refers to the same gate as the survey is not known but Down Farm and the commons around it were right on the parish boundary with Harwell and it is very likely that there was a gate between the two parishes, particularly for moving sheep and cattle. Old parish boundaries were usually delineated by hedges, many of which were mentioned in the old charters and could be regarded as some of our oldest monuments.

One of the earliest surviving documents to include field names is the dowry granted to Clarice in 1367 on the death of her husband Richard de Windsor, the lord of the manor of West Hagbourne. Clarice de Windsor received a total of 91 acres of arable land belonging to the manor. The dowry identifies each piece of this land by size and name and where it lay in relation to the manor:

24½ acres in the Southfeld on the east side
40 acres above the Weye Forlong
3¼ acres in the Brokforlong towards the east
3 acres at Renydche by the high road towards the west
10 acres 1 rood 13 perches 6ft at Roggerscherd
3½ acres 26 perches 12ft at Nicholasforlong
3 acres above Nicholasforlong towards the west

As well as the arable land, Clarice was also entitled to: 1 acre of meadow and over 1½ acres of pasture in the Estmede; 4 acres of meadow in the Westmede; a share of the ox pasture in the Estmede and a third of the annual income from pasture on the Doune. According to the law, a widow was entitled to the tenancy of one third of her husband's land for the rest of her life. Therefore one can assume that the amount of land awarded to Clarice in her dowry represents one third of the total holdings of West Hagbourne manor in 1367.

A *forlong* refers back to the Anglo Saxon farming system in use in Berkshire in the tenth century and originally meant the length of the furrow in a common field. 'Field' is an Old English word which comes from the Saxon *feld,* meaning open land. Clarice's dowry included land she received in the Southfeld to the east of the manor. The dowry also lists all the tenants of the manor and how much rent they paid. One of these was Thomas Stotland who paid 2s a year to the manor. It is believed that the area around the Horse and Harrow Inn, known as Scotlands Ash, is derived from his name. There is also a gate of the same name beside the toll house on the Inclosure Map of 1843. Scotlands Ash appears on the Craven Estate map of 1775, and is one of the few features to be named on the first one-inch Ordnance Survey map of Berkshire, printed in 1830. It could well be the same piece of land which Thomas Stotland rented from Clarice de Windsor in 1367.

Names can tell us a lot about a field's history. The Wet and Dry Moors at the end of Moor Lane were named after natural features, whilst Nicholasfurlong and Roggerscherd took the names of their owners. When later fields were cut, they were known as Seven Acre Piece, Fifteen Acres and so on, according to their acreage. Some names were derived from features on the landscape, such as a gate or pond, which may no longer exist, so that finding these references in old documents gives us some idea of how the land may have appeared hundreds of years ago.

Further documentary clues to the evolution of West Hagbourne names come some 250 years later with the 1662 legacy of William Tyrrell, described earlier in this chapter. Most of the land in the village was then still farmed in the strip system though a little had been enclosed. The land William Tyrrell left to the poor of West

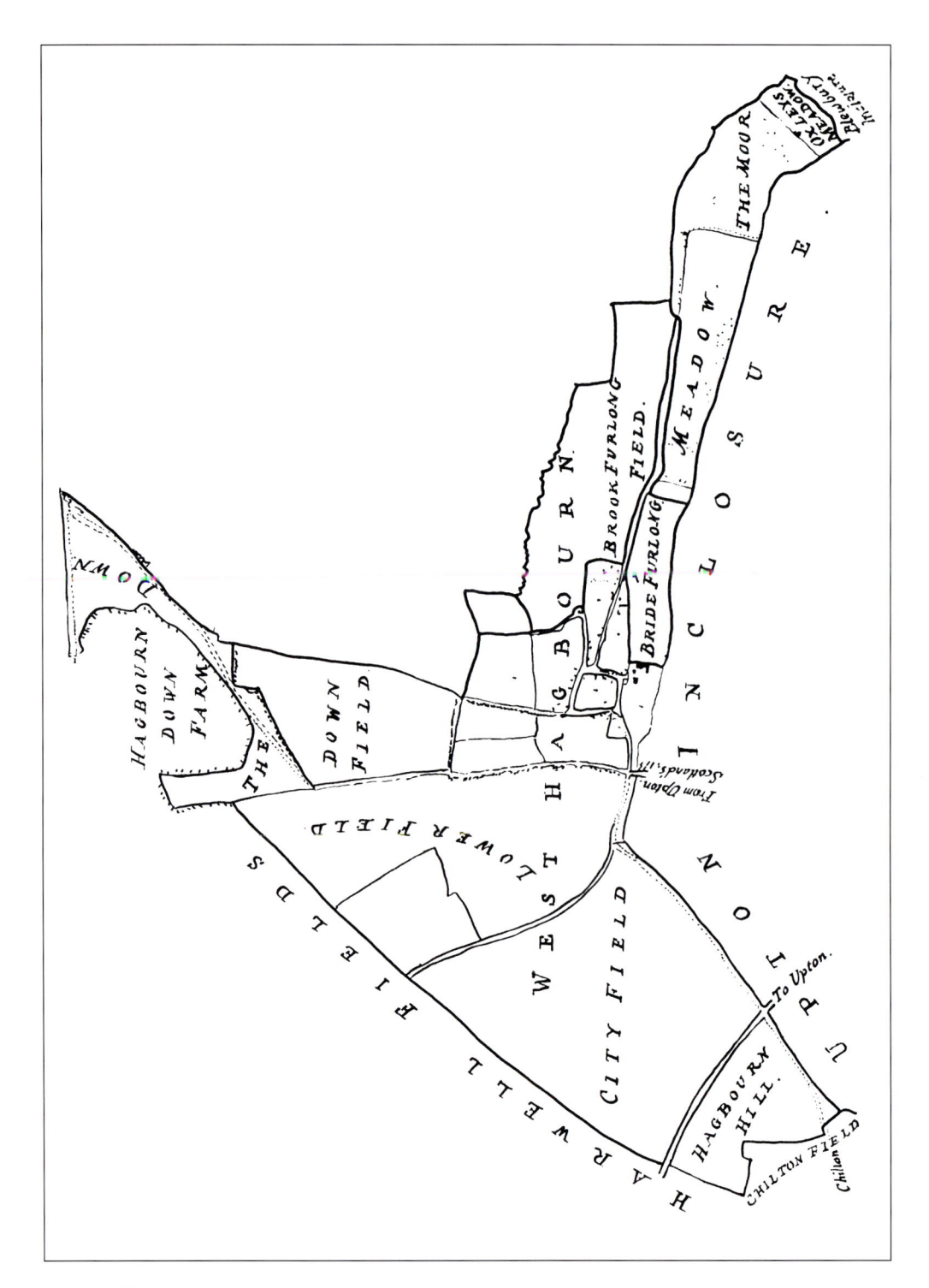

Craven Estate map, 1775

Hagbourne was spread throughout the open fields as follows:

Three roods on a furlong called the Therne
Half an acre on Church Furlong
One acre in the Sitches
One rood upon the Black Hill
Half an acre in Benshole or Bunshill
One rood in Langlands
One rood in Elder Furlong
One rood in Brook Furlong
Half an acre in Chitborough Furlong
One rood in Stony Lands
One rood in ditto
Half an acre in Meer Furlong
One rood of meadow in West Hagbourn Mead

Some of the fields named in Clarice de Windsor's dowry appear again in William Tyrrell's will. Brokforlong has become Brook Furlong by 1662, whilst Mead is a later rendition of Mede.

Another map, slightly later than the Rocque map mentioned previously, gives an even better idea of where the open fields, meadows, downs and moors of West Hagbourne lay and, even more importantly, what they were called. This was a map drawn up in 1775 to indicate the lessees of the Craven Estate in both East and West Hagbourne. Lord Craven was lord of the manor of East Hagbourne and holder of tithing rights in West Hagbourne. The 1775 map identifies the land from which Lord Craven drew the tithes which the villagers so resented paying. It defines the village boundaries and field names in a much more comprehensive way than both the Rocque map and the one-inch Ordnance Survey which lump all the open fields under "Hagborn Fields" and "West Hagborne Fields" respectively. The Craven Estate map is also a useful comparison with the Inclosure Award plan because it shows the open field system of West Hagbourne before the enclosures were awarded in 1843. The Craven map separated the open fields to the west into five main areas running from north to south: the Down, Down Field, Lower Field, City Field and Hagbourne Hill. City Field is referred to as Hagbourne Field on current Ordnance Surveys. The common land to the east of the manor was divided into Bride Furlong, the Meadow and the Moor leading to Oxleys Meadow (later to become Oxlease and Ashmead).

The earliest known map specific to the village of West Hagbourne is dated 1754. Its exact purpose is unknown but it is very likely that it was drawn up as evidence of an earlier enclosure. The original map is crude by modern standards but has a certain charm with its impressionistic drawings of cottages, farmhouses and the church in the east. Parts of the map have been coloured by hand though the significance of the colours is not clear. It is even more detailed than the Craven Estate map and includes the names of many of the individual strips of land which

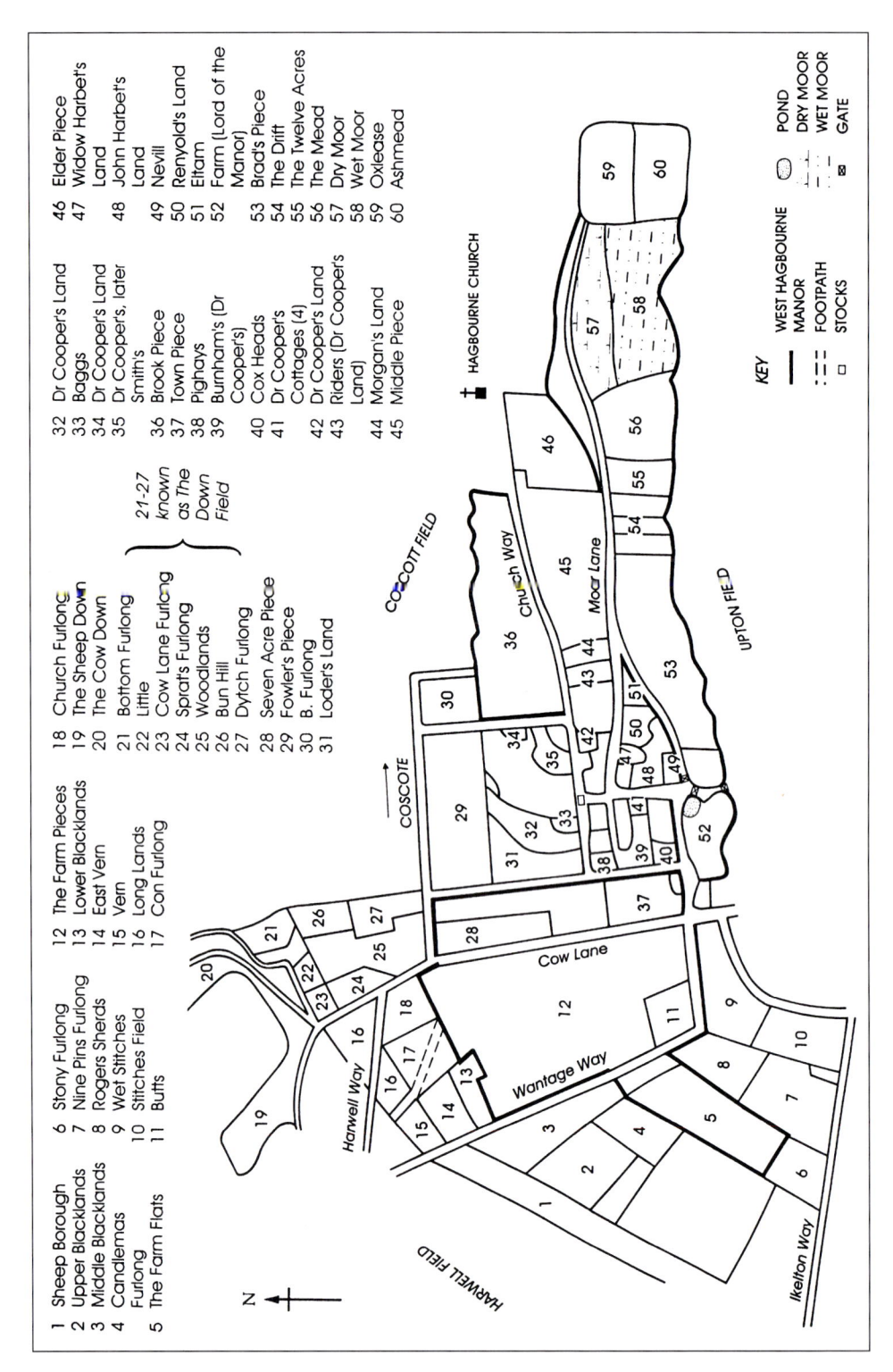

#	Name	#	Name	#	Name
1	Sheep Borough	21	Bottom Furlong	42	Dr Cooper's Land
2	Upper Blacklands	22	Little	43	Riders (Dr Cooper's Land)
3	Middle Blacklands	23	Cow Lane Furlong	44	Morgan's Land
4	Candlemas Furlong	24	Sprat's Furlong	45	Middle Piece
5	The Farm Flats	25	Woodlands	46	Elder Piece
6	Stony Furlong	26	Bun Hill	47	Widow Harbet's Land
7	Nine Pins Furlong	27	Dytch Furlong	48	John Harbet's Land
8	Rogers Sherds	28	Seven Acre Piece	49	Nevill
9	Wet Stitches	29	Fowler's Piece	50	Renyold's Land
10	Stitches Field	30	B. Furlong	51	Eltam
11	Butts	31	Loder's Land	52	Farm (Lord of the Manor)
12	The Farm Pieces	32	Dr Cooper's Land	53	Brad's Piece
13	Lower Blacklands	33	Baggs	54	The Drift
14	East Vern	34	Dr Cooper's Land	55	The Twelve Acres
15	Vern	35	Dr Cooper's, later Smith's	56	The Mead
16	Long Lands	36	Brook Piece	57	Dry Moor
17	Con Furlong	37	Town Piece	58	Wet Moor
18	Church Furlong	38	Pighays	59	Oxlease
19	The Sheep Down	39	Burnham's (Dr Cooper's)	60	Ashmead
20	The Cow Down	40	Cox Heads		
		41	Dr Coopers Cottages (4)		

21-27 known as The Down Field

KEY: WEST HAGBOURNE — MANOR — FOOTPATH --- STOCKS □ POND ⬭ DRY MOOR WET MOOR GATE ✕

Village of West Hagbourne, 1754 (redrawn)

made up the open fields. By referring to the 1754 map and its key, it is possible to work out where some of the land mentioned in Clarice's dowry and land left by William Tyrrell were actually situated.

The land Clarice inherited at Roggerscherd is marked on the 1754 map as Rogers Sherds (8). John Harwood's will referred to it as Rodger's Shade in 1738. A sherd was originally a clearing in a wood and later came to mean 'a gap'. Brook Forlong has been abbreviated to B. Furlong (30) whilst Tyrrell's land at Bunshill had evolved into Bun Hill (26), which was part of Down Field. East of Bun Hill on the north eastern boundary was Witney Wergs, one of several names which have not survived in any form. Wergs comes from the Anglo Saxon word *withig* and refers to the willow obstacles put around the arable land before harvest to prevent cattle from straying on to it. Both Tyrrell's will and the 1754 map refer to Church Furlong (18) though it is not situated anywhere near the supposed site of the village chapel or near Church Path leading to St Andrew's Church in East Hagbourne. It could possibly be associated with the church at Harwell which could easily be reached by a path called Harwell Way in 1754.

Tyrrell's will refers to Stony Lands whilst the 1754 map names Stony Furlong (6) on the upper slope of Hagbourne Hill and adds to the evidence that there was a stone pit there. According to Martha Tyrrell's plea, discussed in Chapter Four, Richard de Windsor granted William Tyrrell the Elder two acres of land "lying at Stone Pit alias Spurwick in Hagbourne". We know that there was once a chalk pit behind the house on Hagbourne Hill. Some of the chalk was used to provide a hard surface for the cattle yard nearby. The chalk pit was gradually ploughed in and by the 1930s it was no longer used but was probably the land called Stony Furlong on Hagbourne Hill. In 1738 John Harwood left his son, Jonathan, a house called Chaulks and two adjoining butts (pieces of arable land smaller than the usual strip). Chaulks may have been named after the chalk pit and could have been the original name of the house on Hagbourne Hill.

On the 1754 map, Tyrrell's Sitches is called Stitches. Wet Stitches and Stitches Field are marked at the bottom of Hagbourne Hill. Stitches can be traced back to the Anglo Saxon word *sica*, meaning a ditch or water course for drainage; an appropriate name for land at the bottom of Hagbourne Hill. *Sica* evolved into syches, then sitches and today that same land at the bottom of the hill is still referred to by local farmers as stitches, by which they mean a drainage ridge or furrow.

The two fields called Long Lands (16 on the 1754 map) were separated by a route called Harwell Way which led to Harwell Field and would have been used by locals to move between the two villages. This path was later known as the Driftway. Langlands Mere lay on the north west boundary, north of Harwell Way. Mere comes from the Anglo Saxon *maere*, meaning "the balk of the long ploughland" but later came to mean a road which developed along a headland. South of the Long Lands were the Verns, later called North and South Vearns. South Vearns Mere was an accommodation road, possibly the footpath marked on the map crossing Con Furlong (17). Vern comes from the Saxon word *fearn*, meaning to mark out land for ploughing. It is likely that the Therne mentioned in Tyrrell's will was a version of Vern. Another old field name which has survived is Goosecoobs, which appeared on the Craven map as Gesoums. It was part of a larger open field called Farm Pieces (12 on the 1754 map).

Shovel Spring, which runs along the boundary with East Hagbourne, is thought to have originated from the Saxon words *Scobban Wyll*. By 1199 it had become Sobewell and later, in a rent survey of 1408–9, was referred to as Scobewell, then Scobba's Spring and finally Shovel Spring. Shovel Spring is part of a whole network of springs, brooks and ditches, some running underground, throughout West and East Hagbourne, linking up with Hakka's Brook on the east side of East Hagbourne village. There was also a field below Shovel Spring at the east end of the parish, called Shobwell Piece. This same field is known today as Shovel Spring by local farmers. Brook Furlong, Brook Piece and Brook Lane take their names from the brook which ran through them all to join Shovel Spring at its source and which still causes flooding in Brook Lane after a rain storm.

As well as field names, the 1754 map provides the first evidence of the village stocks situated in the area known today as The Square in the centre of the village. It also reveals that there were a lot more houses fronting Moor Lane and Main Street between the pond and The Square in 1754 than there are today. Three gates are marked near West Hagbourne manor and one of these dates back to Clarice's time, as her dowry mentions "the pond by the great gate". Some of the paths and well-trodden routes through the village are named on the 1754 map: Church Way, later called Church Path, indicates a time-honoured route to St Andrew's Church in East Hagbourne, whilst Cow Lane inevitably led to the Cow Down and is still known by that name to this day. The Driftway branched off Cow Lane in the direction of Harwell.

However, it is the Inclosure Award and plan which are the best sources for the earliest names of paths and roads in West Hagbourne and whilst some, like Green Gate Lane, Cow Lane and Moor Lane are still in use, the names of many of the public roads have completely changed. Goosecoobs Road, named for the field beside it to the west, was the northern section of what is now York Road, whilst the section of York Road which runs passed York Farm went by the grand name of High Street in 1843. The lower end of York Road, from Green Gate Lane, was called Town Piece Road after the field on its west side (number 37 on the 1754 map). Today's Main Street was known as Pond Road as far as Pond Corner, opposite the pond. It then changed to Village Street as far as The Square, where it joined the High Street. A second pond, called Pill Pond, was situated at the most northern tip of the parish on the boundary with Didcot.

It is not only farmers who have names for the fields but children also invent their own place names. In the days before television, computers and increased traffic on village roads, children tended to roam the fields more freely and most walked to the local school in East Hagbourne along Church Path, which was known to the children as School Path. They had their own names for their secret play places.

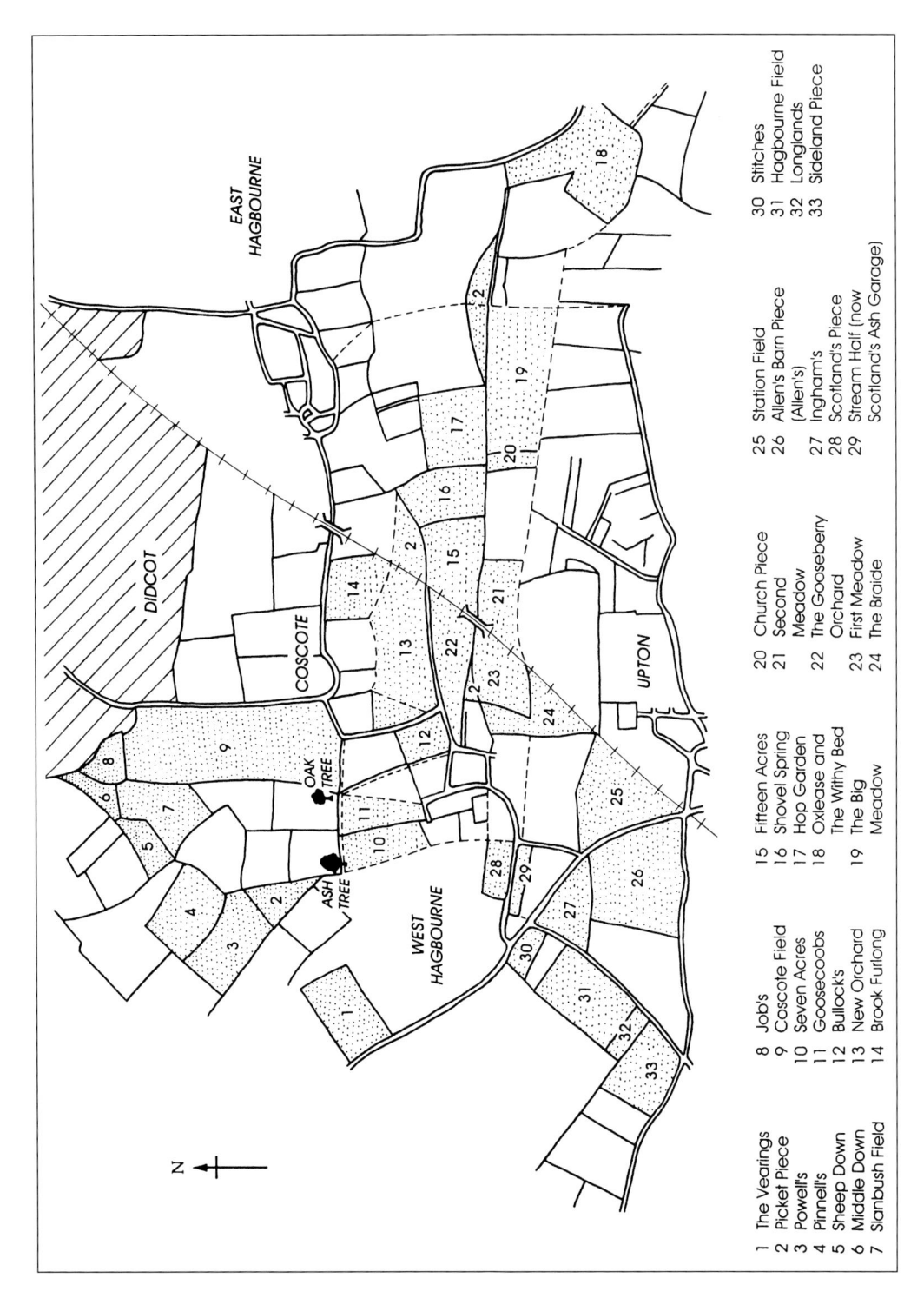

Field names, 2000

Cow Lane, which leads to Harwell from the Horse and Harrow, was "the lane that never ends" and the bushes and trees found there were called "the jungle". Then there was "Lay's Pond" near Manor Farm and "Den's Pond" in Moor Lane with the "growing stone". No one seems to know how that name came into being; perhaps it appeared to grow or shrink according to the height of the water in the pond. Along Moor Lane was always "down the moors" where the "Gypsy Caravan" and "Wipsi's Orchard" were to be found. The once heavily-used path leading from Moor Lane to Upton was known as "the way over the Braide". On the old maps the Braide has been referred to variously as Braid Furlong, Bride Furlong and Brad's Piece – probably all versions of 'broad'.

A map drawn to show the field names used by local farmers today includes many which have appeared in earlier documents going as far back as Clarice's dowry and Tyrrell's will. Many of the names on this map will not appear on any ordnance survey but are well known to those who farm in the area. The oldest are: The Vearings, Sheep Down, Seven Acres, Goosecoobs, Brook Furlong, Fifteen Acres, Shovel Spring, Oxlease, The Braide, Scotland's Piece, Stitches and Longlands. Some of these have their roots in Saxon times whilst others remind us of the natural features of the village with its streams, ditches and wet lands. Some names commemorate villagers who lived several hundred years ago whilst others belong to farming families of today. Most of them are linked with West Hagbourne's farming past and the rural nature of a village now struggling to keep those links alive.

Drawing of milestone on the road between West Hagbourne and Harwell

Sources – West Hagbourne Inclosure Award of 1843

I S Leadam, *The Domesday of Inclosures*, 1517-1518, Longman, Green and Co., 1897.
W E Tate, 'Hand list of English Enclosure Acts and Awards relating to Berkshire', *Bucks, Berks, Oxon Archaeological Journal*, Vol 47, 1943.
Precedents from the Court Rolls of 1660, Berkshire Record Office, Reading. D/EAH E10.
The Rocque Map of Berkshire, 1761. Reissued by H Margary, Lympne Castle, Kent, 1973.
West Hagbourn Inclosure Award, 27 July 1843, Berkshire Record Office, Reading. Q/RDC 39A.
A Plan of the Hamlet of West Hagbourn in the Parish of East Hagbourn and County of Berks inclosed, 1843, Berkshire Record Office, Reading. Q/RDC 39B.

Sources – Roads, Railways and Rivers

Judith Hunter, *A History of Berkshire,* Phillimore & Co. Ltd., 1995.
Michael Bishop, *A Guide to the Byways of East Hagbourne*, The East Hagbourne Parish Council and The East and West Hagbourne Society, Reading, 1980.
B F Lingham, *The Long Years of Obscurity – A History of Didcot, Volume One to 1841*, Didcot Press, 1978.
The Minute Book of West Hagbourne Parish, 4 December 1894 – 31 March 1964, West Hagbourne Parish Council, Oxfordshire.
Turnpike Trusts, Berkshire Record Office, Reading. D/EPT E33.

Sources – West Hagbourne Place Names

Walter de Gray Birch, *Cartularium Saxonicum: A Collection of Charters relating to Anglo-Saxon History*, Whiting and Company, 1887.
Tithe Award, 1841, unpublished, Tithe Redemption Office, London.
Dowry of Clarice de Windsor: *Calendar of Close Rolls, Edward III 1364–1368*, Public Record Office, Kew.
G B Grundy, 'Berkshire Charters', *Berks, Bucks & Oxon Archaeological Journal*, Vol 29, Spring 1925.
Margaret Gelling, *The Place Names of Berkshire*, Vols I, II and III, Cambridge University Press, 1973–1976.
One-inch Ordnance Survey of England and Wales: Oxford and Reading, 1830. Reprint of first edition, David & Charles, 1980.
The last will and testament of William Tirrell the Elder, 1662, Berkshire Record Office, Reading. D/A1 128/42.
Matthias Baker, *A Survey of the Manor and Parish of Hagbourn in the County of Berkshire and also several farms and lands belonging to the right honourable William Lord Craven*, 1775, Berkshire Record Office, Reading.
Map of West Hagbourne, 1754, Berkshire Record Office, Reading.

Will of John Harwood, 15 September 1738, Berkshire Record Office, Reading. D/A1/84/161a.

'Hamilton Bundle', *Chancery Bills and Answers*, 1687, Public Record Office, Kew. C7 337/59.

Brian Lingham, compiler, *Around Didcot and the Hagbournes in Old Photographs*, Alan Sutton, 1990.

Christine Bloxham, 'Pastures Old', *Limited Edition, The Magazine of Oxfordshire*, Newsquest (Oxfordshire) Limited, October 1997.

Chapter Six

The Hagbourne Charities and the Philanthropic Tyrrells

The relief of poverty

The Charitable Trusts Act of 1597 was passed by parliament to stimulate charitable giving. It was a response to the desperate need to alleviate poverty at the end of the sixteenth century. In medieval times the state had not concerned itself with the relief of poverty – that was the province of the church. Part of the pastoral work of the religious orders of the monasteries was to care for the sick, to provide alms houses and food for the poor and temporary shelter to travellers. However, the dissolution of the monasteries in 1536 threw this system into turmoil.

The enclosure of land by the gentry for sheep rearing created unemployment and vagrancy in rural areas such as West Hagbourne, whilst severe land rent rises and inflation also contributed to the general misery of the poor. Also, towards the end of the century, the plague returned, leaving families without breadwinners. To compound matters, the harvests of 1592–6 were bad, causing famine and price rises. There was also a war going on, which meant that discharged soldiers were returning sick or maimed, or else they had simply deserted, exacerbating the vagrancy problem. It became apparent that the increase in homelessness and unemployment required comprehensive legislation if stability and order were to be maintained.

Many of the early acts and laws relating to the poor only served to punish or ostracize people. However, the Elizabethan poor laws of 1597 and 1601 actually began to address these social problems by placing the responsibility of providing for the helpless, aged and sick upon the parish. The laws were to be administered by parish overseers and financed out of a compulsory rate levied upon householders. The parish was also expected to provide work for those genuinely unemployed. Those who refused or avoided work were to be punished.

The administration of these laws relied heavily on the old ecclesiastical organisation of parishes. West and East Hagbourne, together with the Northbourne district of Didcot, were part of the parish of Hagbourne which dealt with both civil and church matters. The parish vestry (vestries being the forerunners of local councils) had to appoint two overseers of the poor to see that the welfare legislation was carried out. They also had to collect the poor-rate which they were empowered both to fix and adjust, and they supervised endowments and other charitable funds. The money raised by the poor-rate was distributed by the overseers according to need. The Poor Laws were administered through the Quarter Sessions, when the overseers had to submit their records to the justice of the peace and account for how they had spent the money raised by the poor-rate.

The overseers were appointed annually from amongst the local parish landowners and usually had some official or legal experience but they were not paid for their work. They met each month with the church wardens on Sunday afternoon in the church, which was often the only building in a village large enough for a meeting, and so their records came to be known as vestry minutes. The law ruled that each parish had to provide shelter for the poor, the aged, orphans and the disabled. It became customary to set aside a house in each village for those who were homeless and although there are no known records for this period it is likely that West Hagbourne had such a dwelling. Needless to say, vagrants were not encouraged to linger in a village in case they became a burden on parish resources. Later, around 1722, parishes were expected to build or rent workhouses to provide work and shelter for the unemployed homeless.

Union workhouses

This system of poor relief continued until 1834 when the Poor Law Amendment Act decreed that parishes should be amalgamated into 'unions' to provide for the poor. These were to be run by Boards of Guardians of the Poor who replaced the overseers. Local parish workhouses were replaced by union workhouses to which people, including children, unable to support themselves were forced to move. No relief was to be given to the able-bodied. The threat of the workhouse became a dreadful fear amongst the poor as they were made as uncomfortable as possible so that inmates would be encouraged to seek work. The union workhouse for Hagbourne was in Wallingford – a long way for poor people in the days before motorised public transport. For the villagers of West Hagbourne to be sent to the union workhouse effectively meant being cut off from family, friends and everything they knew. The workhouse in Wallingford later became a hospital for the elderly but its previous reputation lingered on in the minds of the community. More recently the whole area has been developed for housing and the former workhouse has gone for ever.

One of the people from West Hagbourne who spent some time in the workhouse at Wallingford was Nelly Woodley. Nelly was the daughter of Jabez and Elizabeth Woodley who married on the 3rd of November 1901. Jabez was 50 and Elizabeth was 47 when they married. Nelly was born on the 9th of November 1903. Although she was christened Ellen Elizabeth, she was always known as Nelly. Sadly, her mother died on the 17th of December 1903 when Nelly was barely a month old. As there was no-one to look after her, Nelly was sent to the workhouse in Wallingford. Jabez didn't want his little daughter to forget him so he walked from West Hagbourne to Wallingford and back as often as he could to visit her in the workhouse. Jabez remarried in 1908 and Nelly came home to live with her father and stepmother in a small cottage in Moor Lane.

Origins of the Hagbourne charities

As well as the money raised by the poor laws, both West and East Hagbourne held a pool of money from endowments and legacies which could be shared amongst the needy. Charity Commission records for 1837 show that at one time there were eight parochial charities shared by the two villages. In addition there were two specifically for West Hagbourne and another known as Poor's Land (consisting of four acres of land purchased from several small donations) which was particular to East Hagbourne. The two West Hagbourne charities were those bequeathed by Moses Hawkins and William Tyrrell. The village only benefited from the Hawkins bequest for 58 years, but the Tyrrell legacy continues up to the present day.

The parochial charities, apart from the Richard Creswell and Moses Hawkins Charities, are still in existence, in some form, today. Little is known about some of the original benefactors, though some of the family names are familiar. Many of the bequests were originally in the shape of land or rental charges on land or property. Today they have largely been capitalised and converted into investment units by various funds. The parochial charities originated from the following bequests:

Reynolds's Charity

Nothing is known of Reynolds, the date he made his will or his link with the Hagbournes. He apparently lived in Shinfield and left 20 shillings to be paid annually out of his estate in Wokingham to the poor of East and West Hagbourne.

William Keate's Charity

William Keate of East Hagbourne left 20 shillings for the use of the poor of West Hagbourne to be paid from the rent charge on 14 acres of land known as Breach Furlong in Finmere, Oxfordshire. The date of the will is unknown and could have been that of William Keate who lived in the manor at East Hagbourne in 1539 but it may also have been that of another William who erected the memorial brass to his parents on the chancel wall of St Andrew's in 1617.

Creswell's Charity

In 1675 Richard Creswell left ten shillings to be paid to the poor out of rents from a house, four acres of arable land and one acre of meadow in West Hagbourne. The money was to be distributed annually on St Thomas's Day. By 1837 the house no longer existed and the ten shillings was met mostly by Richard Tyrrell of Harwell and, to a lesser extent, by Francis Woodley of West Hagbourne, both of whom owned strips of land in Hagbourne Fields. Following the Inclosure Award of 1843, the lord of the manor, Mr Aldworth, received large allotments belonging to Tyrrell but it appears that neither he nor his descendants ever paid anything. Woodley's representatives could not be traced. In their report of 1908 the Charity Commissioners concluded that the Charity was therefore lost.

Mary Smith's Charity

In 1718 Mrs Mary Smith left ten shillings for a sermon to be preached annually on the 1st of May in the parish of Hagbourne and ten shillings to buy 20 sixpenny loaves to be given to 20 poor widows in the porch after the sermon had been preached by the vicar. The loaves were sometimes also given to widowers. This sum of 20 shillings was to be paid from an estate in Chalgrove. This bequest was considered as two separate entities – one as an ecclesiastical charity under the churchwardens and the other as an almsgiving (eleemosynary) charity under the parish council. In reality it was still managed by the same trustees.

Eleanor Keate's Charity

In 1719 Eleanor Keate left the rent from her house in Castle Street, Wallingford, for the benefit of the poor of the parish. As well as the house, the property included a yard, outhouses and a small garden. In 1819 the rent amounted to £11 per year with the tenant paying the fire insurance. The house was sold in 1882 for £200 which was invested on behalf of the trustees of the Charity.

Hawkins's Charity

In 1728 Moses Hawkins left all his arable land in Hagbourne Fields to both Moses Hawkins (probably his son) and William Dawes, with the proviso that every Christmas they would give ten shillings to the poor of West Hagbourne for ever. William Dawes bought out Moses Hawkins and later mortgaged the land to Mary Harwood who held it for many years. After her death Mary's son Harry bought the Dawes estate, which included the land in Hagbourne Fields. It then passed through several hands but according to the Parliamentary Returns for 1786 the payment of the ten shillings had, by that time, been withheld. In 1795 the estate was bought by David Dearlove of West Hagbourne.

 The Charity Commissioners pursued the Hawkins legacy and discovered that Dearlove's property had been dispersed amongst several buyers, the largest portion of more than ten acres going to Richard Robinson. The Commissioners obtained an admission from Robinson that he was liable for the yearly rentcharge of ten shillings to the poor of West Hagbourne with a promise that he personally would undertake regular payment in future. However, an inquiry into the Hagbourne charities held in 1908 noted that he never paid any part of the rent-charge and concluded that the Charity was therefore lost.

Harwood's Charity

In 1734 Mary Harwood left £50 which she inherited from her mother, Martha, and £150 of her own, to be invested. The interest was to be distributed annually to the "poor housekeepers" of the parish of Hagbourne by her executor, John Harwood, his heirs and the minister and churchwardens, as they saw fit. John Harwood's heir, Samuel Harwood, a Shrewsbury doctor, bought annuities worth £237, declaring that the interest should be used for the poor of Hagbourne as stated in Mary Harwood's will.

Eaton's Charity

The Eaton Charity was the most valuable of all. In 1772 the Reverend Matthew Eaton's will stated that his real and personal estate was to be sold and the money invested for the benefit of the poor of Harwell, Milton and Hagbourne and also to provide apprenticeships for the poor children of these parishes. It appears that there had been some irregularities in the management of the Charity on the part of the vicars of the three parishes, including the Reverend John Scoolt of St Andrew's, and the trustees took the matter to the Court of Chancery on the 22nd of April 1822. One of the trustees was Job Lousley of West Hagbourne Farm (Manor Farm). The Court decreed that the stock should be invested in the name of the Accountant-General and that future dividends should be divided equally between the parishes of Hagbourne, Milton and Harwell. The distributors were also ordered to keep annual accounts of their receipts and disbursements and these were to be inspected by the three of them annually on Easter Monday. This suggests that the irregularities were more to do with muddle and poor accounting rather than any criminal activity. However, the sums involved were large as the stock was worth £3,180 in 1863 and the dividends and interest came to £95 8s. Hagbourne's share of this was £26 10s per year.

In 1908 the trustees of the Eaton Charity were Job Napper for West Hagbourne, J P Napper for East Hagbourne and Richard Mills representing the vicar. No apprenticeships were awarded after 1860; the practice having become obsolete in the district. Most of the Charity's income seems to have been spent on clothing tickets which were redeemable from the drapers Field and Hawkins of Wallingford who brought up a cart of material to the school in East Hagbourne each January. Some money was given to top up the subscriptions of a clothing club to which nearly 60 villagers belonged. In 1906 and 1907 girls who had held good records of employment for a year were rewarded with dresses costing six shillings.

Widows and widowers were given a larger allowance than those with living spouses. After 1915 other stores in Didcot, Wallingford, Reading and Oxford also supplied goods for distribution by the Eaton Charity. Christmas parcels to the value of one shilling were made up by the village store in East Hagbourne for distribution amongst villagers in West, East and North Hagbourne.

Christopher Elderfield's Charity

The bulk of this Charity was for the benefit of the poor of Harwell but Christopher Elderfield left ten shillings for the parish officers of Hagbourne to attend the audit of the accounts at Harwell church on the first Sunday after Easter to ensure that the trustees did not abuse the Charity. Every tenth year the poor of Hagbourne were entitled to receive half of the year's profits. In 1834 Hagbourne received £29 18s 3d from the rent of the estates at Harwell and South Moreton. This procedure was changed by the Charity Commissioners in 1893 when the trustees were directed to pay the churchwardens and overseers of the parish of Hagbourne a yearly sum of ten shillings and a further yearly sum amounting to one-twentieth of the income instead of one half of the income every tenth year.

John Armstrong's Charity

In 1853 John Armstrong of East Hagbourne left £200 to be invested for the poor of Hagbourne. According to the terms of the will, the bequest was to be distributed under the control of the Reverend Richard Meredith, vicar of Hagbourne; Armstrong's sister, Jane Fairs, and his brother Robert. In order to fulfil Armstrong's wishes an arrangement was drawn up by deed poll in 1864 which allowed the trustees to give the vicar of Hagbourne and his successors the dividends with which to provide the poor with gifts of flannel or blankets. The Reverend Meredith decreed that the blankets would be distributed among poor householders who had resided for four years in East or West Hagbourne. According to the Charity Commissioners' report of 1837, there were about 24 recipients annually and every four years each poor householder received a pair of blankets costing about nine shillings.

Foundation of the Hagbourne Charity

By 1908 all the existing parochial charities, except the Eaton and Tyrrell Charities, were administered by a body of trustees consisting of the vicar, churchwardens, the overseers of the poor and representatives of the parish council of East Hagbourne and the parish meeting of West Hagbourne which did not have a parish council until 1964. However, the parish meeting was given the powers of a parish council under the Local Government Act of 1894. The representative of the parish meeting of West Hagbourne was Ezra Dearlove who was also an overseer. In 1934 the eight parochial charities, known as the Churchwarden's Group, and the Eaton Charity were merged into one, called the Hagbourne Charity. Only the William Tyrrell Charity, which is particular to West Hagbourne, kept its own trustees and continued to be administered separately from the other, merged charities.

The trustees of the charities made sure that the money was used for the poor and needy, as was intended by the founders. In 1837 the total income from all the parochial charities, including the Tyrrell Charity, came to £45. Once the 20 shillings bequeathed to the neighbouring village of Blewbury, as specified in William Tyrrell's will, had been paid, the remainder was distributed at Easter in small amounts varying between five and seven shillings according to the needs of the recipients and whether they were single, married, or had many children. By the beginning of the twentieth century the income was being distributed in the form of coal as well as cash and clothing. The trustees met in January to draw up the list of recipients from among the labourers and widows of East and West Hagbourne and the railway village of North Hagbourne. Twenty three people in West Hagbourne, 54 in East and 25 in North Hagbourne received five hundredweight of coal in 1908 (one hundredweight equalled 112 pounds). A few years earlier there had been as many as 120 recipients, many of them also on poor relief. Two people, who were not householders and had no need of coal, received goods to the value of four shillings which suggests that this was the value of five hundredweight of coal.

Later, the distribution of coal gave way to Christmas boxes for the elderly. In 1933/34 the distribution of money earned from the Hagbourne Charity's investments amounted to £62 (worth over £2000 today). Now the trustees believe it is more appropriate to target specific needs with small, one-off grants of about £20 to meet a particular difficulty, such as special food or medical aids, to make life more comfortable for the bedridden or housebound; reimbursement of travel costs for carers or relatives of the sick or disabled; tools to improve employment opportunities for the unemployed, or items to assist widows with young children.

At the time they were endowed the bequests were generous, but their value today has all but disappeared. However, after more than 300 years since the first endowment, the Hagbourne Charity still exists for the benefit of the residents of West and East Hagbourne and Northbourne.

Hagbourn Benefit Society

During the eighteenth century the working classes began to organise themselves into mutually supportive groups called friendly societies ('box clubs') which provided a very basic kind of social insurance. However, even these societies were only open to those who could afford the contributions and those who couldn't had to wait for the passing of the National Insurance Act in December 1911 to receive sickness and unemployment benefits.

The Hagbourn Benefit Society was established on the 24th of June 1854 and was known as 'The Hagbourn Friendly Society'. The object of the Society was to raise funds through members' subscriptions and donations in order to assist them during sickness and to provide them with a decent burial. There was two types of membership: Honorary Members, male or female, who contributed £5 or more but not less than 10s 6d a year by donations and Assuring Members who were male, between the age of 15 and 40 years and who lived within five miles of the parish church of Hagbourne. Assuring Members paid 2s 6d to enrol and 3d for a copy of the rules.

Sick pay was due on the Tuesday following the day on which the member had declared himself sick, providing that three days had elapsed from the date of the medical certificate. Applications for sick pay had to be made in writing and signed by the surgeon (as GPs were known at the time). On the death of an Assuring Member, a sum of £2 was paid from the fund and 6d from each Assuring Member towards funeral expenses. Honorary and Assuring Members living within two miles of the deceased were invited to the funeral.

The three trustees, the secretary and the treasurer were elected by the members and a Committee of Management, consisting of a minimum of eight people, half of whom had to be Honorary Members, was appointed at the Annual General Meeting. Management meetings were held in the upper school room in East Hagbourne. The names of the elected officers were lodged with the Registrar of Friendly Societies in England. The first trustees of the Hagbourn Friendly Society were Richard Meredith, Joseph Lousley and John Holliday, whilst the secretary was John Lousley.

The Tyrrells, a philanthropic family

There was a time when nearly every child in England was familiar with the name Tyrrell. Sir James Tyrrell was associated with the disappearance and murder of the young King Edward V and his brother Richard, Duke of York, known ever since as 'the princes in the tower.' The murder (almost certainly by James Tyrrell) was thought to have taken place in the Tower of London some time in 1483 under the orders of their uncle who seized the throne and had himself crowned Richard III.

A century later the name Tyrrell – with happier associations – was prominent in Berkshire, especially in West Hagbourne where it is still known to this day through the William Tyrrell Charity. As with many names, the spelling has changed over the years and is often spelled differently even within the same document. The earliest known Tyrrells to live in West Hagbourne were Robert Tyrrold and his wife Agnes who lived in the village in the early sixteenth century. Robert died in 1545, leaving four sons: Richard, who settled in Didcot, William who lived in Drayton and Avery and David who remained in West Hagbourne. David's family eventually moved to Reading where they were weavers and clothiers.

Avery married Alis and died in 1584 leaving at least two children called Robert and William. Robert and his wife Elienor had four sons named Avery, Robert, William and Timothy, as well as two daughters, Elizabeth and Mary. Avery married and had a son, also called Avery. It is likely that William (of the William Tyrrell Charity) never married as there is no mention of a wife or children in his will. Robert's wife was Elizabeth and they had seven children, most of whom were left legacies by their uncle William.

William, the other son of Avery and Alis remained in West Hagbourne and married Elinor (not to be confused with his brother's wife Elienor). Their grandson William and his wife Martha had ten children and were the tenants of the manor of Watlingtons (now Grove Manor Farm). Martha was left a widow in 1685 and took her case to court when the lord of the manor tried to have her evicted. Martha's husband William and their grandson John, who died in 1687 at the age of two, are both buried in St Andrew's Church, East Hagbourne, where their tombstones can still be seen in the floor of the south aisle.

Timothy, the fourth son of Robert and Elienor, moved to London where he became a leather seller. In his will, dated the 11th of August 1656, he left ten pounds to his two brothers William and Avery, ten pounds to his sister Mary Waller, fifteen pounds to his god-daughter Sarah Tirrell and £300 to his niece, Mary Tirrell. His wife Dorothy was pregnant at the time of his death. If she bore a son, the child was to receive £1500 but a daughter would only get £1000. The rest of the estate was to go to Dorothy. All Hallows parish register records the birth of three sons to Timothy and Dorothy: Avery, born in 1647; William, born in 1650; and Timothy, born in December 1656. William died within a year and Avery is not mentioned in his father's will so he too probably died before his father. Timothy, his son, was born four months after his father's death.

As well as these bequests to his family, Timothy Tyrrell also left 20 shillings to the poor of All Hallows, Bread Street, where he lived in London, before he died in 1656. Nor did he forget West Hagbourne, where he was born. He was the first of several Tyrrells to bequeath a legacy to the poor of West Hagbourne to whom he left ten pounds. He also left a further ten pounds for the maintenance of a preaching ministry in West Hagbourne. There is evidence that this ministry continued for at least 127 years since it is mentioned in St Andrew's Glebe Terriers of 1692, 1704 and 1783:

Ten shillings a Year given by Mr Timothy Tyrrell late of West Hagbourn to preach a Sermon on the next Wednesday after the Feast of Saint Bartholemew yearly out of a parcel of Land call'd the Poor's Piece in the Field of Hagbourn.

This implies that the ten pounds Timothy left for this ministry had been used to buy a piece of land in Hagbourne Fields, named Poor's Piece, and that the annual rent of ten shillings from this land was used to preach a sermon around the 24th of August, St Bartholemew's Day.

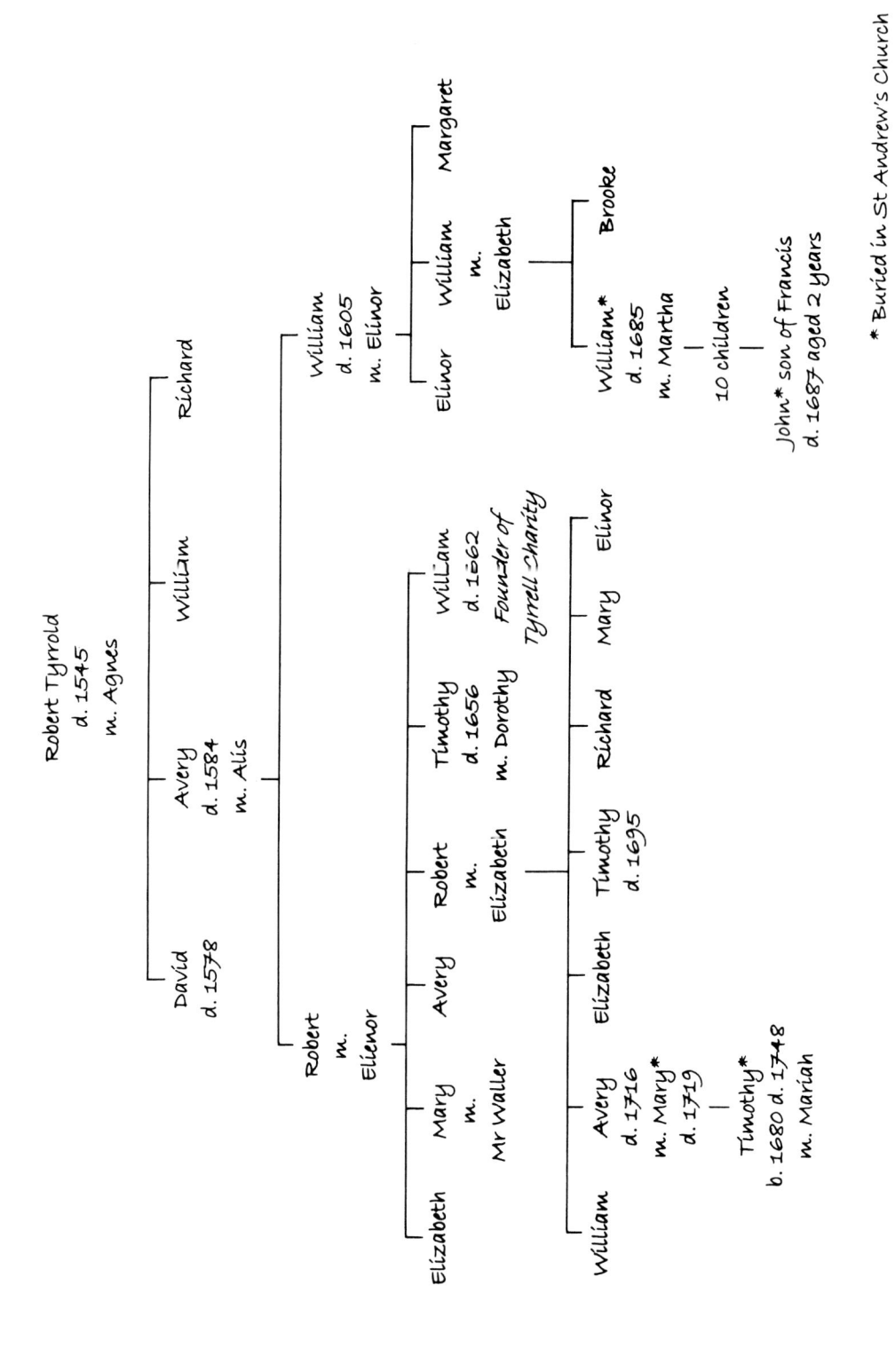

```
                                    Robert Tyrrold
                                       d. 1545
                                      m. Agnes
    ┌──────────────────────┬──────────────────┬──────────────┐
   David                  Avery            William         Richard
  d. 1578                 d. 1584
                          m. Alis
                             │
                          Robert
                            m.
                          Elinor
    ┌──────────┬──────────┬──────────┬──────────┬──────────┐
Elizabeth    Mary       Avery     Robert    Timothy     William
            m.                      m.       d. 1656     d. 1662
          Mr Waller               Elizabeth  m. Dorothy  Founder of
                                                        Tyrrell Charity
                                    │
         ┌──────────┬──────────┬──────────┬──────────┬──────────┐
       William   Elizabeth  Timothy    Richard      Mary       Elinor
                            d. 1695
         │
    ┌────┴────┐
  Avery                                                    William
  d. 1716                                                   d. 1605
  m. Mary*                                                  m. Elinor
  d. 1719                                                      │
    │                                          ┌───────────────┼──────────────┐
 Timothy*                                    Elinor         William       Margaret
 b. 1680 d. 1748                                              m.
 m. Mariah                                                 Elizabeth
                                                              │
                                                      ┌───────┴───────┐
                                                   William*         Brooke
                                                   d. 1685
                                                   m. Martha
                                                      │
                                                  10 children
                                                      │
                                              John* son of Francis
                                              d. 1687 aged 2 years

                                              * Buried in St Andrew's Church
```

Descendents of Robert and Agnes, the first Tyrrells to live in West Hagbourne, 1545–1748

Though some of the Tyrrell family did well in Reading and London, those who remained in West Hagbourne also prospered. Avery, one of the seven children of Robert and Elizabeth and nephew of William of the William Tyrrell Charity, died in 1716. He and his wife Mary have a tombstone inscribed with their coat of arms in St Andrew's Church, East Hagbourne. A report in the *Parish Watchword* for 1898, a forerunner of *St Andrew's Hagbourne Parish Magazine*, described the visit of Avery Tyrrell, parish churchwarden of Horton Slough, who was making investigations about his ancestors as he believed that some of them had once lived in West Hagbourne. One of the Tyrrells had requested in his will that he be buried at the end of his pew in Hagbourne Church. During his visit Avery discovered:

> *... a very handsome slab of black marble on the floor of the tower, with the Tyrrell coat of arms and crest. The latter is singular: a boar's head, with a peacock's tail in the mouth. The first inscription on the slab is to the memory of Avery Tirell, Gent., who died December 11th, 1716.*

This tombstone is no longer visible as it is concealed by tiles which were laid on the floor of the church parish room when it was constructed in 1984. Avery's son Timothy (1680–1748) is also buried in St Andrew's Church. Timothy must have been a wealthy man as he left "a mansion, tenements and freeholds" to his nephew Charles Morgan. However, what he left to East and West Hagbourne is the most interesting part:

> *To the Vicar, Churchwardens and Overseers of the Poor in E. & W. Hagborne forty pounds of lawful money of Gt. Britain in Trust, that they and their successors forever do, and shall, place out the said forty pounds at interest on as good Security as they can and the Interest and produce thereof do, and shall, yearly and every year forever, pay unto some discreet Schoolmistress or Schoolmaster, to be by them chosen to teach ffoure poor Children (and I rather prefer Boys before Girls) of the Parish of East and West Hagborne, that is to say, Two of East and two of West Hagborne (whose parents doth not pay to Church and Poore) to read English thoroughly. Such Schoolmaster or Schoolmistress and Children to be from time to time chosen and displaced by the said Vicar, Churchwardens and Overseers and their Successors as they think fit. But my will is that no child under the age of 5 yeares shall be placed in such school.*

This legacy is referred to in the Bishop's Visitation proceedings of 1783 when John Scoolt, the curate of St Andrew's at the time, made his report on the state of the parish and its activities to the Bishop in Abingdon. Visitations took place during the year of the Bishop's installation and then every following third year. The visitations sought to answer a number of questions concerning the number and frequency of services, the Sunday School, the vicarage, the upkeep of the parish registers, schools, the presence of other chapels in the area, and much else besides.

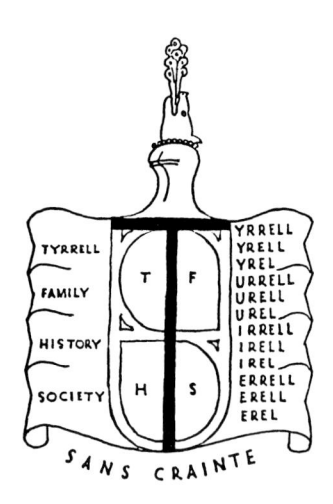

Logo of the Tyrrell Family Society based on the Tyrrell crest

John Scoolt's report to the Bishop stated:

> ...there is no Public School in the Parish. A Devise of 40 shillings per annum was left by a Charitable person for the purpose of putting some poor children to school but the present possessor of the estate withholds it.

This statement implies that 35 years after his death, the will of Timothy Tyrrell was being ignored by his beneficiaries.

Neither the legacy of Timothy Tyrrell who died in 1656, nor the later one made in 1748 by another Timothy Tyrrell, are referred to in the 1837 Commissioners' report on the charities of the Hagbourne parish. This suggests that the wishes of both these men were not carried out for very long even though John Scoolt was aware of the second legacy in 1783.

The Tyrrells went on renting or owning land in West Hagbourne well into the nineteenth century. Records show a Tyrrell paying tithes in 1783, whilst another Tyrrell – Richard – was one of those affected by the Inclosure Award when his strips of land were reallocated in 1843. Indeed, the Tyrrell family name, with all its variations of spelling, has been familiar in West Hagbourne since Robert and Agnes lived there in the early part of the sixteenth century. Today the Tyrrell name is widely known in the district, and roads have been named after the family in neighbouring villages. The Tyrrells have even set up their own family history society.

The William Tyrrell Charity

The Tyrrell who has had the most influence on the fortunes of West Hagbourne was William Tyrrell the Elder who founded the charity which still bears his name.

He was the great grandson of Robert and Agnes, the first Tyrrells to appear in village records when the name was spelled Tirrold. William died in 1662. In his will, dated the 16th of September 1662, he remembers not only his family but also the poor people of West Hagbourne and Blewbury. The following is a summary of William Tyrrell's bequests and includes the extracts most relevant to West Hagbourne and to his direct descendants. The name Tyrrell follows the same spelling as the original will which is held at the Berkshire Record Office. At the time this will was written, the word 'cousin' was often used for any relative; the finer distinctions of nephew and niece came into common use later. The modern term has been added in brackets to indicate the true relationship between William and his beneficiaries and also to avoid compounding the confusion which can arise when each generation uses the same Christian names. Even William Tyrrell has used the term 'Elder' in his will, probably to distinguish himself from William Tirrold the Younger.

> *I William Tirrell the Elder of West Hagborne in the County of Berks Yeoman being sick of bodie but of good and perfect memorie (God be praised) doe make and declare this my last Will and Testament... to be buried in the parish Church of Hagborne aforesaid*

> *Item I doe Give and devise unto my Brother Avery Tirrell All that my House and Lands in Blewbery in the County of Berks with the appurtenances for and during the terme of his naturall life. And after his decease I doe Give and devise the said House and Lands with the appurtenances in Blewbery aforesaid unto my Cousin [nephew] Avery Tirrell Sonne and heir of my said Brother Avery and his Heires for ever*

> *Item I doe Give and devise unto my Cousin [nephew] William Tirrell Sonne of my Brother Robert Tirrell and his Heires for ever All that my Messuage or Tenement and two yard lands with the appurtenances situate lying and being in West Hagborne aforesaid*

> *Item I doe Give and devise unto the Poore of Blewbery aforesaid for ever The yearly rent or sume of twentie shillings of lawful money of England to be issuing and payable unto them out of my Quarterne of a Yard lands which I lately purchased of William Bone lying and being within the Fields and precincts of West Hagborne*

> *Item I doe Give and devise unto the Poore of West Hagborne aforesaid for ever the remainder of the rents issues and profitts of my said Quarterne of a Yard and I Will that my guifts to the Poore of Blewbery and West Hagborne as aforesaid shall be settled and assured unto them according to the advice of learned counsel in the Law.*

A yard was the English name for a virgate – a land measurement of about 30 acres. However, it was a variable measurement: in Didcot it equalled 16 acres; in

1902 West Dapdune Charity

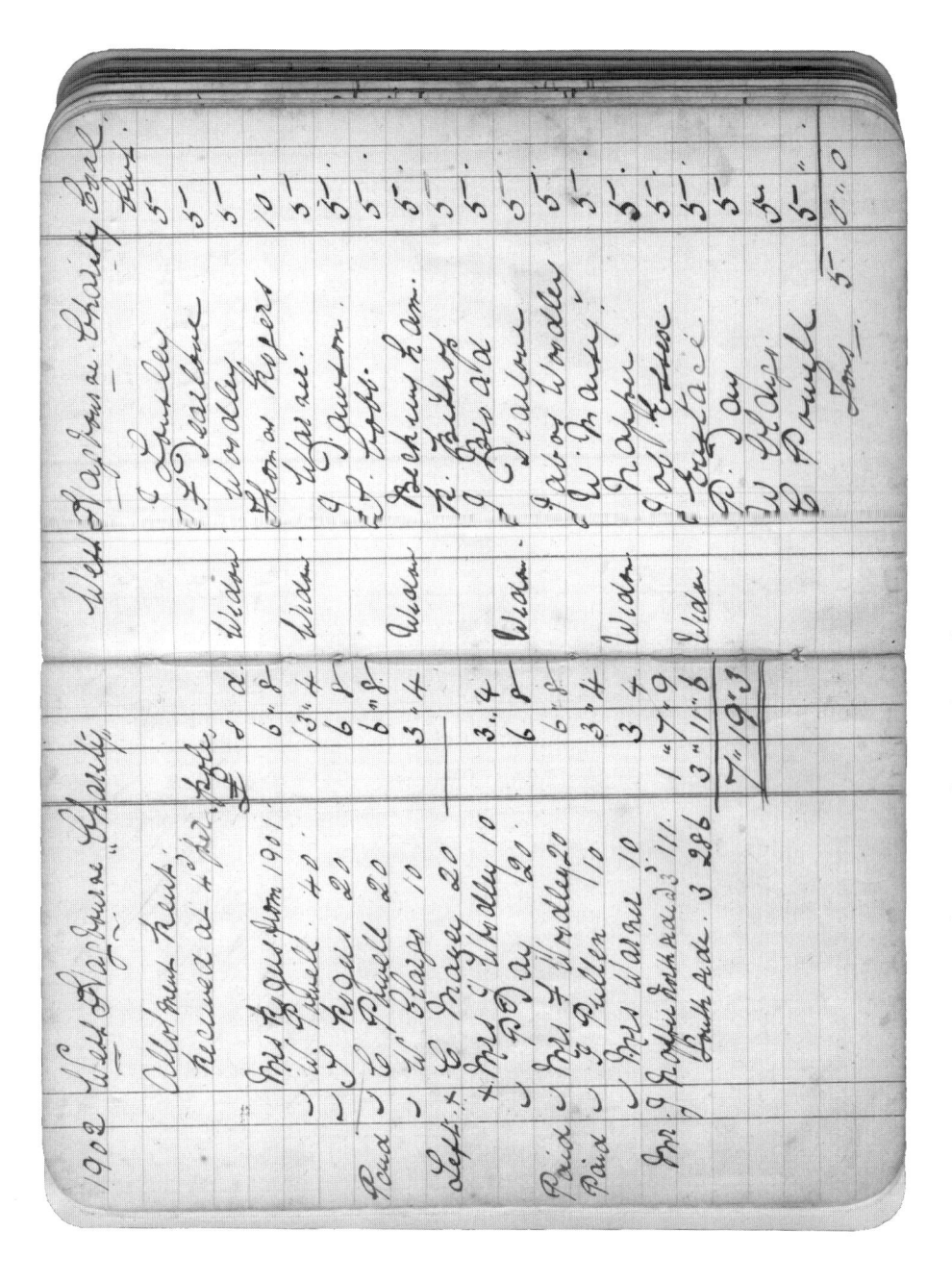

		£ s. d.
Allotment Rents		
Received at ½ per ½ year		
Apl.	By Qd. from 1901	6. 8
	W. Tyrrell 40	13. 4
	L. Rydd 20	6. 8
Paid	E. Puzell 20	6. 8
	W. Mayer 10	3. 4
Sept.	E. Mayer 20	
+Mrs J. Woolley 10		3. 4
	P.O. ay 20	6. 8
Paid	Mrs J. Woolley 20	6. 8
Paid	J. Puller 10	3. 4
	Mrs Walker 10	3. 4
Gor.	Goodwin from field 3. 111.	1. 7. 9
	Bath Acre. 3. 286	3.11. 6
		7. 9. 3

West Dapdune Charity Egal

	E. Lander	5 -
	T. L. Dearlove	5 -
Widow	Woolley	5 -
	Thomson Rogers	10 -
Widow	Lipscombe	5 -
	J. Lawson	5 -
	E. D. Lobb	5 -
Widow	Beckingham	5 -
	R. Bethey	5 -
	J. Burall	5 -
Widow	Dearlove	5 -
	Mrs J. Woolley	5 -
Widow	W. Danby	5 -
	R. Organ	5 -
	O. J. Lawson	5 -
	E. Eustace	5 -
	R. Day	5 -
	W. Lobb	5 -
	L. Pringle	5 -
	Sons	5. 0. 0

The William Tyrrell Charity account of income and expenditure for 1902

Harwell 27 acres; in Blewbury 30 acres; in East Hagbourne 20½ acres and in West Hagbourne 20 acres.

William Tyrrell's will then goes on to itemise the individual bequests to his family: mainly his nephews and nieces. He also bequeathed three sheep to his godson William Tirrell, son of William Tirrold the Younger. William Tirrell, the son of his brother Robert, was appointed sole executor whilst his "loving friends" William Tirrold of the Vale and Avery Tirrold son of his brother Robert were to be supervisors and overseers of the will. They were to be paid ten shillings each for their trouble by the executor. The will was signed by William Tirrell the Elder in the presence of Avery Tirrell and William Holt.

In 1662 most of the land in the village was still farmed by the strip system though some had been enclosed. The land William Tyrrell left to the poor of West Hagbourne amounted to a total of five and a half acres and was spread throughout the open fields as described in the previous chapter.

There are no known records regarding the administration of the Charity for the period immediately following Tyrrell's death but the Charity Commissioners' report of 1837 informs us that from 1832 all the land belonging to the Tyrrell Charity was let out to Mr George Napper for a term of eight years at an annual rent of eight pounds. This suggests that in the intervening years, the land had continued to be rented out and the wishes of William Tyrrell had more or less been carried out. George Napper obtained the letting through auction when the previous tenant left the parish, having become bankrupt. The Napper family have rented part of the Tyrrell Charity land ever since.

A few years later in 1843, the Inclosure Award for West Hagbourne was drawn up, and the remainder of the open fields was finally enclosed by law. This document contained a plan showing how the land had been apportioned (see page 72). For example, William Tyrrell's original strips were exchanged for a single plot, assigned on the plan as "An Allotment to the Poor". This was situated at the bottom of Hagbourne Hill, the old road to Chilton forming a boundary on the south eastern side. Although the Award does not mention Tyrrell by name, it refers to the "Common Lands in West Hagbourne" of the "Churchwardens and Overseers". This was clearly a reference to the Tyrrell bequest, since this was the only piece of land of any size under their jurisdiction in West Hagbourne. This particular parcel of land measured three acres, three roods and six perches, which was over one acre less than the original bequest. A perch, also known as a pole, was an old measure of land equal to 160th of an acre. There were 40 perch to a rood and four roods to an acre.

We know that careful accounts of income and expenditure were kept from at least 1896 as two account books belonging to the Charity are still in the hands of the trustees. These account books, dating from 1896 until 1957, list the names of those who rented land and allotments, the amount of land, and the income from that land. They also detail the expenditure, including the amount of poor relief paid and to whom; the amount of coal distributed each year and the names of the recipients; the coal bill for the year; rates; and any other expenses incurred, such as stamps. Each year one pound was faithfully paid to Blewbury, following the instructions of William Tyrrell's will.

These account books are a fascinating record of the time as they provide the names of many people who have lived in the village in the last 100 years. Familiar family names such as Bishop, Dawson, Dearlove, Lousley, Napper, Powell, Pullen, Warner and Woodley appear over and over again, while others appear only once. As time goes on, it is the widows who become the recipients, reflecting the early deaths of many of the village men. We also learn that not only did the Nappers rent Tyrrell land, but they were also coal merchants at one time. In the financial year 1897/98 Jos Napper sold the Charity seven tons and nine hundredweight of coal which was distributed to 24 villagers. The Nappers continued to deliver coal for the Charity for many years, the last distribution being in 1935.

By 1907, when Ezra Dearlove was the sole trustee of the Charity, about one acre of land was let out as ten allotments at four pence per pole whilst Jos Napper rented the rest at three pence a pole. The total income for the Charity from those rentals was £8 5s 3d. Napper's land consisted of two plots separated by a path of some kind. In the account books the income for the two plots was always listed separately and they were referred to as the north and south sides, the latter being the larger. The size of the south plot remained constant but the rental from the north side fluctuated as the number of allotments rented out also changed over the years.

It is possible to deduce the size of the Tyrrell Charity land in 1907 from the annual rent received for the allotments and the two plots. The amount of land rented as allotments was one acre and twenty poles; the south plot measured one acre, three roods and six poles, whilst the north side was smaller at three roods and eleven poles. As the path between the two plots was included in the acreage, the total size of the Tyrrell Charity land in 1907 amounted to three acres, two roods and thirty seven poles – much the same as it had in 1843 at the time of the Inclosure Award.

The Tyrrell land continued to be managed in much the same way until 1922 when the account book reveals a shift in the way the land was rented out. From 1922 there is no further mention of the south side but the north side continued to be rented out as a separate plot to J F Napper. The amount of land rented by Napper in 1922 was one acre, one rood and six poles – over one acre less than when the land was rented out as two plots in 1920. The total amount of Tyrrell land in 1922 consisted of three acres and three poles – more than half an acre less than in 1907 and nearly two and a half acres less than the original amount of land that William Tyrrell left in 1662.

The Tyrrell Charity land has continued to be let out in a similar fashion ever since, with some rented as allotments to the villagers of West Hagbourne, whilst the rest is rented out as a single piece to Joe Napper, a descendant of the earlier George Napper. The amount of land was again reduced when the Berkshire

County Council bought 470 square yards of the Charity's land during the realignment of the A417 in the late 1960s. The £30 from the sale of this land was invested with the Charities Official Investment Fund.

The nature of the way income from the Tyrrell Charity has been distributed to the poor has gradually changed over the centuries. The annual distribution of coal continued until 1935. After the second world war money was given instead of coal and gradually, as the Charity income decreased because fewer allotments were being taken up by the villagers, gifts of money became less and less frequent. Once all the distributions, including poor relief, had been made, there was usually very little left to be carried over to the next financial year which started on the first of April. Often there was less than a pound remaining, indicating that the trustees were required to distribute most of the Charity's income each year. Eventually there were no really destitute people in the village, so a new criterion for giving was introduced which was to make a gift at Christmas to the pensioners in the village. In 1990 for the first time, the Tyrrell Charity, with the help of the Pumpkin Club, gave a Christmas lunch at the Horse and Harrow for all the pensioners in the village. Again, in 1997 and 1998, the Charity contributed to a party for past and present residents of West Hagbourne.

The Charity land was invaded by gypsies in 1992 and some of the funds were spent on removing them and buying a new gate for the land. In 1993 Mrs Isobel Walmsley left £250 to the William Tyrrell Charity, the first bequest since William Tyrrell founded his Charity. Mrs Walmsley lived in the village for many years and a Prunus tree has been planted in the garden by the bus shelter in her memory. The yearly "twentie shillings of lawfull money" which William Tyrrell left for the poor of Blewbury was paid until 1993 when it was agreed by the Charity Commission and the trustees of Blewbury and West Hagbourne that a final, one-off payment of ten pounds would be given to Blewbury.

Administration of the Tyrrell Charity

Nowadays the Charity is administered locally by trustees who must live in West Hagbourne. Up until 1931 the Charity had been managed according to an order made by the Charity Commissioners on the 17th of November 1896. Under the new Local Government Act of 1894, all small charities in the country were listed, and came under the overall supervision of the Charity Commissioners. Following an application made to the Board of Charity Commissioners, dated the 31st of March 1931, which was signed by Archibald Napper, publican, and Ernest William Allen, farmer, a new scheme for the regulation of the Charity was ordered by the Board, following agreement with John E Lay, the then chairman of the parish meeting of West Hagbourne, and the trustees of the Charity itself. The trustees at that time were the churchwardens of East Hagbourne, and Frank Napper, farmer, of Ivy Cottage.

The West Hagbourne Inclosure of 1843 had erroneously allotted the trusteeship of the Charity to the churchwardens and overseers of East Hagbourne. Later, under an order made by the Charity Commissioners in 1896, the parish meeting of West Hagbourne was authorised to appoint an additional member to the governing body. In reality, the Charity had always been managed by trustees from West Hagbourne and for many years Ezra Dearlove had been the sole representative from the parish meeting of West Hagbourne. The 1931 application was clearly an attempt to correct the error made in the Inclosure Award and to take the management of the Charity legally away from the churchwardens of East Hagbourne and place it in the hands of West Hagbourne. Under the new scheme, the Charity was to be administered and managed by a body of trustees consisting of three "competent" persons to be appointed by the parish meeting of West Hagbourne for a term of four years. The first three people to be appointed trustees from West Hagbourne were Mr F Napper of Ivy Cottage, Mr D Napper of Grove Farm and Mr E W Allen of York Farm. The scheme clearly laid out how the income was to be spent:

> *The yearly income of the Charity shall be applied by the Trustees in supplying Clothes, Boots, Linen, Bedding, Fuel, Tools, Medical or other aid in Sickness, Food or other articles in kind to such poor persons resident in the Ancient Township of West Hagbourne and not in receipt of Poorlaw relief other than medical relief.*

The scheme also permitted the trustees to let out Tyrrell Charity land as allotments, subject to the provisions of the Allotments Extension Act of 1882.

The Tyrrell coat of arms

Annual accounts were to be submitted to the Charity Commissioners and published according to the provisions of the Charitable Trusts Acts. Trustees were not allowed to hold any interest in property belonging to the Charity and were not to receive any remuneration or income through their position as a trustee. The schedule of the scheme identified the Tyrrell Charity land as follows:

A piece of land, situate in the Parish of West Hagbourne and bounded on the South East by the Chilton Road, on the South by the Pumping Station, on the North by land belonging to Messrs. Morland and Company and on the West by land belonging to Dennis Napper, containing 3a. 3r. 17p. or thereabouts, and now let in allotments.

The Order was signed and sealed on the 8th of September 1931 and the account book shows that the stamp duty paid on it was ten shillings. By their own admission, the Commissioners did not actually measure the land in 1931 and since the income from the allotments then was considerably less than in 1922 and as there is no evidence to suggest that the Charity had obtained more land in the meantime, one has to conclude that the "3a. 3r. 17p. or thereabouts" quoted in the 1931 schedule was exaggerated by more than half an acre. The Tyrrell Charity has been run according to the 1931 scheme ever since, although, as we have seen, the way the income has been dispersed has altered according to the changing needs of society and potential recipients.

In previous centuries, when abject poverty, poor housing and the workhouse were the lot of many, charities were vital for providing the basic necessities of life. With the advent of the welfare state following the second world war, people are, on the whole, better off and state benefits help those who are not. The need for local charities to provide a basic standard of living has diminished. However, as people continue to live longer and the burden on the state increases, charities continue to play an important role in society, albeit a very different one than they played in 1656 when Timothy Tyrrell left ten pounds to the poor of West Hagbourne. The funds raised by charities today are more focused on supporting a particular group, such as animal welfare, the blind, medical research, or third world countries and people can choose which charity they wish to support. However, we are still encouraged by these charities to make legacies in their favour, just as people of West Hagbourne have been doing since the late Middle Ages.

Sources – The Hagbourne Charities and the Philanthropic Tyrrells:

G R Elton, *England under the Tudors*, The Folio Society, 1997, pp186–187, 255–256.
Endowed Charities (County of Berks.), Berkshire Record Office, 1908, pp 725–737.
Max Beran, *A financial history of Hagbourne parish charities*, Hagbourne Charities (unpublished), 1998.
B F Lingham, *The long years of obscurity – a history of Didcot, Volume One to 1841*, Didcot Press, 1978.

'Inquiring concerning charities', *Charities and Education*, Vol IV, 1815–1839, p163.

Roy Porter, *England in the Eighteenth Century*, The Folio Society, London, 1998.

'Rules and Regulations of the Hagbourn Benefit Society', *Social and Industrial Questions 1879–84*, The British Library, London.

Will of Timothy Tyrrell, Gent., of West Hagbourn, 1656, Bodleian Library, Oxford. D/A1/130/111.

Glebe Terriers, 1692, 1704 and 1783, Trowbridge Record Office, Wiltshire.

The Bishop's Visitations, 1783, Trowbridge Record Office, Wiltshire.

Tyrrell Family History Society, Marcham, Oxfordshire.

Parish Watchword, 1898, St Andrew's Church, East Hagbourne.

The last will and testament of William Tirrell the Elder, 1662, Berkshire Record Office, Reading. D/A1 128/42.

Tyrrell Charity account books, 1896–1957. Held by the trustees of the Tyrrell Charity, West Hagbourne.

Scheme, including vesting in official trustee of charity lands, Charity Commission, 1931. Held by the trustees of the Tyrrell Charity, West Hagbourne.

The minutes of the annual assembly of the West Hagbourne parish meeting, 1932, Parish Clerk, West Hagbourne.

West Hagbourn Inclosure Award, 27 July 1843, Berkshire Record Office, Reading. Q/RDC 39A.

A Plan of the Hamlet of West Hagbourn and County of Berks, inclosed, 1843, Berkshire Record Office, Reading. Q/RDC 39B.

Chapter Seven

Church and Chapel

... bells summon the people of West Hagbourne, a village only one mile to the west which has no church presumably because it was too good to need one rather than too bad to desire one.

R P Beckinsale, 1951

The parish church of St Andrew

The church of St Andrew is the parish church of West and East Hagbourne. Both villages have existed within its ecclesiastical parish for centuries during which time many villagers from West Hagbourne have been married, christened or buried there. The church helps to bring the two villages together through worship, church fund-raising events such as the annual village fête and by educating the children of both villages at the Hagbourne Church of England School. St Andrew's has played such a central role in the life of the village that East Hagbourne has often been called Church Hagbourne.

Although St Andrew's is situated in East Hagbourne, its ties with West Hagbourne go right back to its very beginning. When William the Conqueror redistributed land and property after 1066, he allowed the Norman priest Reinbald, a former chancellor of Edward the Confessor and dean of the collegiate church at Cirencester in Gloucestershire, to continue to hold the manor and church of East Hagbourne. The church at Cirencester was rich even before the Conquest and Reinbald received a hefty stipend from church revenues. In 1117, William the Conqueror's son, King Henry I, founded the abbey of St Mary for the Augustinian canons at Cirencester. The abbey took 14 years to complete and replaced an earlier Saxon church. It is not to be confused with the church the Normans built a little to the south of the abbey to compensate for the loss of the Saxon church. This became the parish church of Saint John Baptist which today dominates the ancient market town of Cirencester.

Augustinian monasteries began to proliferate during the reign of Henry I and Cirencester Abbey became the richest of all the Augustinian properties. It received generous royal endowments and accumulated great wealth from tithing rights, including those of West Hagbourne. Henry I, having first obtained Pope Innocent's permission, endowed the abbey at Cirencester with all the late Reinbald's extensive estates which included not only the manorial land and church of East Hagbourne, but also the tithes and chapel of West Hagbourne. This charter was issued in 1133 and was subsequently confirmed by successive kings, including Stephen (1139), Henry II (1155), King John (1199) and Edward III in 1337. The part of the charter referring to the Hagbournes reads as follows:

In Bershyr'... Hakeburnum cum xi hidis terris, et iii virgates terre, et ecclesiam eiusdem ville, cum capella et x^{mis} alterius Hakeburnum

The words "cum capella et x^{mis} [decimis] alterius Hakeburnum" (with the chapel and tithes of the other Hagbourne) refer to West Hagbourne and confirm that the village did have its own chapel in the twelfth century. This makes the chapel at least contemporary with the original twelfth century nave and chancel of St Andrew's. It is thought that these were built on the foundations of an earlier, eleventh century, Saxon church. The chapel in West Hagbourne could well have been built at the same time as the nave of St Andrew's and it is not unreasonable to conjecture that there may also have been an earlier Saxon church in West Hagbourne. Christianity had become a strong, unifying influence during the Anglo-Saxon period and medieval communities, both large and small, expressed their identities through the building of churches.

West Hagbourne's chapel was known as a 'chapel of ease', that is to say a second place of worship forming a local extension to St Andrew's under the auspices of the abbots of Cirencester. It would have been a small structure, probably of roughly hewn stone, built on the single-cell plan which was common throughout the Middle Ages in rural areas of England. The traditional site of the chapel has always been to the north east of Manor Farm on land behind the house known today as Chapel Hayes. Apart from the charters, the only other written reference to a chapel in West Hagbourne appears in a letter written in 1836 by Job Lousley to John Richards who was attempting to write a history of Berkshire at the time. Job Lousley (1790–1855) was a wealthy farmer, well known in antiquarian circles, whose family rented West Hagbourne Farm from J B Pocock, lord of the manor in 1814. In his letter he told Richards that West Hagbourne had once had a chapel of ease which had been destroyed at the time of the Reformation. It is more likely that the tiny chapel fell into ruin through the lack of a priest when the abbey at Cirencester was dissolved by Henry VIII and subsequently destroyed in 1539–40. The fact that St Andrew's Church was not disturbed would also suggest that the chapel fell into a state of neglect after the Reformation rather than being actively destroyed.

The supposed site of the chapel is marked on an Ordnance Survey map of 1876. When the first parish maps were drawn up, the cartographers obtained the names of the paths, roads and fields from the inhabitants. Therefore it is most likely that the information concerning the site of the West Hagbourne chapel was obtained from local families. Once the ground had been consecrated it tended to remain so, as was the case at Cirencester and the Hagbournes where Norman churches were built on the sites of previous Saxon churches. It seems that this tradition was carried into the twentieth century in West Hagbourne as a previous inhabitant remembers a priest coming every year to bless the ground where the chapel is believed to have once stood.

The abbey at Cirencester may have been destroyed in 1539 but the tithes still had to be paid. In fact, tithes had been paid on the manor of West Hagbourne since the days of William de Windsor. An annual pension of 26 shillings was paid to the abbess and convent of St Mary, Winchester, from the manorial tithes of West Hagbourne. In 1260 there was a dispute between the abbess of St Mary and the abbot of Cirencester because the tithes had been withheld. The bishop of Salisbury settled in favour of the abbess and ordered the abbot of Cirencester to pay 20 shillings a year from the West Hagbourne tithes. At the height of Cirencester Abbey's powers, West Hagbourne's contribution amounted to one tenth of all produce and included wheat, hay, wool, lambs, hens and pigs. The village also had to pay tithes on the fines levied by the manorial courts, the rents from the manors, the wages earned by tenant farmers, and even the tolls paid at the Sunday markets. At the time of the Dissolution the total value of the tithes paid by the Hagbournes to the monastery at Cirencester from all these sources was £92 9s 10d; a considerable sum in 1539. The Lysons brothers, in their 'Magna Britannia Berkshire', refer to "the great tithes of East and West-Hagbourne" which belonged to the abbey at Cirencester. The "great tithes" were the major crops. The fact that the tithes were so valuable shows just how fertile and productive the land was at that time.

There still exists today a faint link between the Hagbournes and the abbey of long ago. The last abbot but one was Abbot John Hakebourne, almost certainly a descendant of a Hagbourne family and possibly a relative of the priest, Richard de Hakebourne, whose half-effigy was observed on an early fourteenth-century cross in Merton College chapel, Oxford, by John Field, the Vicar of Benson, in 1889. Abbot Hakebourne donated the beautiful fan-vaulted ceiling of St Catherine's chapel in the parish church at Cirencester in 1508 and one of the roads made at the edge of the site of the abbey is named in his memory.

The south aisle and chapel

West Hagbourne's close involvement in the building of the church of St Andrew continued in the fifteenth century with the extension and rebuilding of the south chapel and aisle by John York and his wife Clarice of the manor of West Hagbourne. We know this from the inscriptions on three brasses commemorating Clarice de Windsor and the York family, now set in a single stone on the wall of the south aisle. The first brass belongs to Clarice de Windsor, whose story has been told in Chapter 3.

**Hic jacet Claricia Wyndesore quonda dna de Westhakburn
et uxor Johis York que sieri fecit ista capella que obijt
xxij die Marcij a° dni M° CCCC° iij° cui' aie ppiciet' ds Amen**

The Clarice de Windsor brass above, with the Latin wording from Berkshire Monumental Brasses *below. This can be translated as:* Here lies Claricia Wyndesore one time Lady of Westhakburn and wife of John York who caused this chapel to be built and died on the 22nd day of March in the year of our Lord 1403 on whose soul God have mercy, Amen.

The second brass commemorates Clarice's second husband, John York, and states that he was the founder of the aisle and died on the 15th of July 1413.

The third brass records the deaths of John, the son of Clarice and John York, and their daughter-in-law Joan in 1445. The inscription implies that they both died at the same time, or at least in the same year.

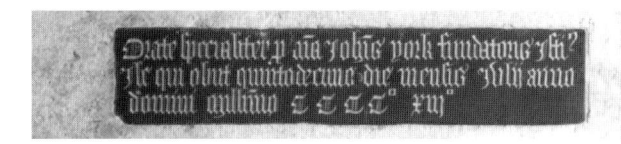

**Orate specialiter p. aia Johis York fundatoris Isti
Ile qui obijt quinto decimo die mensis Julij Anno
domini millimo CCCC°xiij°**

The brass of Clarice's husband, John York, above, with the Latin wording from Berkshire Monumental Brasses *below*

**Orate specialiter p aiabz Johannis York et Joha=
ne uxoris eius qui obierunt quinto die mes'
Septembris anno dni millimo CCCCxl° quinto**

The brass of Clarice's son, John, and her daughter-in-law Joan, above, with the Latin wording from Berkshire Monumental Brasses *below*

These brasses help to date the south chapel and aisle to the fifteenth century. The building work would have been completed after the deaths of Clarice and John, probably under the supervision of their son, John York, who died in 1445. In his architectural history of St Andrew's, Dr J W Walker takes the view that John York rebuilt an existing south aisle by widening the aisles of both the nave and chancel to include the whole south side of the church which was then given a new wall and a flat panelled roof. On completion of the new structure the old walls and lean-to roof were removed. The roof of the south aisle was renewed in the seventeenth century. Clarice's chapel replaced one which was built when the chancel and original south aisle were first extended in the thirteenth century.

Walker suggests that Clarice and John York, as lord and lady of the manor of West Hagbourne, rebuilt the chapel and had the south aisle extended so that they could found a chantry in the chapel. Chantry chapels became common towards the end of the thirteenth century in parish churches. Individual benefactors would endow an altar in their parish church in the hope of securing salvation in the next life for themselves and their family. Wooden screens were built to separate the chapel from the chancel and the grooves can still be seen on the capitals where the screens were fixed. To all intents and purposes this became a private pew for the York family. In order for the officiating chantry priest and the family in the chantry chapel to see what was happening at the high altar, a squint, or oblong opening, was pierced through the western end of the south chancel wall of St Andrew's.

The three brasses commemorating Clarice and the Yorks on the wall of the south aisle have not always been in that position and they have caused considerable confusion to church historians because they have been moved on at least two occasions. When the herald and antiquary Elias Ashmole (1617–1692) paid a visit to St Andrew's during his visitations of 1665–66, he noted that Clarice de Windsor's gravestone was lying in the north side of the chancel and that there was a brass effigy of a woman above the inscription. He did not mention the other two York brasses.

The Oxford scholar Thomas Hearne (1678–1735), who kept copious notes and diaries about his travels around his native Berkshire, also visited St Andrew's sometime before 1716. He too observed Clarice's gravestone but by then only the lower part of her effigy remained, the rest having broken off. Hearne believed that this had occurred accidentally rather than being deliberately damaged during the Civil War: "…'twas not convey'd off by the Rebells, or other disaffected People, this being one of the Churches that escaped their Malice". Hearne is quite clear on the position of Clarice's brass in "a Chapell in the North side of the Chancell under the North Wall". Later historians have taken Ashmole's sighting of the brass in the "north side of the chancel" to mean that she lay in the chancel. Hearne saw her brass inscription with the remains of her effigy some 50 years later in the north chapel. If the brass of Clarice was transferred from the chantry to the north chapel sometime after Ashmole's visit, the effigy could have been damaged during that move.

Both Ashmole and Hearne assumed that Clarice's brass was in its natural resting place. When Professor Nikolaus Pevsner, the influential art historian of the first half of the twentieth century, visited St Andrew's during his research for his series 'The Buildings of England', he observed the brasses of Clarice and John York on the north side of the church. He found this "eminently interesting" as he dated the north chapel and aisle very firmly in the architectural period known as Decorated (1277–1377) whilst the dates on the brasses of Clarice and John York contradicted his dating. Pevsner therefore realised that Clarice could not have built the north chapel and John York could not have founded the north aisle, despite the inscriptions on their brasses indicating that they did.

Visiting the church in 1912, Charles Keyser, a considered authority on church murals, found all three brasses together on the floor of the north aisle whilst H J Morley recorded that the three brasses were all on one stone in 1922. Several church guides have been written during the twentieth century which provide conflicting evidence as to the various positions of these brasses in the chantry, the north aisle or the north chapel. Whatever the exact sequence of events, there are enough reported sightings to surmise that Clarice de Windsor's brass and effigy were moved to the north chapel from their original place in the south chapel, possibly via the chantry, at some point towards the end of the seventeenth century or very early in the eighteenth. Her effigy was by then lost and her commemorative brass was later moved to the floor of the north aisle to join those of her husband and son. These had also been moved from their original places in the south aisle. This latter move could have occurred during the major restoration work which took place in 1860. We can be grateful to Ashmole – commonly regarded as the "first historian of the county" – for recording the existence of Clarice de Windsor's effigy before it disappeared for ever.

In April 1939, Margaret, Viscountess Dillon proposed that the south chapel (now the Lady Chapel), then used as a choir vestry, should be restored. The transfer of the three York brasses from the north aisle to their proper place in the south aisle was part of that restoration. Why they were moved from the south chapel and aisle in the first place will never be known but it is fitting that they should be back where they belong.

When Pevsner visited St Andrew's he dismissed the octagonal font in the south aisle as being "nothing special". It is in fact very special to West Hagbourne because it demonstrates its close links with the church and is a further example of West Hagbourne's contribution to the fabric of the parish church of the two Hagbournes. The font dates from the early fifteenth century which makes it contemporary with the south aisle and chapel built by Clarice and John York. It also bears four painted shields, three of which are the coats of arms belonging to the families of Clarice de Windsor and the Yorks, whilst the fourth shield bears the cross of St George. The dating and position of the font in the south aisle and the coats of arms of their respective families provide pretty conclusive evidence that the font was also the work of Clarice and John York. The font can be regarded as an integral part of the massive reconstruction of the south aisle of St Andrew's church on which they embarked almost 600 years ago.

The font is octagonal and each face has a quatrefoil, four of which contain the shields. Alternating with the shields are foliated bosses in the shape of roses. The coats of arms belong to the families of Drokensford, Windsor and York, Clarice being the link between them. She was born into the Drokensford family and was a distant relative of John Drokensford, the Bishop of Bath and Wells (1309–26). Her first husband was Richard Windsor, a direct descendant of the first constable of Windsor Castle and her second husband was John York.

L: Octagonal font showing shields and foliated bosses. R: From top to bottom: York, Windsor and Drokensford shields

The family shields have been simplified on the font but they have been reproduced in their full glory in three of the lights in the window of the south chapel. In 1939, Viscountess Dillon gave 'The Window of Vision' in the south chapel in memory of her brother Sir Frances Ffolkes, whose arms are at the foot of the window. It was designed by her son, Mr Tracy Philips. The Drokensford, York, Windsor and Dillon coats of arms make up the four top lights in the window which was incorporated when the Lady Chapel was restored in 1939. The shields on the font were also repainted at the same time.

Two of these shields appear again on the exterior of the west window of the tower. At the bottom of the external hood moulds are two very worn shields on which can just be made out the coats of arms of the Yorks and Drokensfords. The present tower dates from the first quarter of the fifteenth century and is compatible with the dating of the reconstruction of the south aisle by the Yorks. Perhaps this is why the coats of arms of the families of Clarice and John York were chosen to grace the exterior of the tower. Whatever the reason, it seems appropriate that they should appear on the west side of the church facing towards West Hagbourne where they lived as lord and lady of the manor.

The south chapel window   *The shields on the west window*

The manorial families of West Hagbourne were not the only ones to be buried in St Andrew's. The gravestones and memorials of many other families down the centuries can be found on the walls and floors of the church, as well as tombstones whose inscriptions were obliterated long ago in the churchyard. There are Harwoods, Loders, Tyrrells, Dearloves and others, long forgotten. Interestingly, quite a few have ended up in the south aisle or in the south side of the churchyard. One of the most notable of these West Hagbourne families was the Aldworths.

Alice Aldworth, whose brother and husband are buried in the south aisle, died in 1545 and has been credited with leaving 16 pence for a bell in the parish church of Hagbourne. This information has been repeated in several published articles about the history of the church. However, this story is a misinterpretation of what was actually written in her will. Alice Aldworth did refer to the bells of Hagbourne but there is no mention of the purchase of any bells and it is unlikely that 16 pence would ever have been enough to buy them. The item about the bells appears in her will with a list of instructions about burial arrangements and most likely means that she was leaving 16 pence for the church bells to be rung at her funeral:

> *And my body to be buried in the Church yard by the sepulchres of my ancestors at the south end of Hagborne. Item I bequest to sarum [diocese] 2d. Item to the bells of Hagborne xvid [16d]. Item to Sir John Parker to pray for me and my friends six pounds. Item I will have at my burial ten priests....*

Detail of the Drokensford coat of arms

Detail of the York coat of arms

According to a document produced in connection with the restoration of the bell-cote in 1985, a sanctus bell has been rung at St Andrew's since 1490 so Alice Aldworth could not possibly have donated this bell to the church. The present sanctus bell was cast sometime in the seventeenth century. The tower now hosts a set of eight bells, the oldest of which dates back to 1602, more than 50 years after Alice's death. The bells she requested to be rung at her funeral were probably the bells installed when the tower was rebuilt early in the fifteenth century. These started to be replaced in the seventeenth century. Today the bells of St Andrew's are famous for their musical peals and have been rung by enthusiastic bell ringers over the ages to call people to worship.

Another brass in the church remembers the men and women from the Hagbournes who made the ultimate sacrifice in the two world wars. Their names are inscribed on a brass plaque on the wall next to the north door. The men from West Hagbourne were Anthony Allen, Leslie Denning, Kerry Ryan and Frederick Bulter who all died in the Second World War. There have been many contributions to St Andrew's by villagers of West Hagbourne, including a shepherd's crook given by Anthony Allen of York Farm at the beginning of the War. Sadly, he was killed in action in 1943. Not only is the shepherd's crook a very apt symbol of the vicar's role as the shepherd caring for his flock, but it is also a reminder that the parish church of St Andrew's has always been at the centre of a productive farming community which, over the centuries, has sustained kings, abbots and manorial barons.

Religious observance in the Hagbournes

The proceedings of the Bishop's Visitation to St Andrew's in 1783 is full of insights into the practice of religion in West and East Hagbourne during the eighteenth century. Visitations took place during a new bishop's installation year and every three years following. The Bishop himself did not personally visit every church within his diocese but relied on the local clergy to make reports concerning church services, the activities of the Sunday School, the state of the vicarage, upkeep of parish registers and all the other myriad responsibilities held by a parish priest.

The curate of St Andrew's in 1783 was John Scoolt (sometimes spelt Schultes or Shultz) who was also rector of the chapel at Sotwell and served St Leonard's Church in Wallingford where he lived at the time. We learn from his report to the Bishop of Abingdon that there were prayers and preaching twice every Sunday at 10.30am and 2.30pm at St Andrew's. Divine Service was held at Christmas, Easter, Whitsuntide, the two holidays immediately following each festival and on Good Friday. Scoolt pointed out to the Bishop that he held Divine Service as a mere curate since he was not, at this time, the incumbent of St Andrew's. The Holy Sacrament was given at Christmas, Easter and Whitsuntide when he estimated that about 50 people received communion. The young people of the village had catechism classes every Sunday afternoon between Easter and Whitsuntide. The births and burials register had been duly kept since 1661 whilst the marriage register was maintained according to the law. The two church wardens were appointed annually on the Tuesday of Easter Week, one being chosen by the parishioners, the other by the minister. In his report the Reverend Scoolt paints a picture of a dutiful, law-abiding, God-fearing community in which everyone attended church services regularly; where there were no Papists, nor any Papist priest, school or meeting place; and where there were no members of other sects in the parish.

John Scoolt's Visitation report also tells us quite a lot about himself, his personal views and what it was like to be a parish priest at that time. Apparently it was not much of a living for a curate working in a poor rural community as no money was given at the offertory and the only augmentation he received was 20 shillings a year from the legacies of Timothy Tyrrell (1656) and Mary Smith (1718) for the purpose of preaching two sermons. The details of these legacies are covered in Chapter Six. Some years later, in 1801, by which time he had become the incumbent of St Andrew's (1791–1823), John Scoolt complained that his 'cure', or living, barely kept him and that the vicarage was in a poor state of repair. He moved into the vicarage in East Hagbourne with his family in December 1791 when he became the incumbent priest of the parish.

The curate Scoolt also observed that the charitable benefactions were not properly settled and were in danger of being lost. He was probably referring to the charities of Richard Creswell and Moses Hawkins which were eventually dissolved. However, his words probably came back to haunt him many years later when he was one of the three vicars responsible for the Eaton Charity which benefited the poor of Hagbourne, Milton and Harwell. The trustees claimed irregularities in the management of the Charity and took the matter to court in 1822. Job Lousley of West Hagbourne was one of the trustees and appears to have been a leading light in getting the case to the Court of Chancery which took action to secure the Charity's capital and, among other things, ordered the Reverend Scoolt to pay £31 16s into the bank in the name of the Accountant-General. The villagers of Hagbourne were so grateful to Job Lousley that they presented him with a silver mug inscribed:

> *The Vicar's Cup... presented by 120 Poor Persons of Hagbourn to Job Lousley, Churchwarden, in gratitude for... recovering their Property from the hands of a Rapacious and Dishonest Vicar who had long been in the habit of defrauding them of the same...*

It seems unlikely that the Reverend Scoolt was actually involved in any criminal activity or he would have been punished accordingly by the court. It seems more probable that he was negligent in his duties towards the management of the Charity and did not ensure that the money from the Charity's investments was distributed according to the spirit of the bequest. Also, there were two other priests from Milton and Harwell who shared responsibility for the administration of the Eaton Charity so Scoolt could not be held solely accountable for what had gone wrong. However, after years of living in poverty, poor housing conditions and feeling put-upon and overworked, perhaps he was tempted to augment his stipend with some of the Charity's considerable proceeds.

One thing that is clear from the inscription on Job Lousley's mug is that the Reverend Scoolt was not popular with his parishioners and in some of his writings he comes across as a prejudiced, bitter, arrogant and even aggressive man. He was intolerant of other religions as his Visitation report showed and he was very much against the Methodists. He had chased a group of them out of their chapel in East Hagbourne and put their leader to flight. However, the Methodists lived to fight another day as the Primitive Methodist Chapel in East Hagbourne continued to serve both villages well into the twentieth century. Scoolt held a postgraduate degree and he was dismissive of less educated men. He thought all the clergy should "drive back the self-ordained preachers to their anvils and lasts". However, not every vicar was as ruthless as the Reverend Scoolt in putting down other denominations and gradually non-conformity became acceptable. As early as 1660 there had been a Presbyterian minister by the name of John Sayer in the Hagbournes.

Worship in West Hagbourne

Although West Hagbourne lost its chapel of ease after the Reformation, it was not without its own places of worship. Several chapels seem to have sprung up in Moor Lane. One of these was recorded on the Inclosure Award of 1843, together with a house belonging to Mr Robinson. In 1832, permission was given at the Quarter Sessions for a house owned by Moses Beavis (Bovis) to be used as a chapel. This house was on the opposite side of Moor Lane and is known today as Enard Cottage. The Reverend Edwin George Bullock (known locally as Father Antony) bought the house from Beavis's son in 1902 and continued to maintain the chapel which was outside the house itself. Two years later he bought the house next door, now called Thatch Cottage. According to a sale notice of 1895, one of the rooms of this house was being used as a chapel at the time of the sale and Father Antony continued to do the same until the day he died. In his will he referred to the two chapels as the exterior and interior chapels and appears to have said Mass in both.

In 1900 it was noted that the children of West Hagbourne were not attending Sunday School so a group was started in the village and held each Wednesday afternoon. Villagers also worshipped together in their homes. According to St Andrew's Parochial Magazine of 1897, a service was held each Tuesday at 7.00pm in Mr Warner's house. A suggestion was made and recorded in the same magazine that West Hagbourne needed a mission room. Mr Aldworth, owner of Grove Manor Farm, offered land and Mr Eli Cauldwell of Manor Farm promised to draw up plans. Some money was given by well-wishers but there was little response to an appeal made to the villagers and this proposal unfortunately came to nothing.

This was perhaps the closest West Hagbourne ever came to having its own village hall.

The unique practice of holding communion and other religious services in private homes still continues today. It has brought people together and has always been enthusiastically supported by a succession of vicars. For example, the Reverend G R Wells took Holy Communion in the home of Mr and Mrs Butler in York Road on the evening of the 25th of July 1974. It is of great credit to those people who started the practice over 100 years ago and is much appreciated by those who do not find it easy to get to church.

The days of religious intolerance, as shown by the likes of the Reverend Scoolt, are now over and instead churches are eager to work together whenever possible. The parish looks beyond its own needs to the wider world and to poor communities in other countries. St Andrew's may stand as a historic monument to the past but it is also very much part of the present. The sanctus bell still calls worshippers to church and the sound of the bells continues to float across the fields to West Hagbourne, just as it did hundreds of years ago.

The bell-cote, restored in 1985

Sources – The parish church of St Andrew

R P Beckinsale, *Companion into Berkshire – the History, Peoples and Places of England's Royal County*, Methuen, 1951.
Sir William Dugdale, *Monasticon Anglicanum*, Vol 6, Part 1, (new edition), James Bohn, London, 1846.
Charter of Henry I, July 1133, reproduced in C D Ross, *Cartulary of Cirencester Abbey*, Vols I and III, 1964. Bodleian Library, Oxford.
Canon J A Lewis and Canon H S Ringrose, *Parish Church of Saint John Baptist, Cirencester*, (revised booklet) Cirencester Parish Church, Jarrold and Sons Ltd, 1989.

Colin Platt, *The Parish Churches of Medieval England*, Chancellor Press, 1995.
Job Lousley's letter: John Richards, *Berkshire Collections, Parochial Memorials*, Vol II, G to Y, 1837, British Museum. Additional Manuscript 28.664.
Blessing of the ground: Guy Napper of Upton recounted this story to Fred and Edna Scott of Chapel Hayes, West Hagbourne in the 1970s.
Daniel and Samuel Lysons, *Magna Britannia Berkshire*, with a new introduction by Jack Simmons, E P Publishing, 1978.
Effigy of Richard de Hakebourne: John Edward Field, 'The Monumental Brasses of Berkshire', *Quarterly Journal of Berkshire Archaeological and Architectural Society*, No 1, April 1889, p51.

Sources – The south aisle and chapel

Brass inscriptions reproduced from: H T Morley, *Monumental Brasses of Berkshire – 14th to 17th Century*, Berkshire Archaeological and Architectural Society, Reading, 1924.
J W Walker, *The Architectural History of East Hagbourne Church*, 1925.
Elias Ashmole, *The History and Antiquities of Berkshire*, William Carnan, London, 1719.
Simon Townley, 'Berkshire', *English County Histories – A Guide*, C R J Currie and C P Lewis (eds), Alan Sutton, 1994.
Thomas Hearne made references to the monuments in St Andrew's Church in his edition of W Roper's *Life of More*, 1716, Bodleian Library, Oxford.
D W Rannie, (ed.), *Hearne's Remarks and Collections*, Vol LX, Oxford Historical Society, Clarendon Press, 1901.
Nikolaus Pevsner, *The Buildings of England: Berkshire*, Penguin Books, 1966.
Charles Keyser, 'Notes on the Churches of Steventon, Harwell, Didcot and Hagbourne' read before Berks. Archaeological Society, 28 March 1912, printed in *Berks, Bucks and Oxon Archaeological Journal*, Vol 18, No 4, January 1913.
Guide to the Parish Church of St. Andrew, East Hagbourne, ed. by E T Long for Berkshire Archaeological Society, East Hagbourne Parochial Church Council, c1938.
St Andrew's East Hagbourne Record of Church Furnishings, The National Association of Decorative and Fine Arts Societies, 1994.
St. Andrew's Church, East and West Hagbourne, A Short History, ?1971. Re-issued as *The Story of Hagbourne and the Church of St. Andrew*, 1977.
S P Spokes, 'Coats of Arms in Berkshire Churches', *Berkshire Archaeological Journal*, Vol 39, No 2, Autumn 1935.
E F Greening Lamborn 'The Armorial Fonts of the Oxford Diocese', *Berkshire Archaeological Journal*, Vol 45, Part 2, 1941.
Will of Alice Aldworth of West Hagbourne, 7 September, 1545, Public Record Office, Family Records Centre, London.
Leaflet possibly used in bell-cote appeal, 1983. In the keeping of the vicar according to *St Andrew's East Hagbourne Record of Church Furnishings*.
Sanctus bell: *Berks, Bucks and Oxon Archaeological Journal*, Vol 18, No 4, January 1913.
N H Balshaw, *Change ringing at St Andrew's Church, East Hagbourne*, leaflet published by The Hagbourne Society of Change Ringers, 1994.

Sources – Religious observance in the Hagbournes

Bishop's Visitation, 1783, Wiltshire Record Office. D1/56/3.
Bishop's Visitation, 1801, Wiltshire Record Office. D1/56/4/2.
Job Edward Lousley, 'Job Lousley (1790–1855) of Blewbury and Hampstead Norris', *Berkshire Archaeological Journal*, Vol 63, 1967–8, pp57–65.
William Page and Rev. P H Ditchfield, (eds), *The Victoria History of the County of Berkshire*, Vol 3, 1923.
W H Summers, *History of Berkshire and South Buckinghamshire and South Oxfordshire Congregational Churches*, W J Blackett, 1905.
Quarter Sessions, 1832, Berkshire Record Office, Reading.

Sources – Worship in West Hagbourne

West Hagbourn Inclosure Award, 27 July 1843, Berkshire Record Office, Reading. Q/RDC 39A.
St Andrew's Parochial Magazine, 1897, Oxford Central Library for Local Studies.

Chapter Eight

West Hagbourne in the Nineteenth Century

The Census

The first census was taken in Britain on the 10th of March 1801. In the eighteenth century there had been considerable uncertainty concerning the size of the population of Britain, and whether it was diminishing in relation to its old enemy France. At that time the population figures were collated from the Anglican birth, marriage and death registers kept in every parish in England since Elizabethan times. Over the course of the eighteenth century, other countries such as Denmark, Sweden, Norway, Spain and Holland initiated censuses, but all attempts to follow suit in Britain came to nothing until 1800, when the Population Bill was passed. When the first census was taken in 1801, it was revealed that the population of England and Wales was 9.168 million, whilst in Scotland it was 1.599 million. Though simple, the first census was considered to be "a milestone in the provision of statistical data".

Since 1801, a census has been taken every ten years, except in 1941 when the country was at war. The early censuses, taken between 1801 and 1831, were mainly concerned with population figures, though there was a rough classification of occupations into agriculture, manufacturing, commerce and handicrafts. These categories were gradually extended over the years to include professional, retail trades and industrial labour. Names were recorded for the first time in the 1841

YEAR	1801	1841	1851	1861	1871	1881	1891
Number of houses	39	46	43	38	39	40	34
Unoccupied houses	1		3	2	3	1	4
Number of people	196	239	209	164	181	162	157

Above: Details of houses and population from the census returns of West Hagbourne between 1801 and 1891. Right: Nineteenth century occupations. Many people, particularly publicans, had more than one occupation and this is indicated by italics. Brackets are used where more than one occupation is counted in the same box

OCCUPATIONS	1841	1851	1861	1871	1881	1891
Agricultural labourer	53	46	34	41	22	30
Annuitant, ie pensioner (Apprentice)		1		(1)		
Baker (Basket maker)	1	3 (1)	1			
Carpenter	3		2			
Carrier	1		1		1	
Carter			6	3	6	
Char woman (Parlour & housemaid)		1			(2)	1
Children under 14 years	101	84	51	56	52	53
Coachman/*Servant*					1	
Engine driver/ *Agricultural labourer*				1		
Farm bailiff					1	
Farmer	4	6	5	4	4	2
Fogger, ie cowman				1		
Fruit dealer (Fund holder)			1 (1)			
Gardener/*Domestic servant*					1	
Grocer (Small shopkeeper)				2	2	2 (1)
Groom/*Gardener*				1		
Groom (Horse dealer)			1		1	2 (1)
Housekeeper (Laundress)				1 (1)	(1)	3
Independent means						5

OCCUPATIONS	1841	1851	1861	1871	1881	1891
Labourer - general					2	
Landlady of lodging house						1
Licensed hawker						1
Maltster (Maltster's wife)	1	1				(2)
Nurse					1	
Pauper (Painter & glazier)	2	8	7	2		(1)
Plough boy		1		1		
Police officer				1	1	2
Publican	1	1	1	1 (1)	1	
Publican/*Blacksmith* (Publican/*Bricklayer*)						
Publican/*Farmer* (Publican/*Wheelwright*)	(1)	1				
Railway labourer (Railway station worker)					3 (1)	2
Railway worker - temporary					53	
Rat catcher (Sawyer)	(2)	(1)		1		
Seamstress/*Needlewoman*		1			2	
Servant, incl. Cook & Domestic servant	8	8	4	7	7	4
Servant on farm - male	6	6		2	5	
Shepherd (Shepherd boy)	3	1 (1)	3 (1)	2	5	1
Supported by children						6
Toll collector	1	1				
Wheelwright/*Carpenter*				1	1	

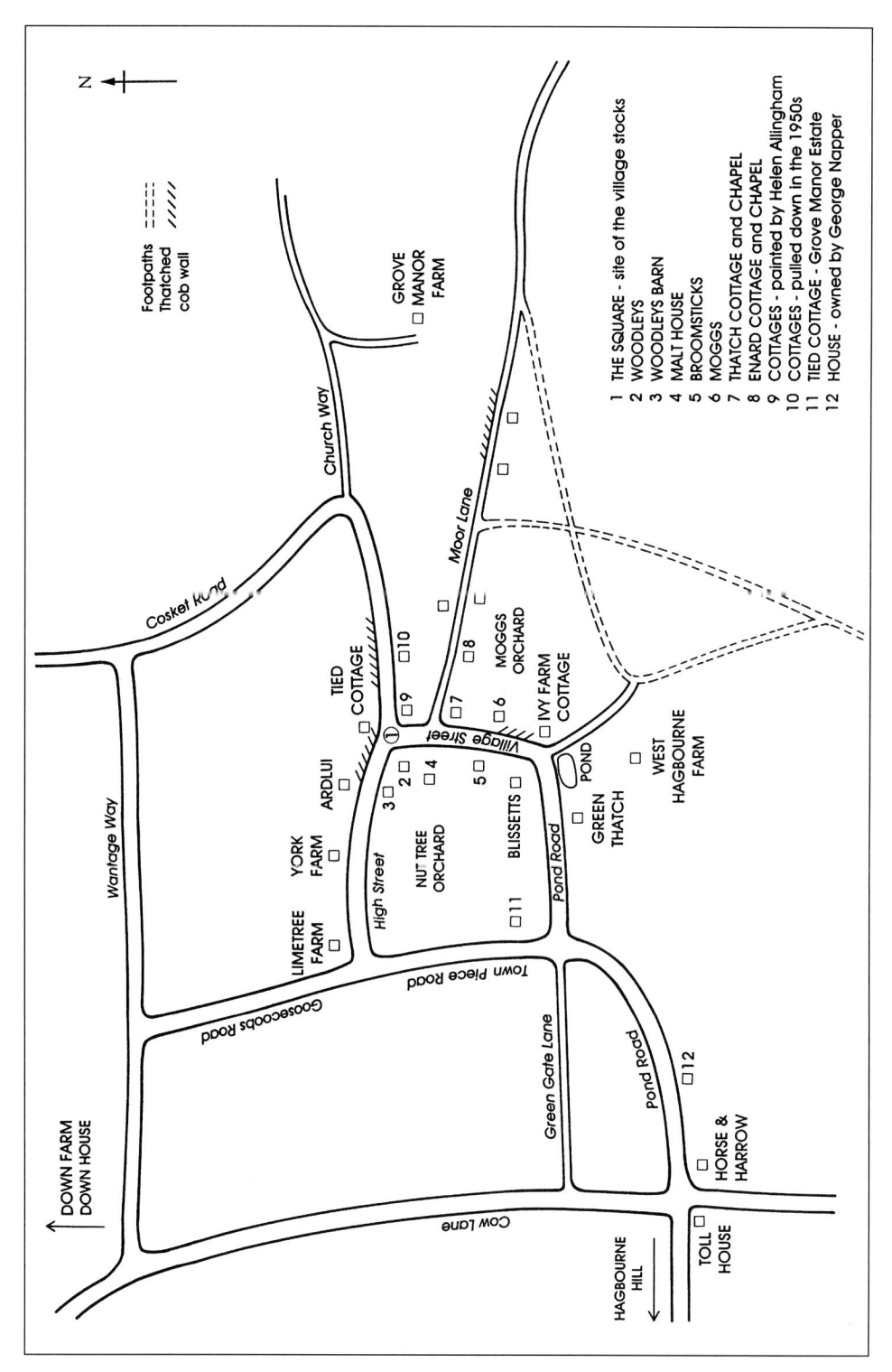

Map of West Hagbourne, showing the route which the enumerator Francis Shepherd may have taken on the 31st of March, 1851

Key:
- Footpaths
- Thatched cob wall

1. THE SQUARE - site of the village stocks
2. WOODLEYS
3. WOODLEYS BARN
4. MALT HOUSE
5. BROOMSTICKS
6. MOGGS
7. THATCH COTTAGE and CHAPEL
8. ENARD COTTAGE and CHAPEL
9. COTTAGES - painted by Helen Allingham
10. COTTAGES - pulled down in the 1950s
11. TIED COTTAGE - Grove Manor Estate
12. HOUSE - owned by George Napper

census. Ages up to 14 years were recorded exactly, whilst ages above 14 were rounded down to the nearest multiple of five.

The census was carried out by dividing the country into registration areas, which in turn were divided into smaller districts of between 25 and 200 inhabited houses. An enumerator was appointed to collect the information. Householders filled out their own census forms if they could, otherwise the enumerator helped them. He then entered the information into books to be deposited at the Land Registry in London. Today, these censuses are available to the public and are a valuable source of information for researchers of family and local history.

A close look at West Hagbourne's census return for the year 1851 can tell us a lot about the people who were living in the village in the middle of the nineteenth century. In 1851 the census took place on the night of the 30th of March. By then, Queen Victoria had been on the throne for 14 years and industrial development was gaining momentum all over the country, but little had disturbed the pattern of rural life in West Hagbourne.

The baker, Francis Shepherd, was the enumerator for West Hagbourne in 1851. Based on the return he made, one can imagine how he may have gone about his task, what he may have been thinking and what he found, as he went around the village collecting his census information on the morning of Monday, the 31st of March. The street names in his story are those which were in use in West Hagbourne in 1851 and all the people named appear on the census return. However, the following story is a fictionalised account of Francis Shepherd's day.

Census day in 1851 – Francis Shepherd's story

It was a long and busy day for Francis Shepherd. He took his responsibilities seriously and although he had done the job once before in 1841, it was different this time. Ten years ago his six children were all living at home and they had helped him in his bakery but now, at the age of 52, he lived alone. Also, there was much more information to record this time, such as exact age, place of birth, marital status and the relationship of each person to the head of the household. The number of lunatics, blind, deaf or dumb people also had to be recorded, but fortunately he found none of these in West Hagbourne.

It was also a tiring day, as he had to cover quite a distance. Although there were only 43 houses in the village, they were as far apart as the top of Hagbourne Hill to the south, and Down Farm and the inn at Down House across the fields to the north, on the boundary with Didcot. Luckily for Francis, three of the houses were empty and did not require a visit from the enumerator.

In 1851 farming was the main occupation, with 44 men classed as agricultural labourers. Therefore, Francis Shepherd decided to begin by collecting the census returns from the larger farms. First, however, he visited the houses on Hagbourne Hill whilst he was still feeling fresh. He remembered that in 1841 he had left the hill until last and had found it hard going then, when he was ten years younger.

The first farm he visited was West Hagbourne Farm (now Manor Farm) where Joseph and Hannah Lousley employed 12 men to work on 240 acres of arable land. When Francis went there to collect the census return, there were nine children – all boys – at home on the previous night, as well as three servants, who all lived in. Men, as well as women, were employed as servants in those days. After leaving West Hagbourne Farm, Francis went across to nearby Ivy Farm Cottage where Joseph's mother, Sarah Grimshaw, lived.

The next farm Francis Shepherd visited was Grove Manor, a much larger farm of 385 acres. In 1851 it was leased to Robert Smith and his wife Elizabeth, who employed 18 labourers. Robert and Elizabeth were a young couple with two small children and Francis noted on the census return that three servants lived in. Robert Smith was born in West Hendred but his wife came from London. Francis mused to himself as he left the house, situated on the edge of the village, that she probably found rural life rather quiet and isolated compared with London.

On leaving Grove Manor Farm, Francis retraced his steps back to the centre of the village along Church Way, a route he usually only followed on Sundays when he attended the morning service at the parish church in East Hagbourne. As he walked along, he met the char woman, Naomy Norris, on her way to Grove Manor Farm. He continued down the High Street to York Farm, where the tenant,

Ivy Farm Cottage was built in the eighteenth century opposite the village pond. This photograph was taken about 1900 and today, a century later, the house appears remarkably unchanged. The railings were still there in the early 1930s and were probably removed during the Second World War

Photograph of York Farm taken from the Square in the early 1900s

This cottage belonged to Grove Manor Estate and had many tenants, including Mary Ann Woodley, photographed here in about 1908, holding the hands of her two grandchildren Wipsi and Alice Powell. The identity of the other boy is not known. The cottage fell into disrepair and was eventually pulled down

John Bullock, employed seven workers on the 140 acre farm. John and his wife Sally lived there with their five daughters. Francis noted that none of them were married, though the eldest was 24 years old. York Farm became known locally as Bullocks, as villagers often referred to a house by the name of the occupier.

On leaving York Farm, Francis went next door to Lime Tree Farm to record the details of Joseph and Isaac Dearlove, father and son, who farmed 43 acres. They employed two men and a plough boy called Stephen Essex, aged 15. Francis then headed north along Goosecoobs Road until he reached a footpath called Wantage Way, where he turned left and continued to Cow Lane. On the way, he met a few farm labourers heading back to the village for their dinner. At the end of Cow Lane, Francis took the well-worn track through the Sheep Down until he reached Down Farm where Henry and Sarah Thomas and their house servant, Sarah Bennett, were the occupants. Henry Thomas was farming the land himself but he probably employed casual labour at harvest time. Francis recalled that when he came up here on the previous census day, in 1841, the Sheep and Cow Downs were still common land used by the villagers to graze their livestock.

From Down Farm, Francis had quite a hike across the Cow Down and a couple of fields until he reached Down House, a small inn (later called the Wheatsheaf) on the very edge of the parish. There he treated himself to a well-earned rest. He had built up a thirst, and his throat was dry after talking to so many people in one morning. He chatted briefly about the census return with the publican, James Lyford, and his wife Miriam, but they were quite busy as the place had filled up with travellers from the nearby Wallingford – Didcot – Faringdon turnpike. It was not long before he headed back down Cow Lane to the centre of the village to collect the rest of the returns from those not so directly connected with the farms.

From Cow Lane he took the short cut down Green Gate Lane to Town Piece Road and collected the census from the thatched cottage on the corner of Pond Road (now Main Street). The cottage was set on about $2\frac{1}{2}$ acres of land, comprising an orchard and paddock which was later sold off in small lots to neighbouring landowners in the twentieth century.

Francis continued along Pond Road to see Francis Redwood who lived with his family at the cottage by the pond, known today as Green Thatch. Francis was an agricultural labourer, whilst his 21 year old son, John Redwood, was a basket maker. His skills were in great demand as baskets were widely used in West Hagbourne's extensive orchards at fruit picking time. He also made the large sieves used to pack the fruit ready for transporting to the fruiterers. The fruit was layered between stinging nettles and paper which protected the fruit from bruising whilst in transit. The Redwoods continued to live at the cottage until the 1900s, followed by a succession of tenants, including the Randells who ran a sweet shop there.

Francis then crossed Pond Road to call on the families living in the cottage, now called Blissetts, on the corner opposite the pond. The original building was already over 200 years old when Francis Shepherd called to collect the census returns. A timber-framed building incorporating a brick-built chimney, it has been

Green Thatch has been considerably extended since this photograph was taken

The thatch over the front porch has been replaced by tiles and the door on the right has disappeared since this photograph of Blissetts was taken in 1910. Otherwise, the outside appearance of the house has remained largely unchanged © CROSSLEY

Moggs Cottage about 1910. Thatch Cottage is the house on the left of the photograph and part of the adjoining thatched cob wall can be seen on the right
© CROWN COPYRIGHT. NMR

described as a typical Berkshire house of the early seventeenth century. Various additions have been made over the centuries and it is believed that it could have been made into three cottages at one time, particularly in the light of the recent discovery of evidence of a third staircase. These cottages were later converted into a single dwelling, probably named after John Blissatt of Aston Upthorpe, who was one of the owners in 1665. The property was part of the Windsor manor until Richard de Windsor sold the estate in 1661.

Francis then turned into Village Street for the second time that day. He walked along beside the cob wall which fronted Moggs Orchard between Ivy Farm Cottage and the house once known as Moggs (now Wycherts). Today this is the only remaining bit of thatched wall in the village, but Francis went past at least three others that day: one in Moor Lane near the small pond by Grove Manor Farm, one in the Square next to York Farm Cottage, and the third at the eastern end of the High Street leading towards Grove Manor Farm. A tiny section of this latter thatched, cob wall is just visible on the right, behind the wedding party in the photograph on page 178.

Sophia Broad and Sarah Powell at the gate of the two cottages now called Broomsticks, about 1914. Sophia, always known as 'Aunt Soph', was born in Moor Lane in 1867. She moved to one of the cottages at Broomsticks with her seven children when she was widowed in 1913. Aunt Soph became a familiar sight, sitting by the front gate chatting to passing villagers, always wearing a long skirt and black boots

Next, Francis Shepherd stopped to collect the census returns from Moggs, which was then two three-storey thatched dwellings and had its own bread oven. The thatch did not survive and was temporarily replaced by a tin roof until John Lay bought the two cottages in 1959, converted them into one dwelling and had the roof tiled. The name was changed to Wycherts in the twentieth century.

Francis then crossed the road to pick up the census returns from the two semi-detached cottages now converted into one house known today as Broomsticks. From there he continued up Village Street to visit John Hale, a retired maltster. In later years, maltsters' wives also took on this job. Francis had to pass through the solid gates at the entrance to Nut Tree Orchard where the malt house then stood. The orchard later became part of the garden of the neighbouring house called Woodleys and the gates remained long after the malt house was demolished. These gates survived well into the twentieth century, long after the malt house had disappeared. Nut Tree Orchard was renowned in the village for its Bramleys and superb Newton Wonders but there were no windfalls to distract Francis at this time of year.

Photograph of Thatch Cottage taken early in the twentieth century when the roof was being rethatched. The door on the right was the entrance to Father Antony's chapel

    The next stop for Francis was the dwelling known today as Thatch Cottage on the corner of Moor Lane and Village Street. Although he did not need to write it on the census return, Francis made a mental note of the Sun Insurance number 34706 above the door whilst he waited for someone to answer his knock. John Norris, a farmer who once owned the dwelling, had taken out the fire insurance policy in 1774. The property was later owned by the Lousleys and when they sold it to Robert Smith Langford in 1895, one of the rooms was being used as a chapel. This may have attracted Father Antony to the cottage, which he purchased in 1904 and continued to use the chapel for services. This was the second house which Father Antony bought in West Hagbourne. His story is told in Chapter 11.

    On leaving Thatch Cottage, Francis Shepherd turned into Moor Lane, at one time known as Norris Lane after John Norris. Francis was glad that it was a dry spring as the lane could be very muddy during the winter. He called at five homes in Moor Lane, one of them being that of the Broad family, where Eve Broad was a seamstress who had patched many a shirt of his to make it last a little bit longer. Francis also collected a census return from Moses Beavis and his wife Letitia. Their son George, a farm worker like his father, also lived at home. The house, now called Enard Cottage, was two dwellings at one time, and according to the vernacular architect Chris Currie, dates back to the Medieval period. Moses Beavis incorporated a chapel into the property in 1834. Francis had never attended a service there as he preferred to worship at the parish church in East Hagbourne where he had been baptised. The chapel continued to be used by Father Antony

Front view of the property once owned by Moses Beavis, just before restoration in 1953. This house in Moor Lane is now called Enard Cottage

Rear view of Enard Cottage after modernisation

when he bought the property from George Beavis in 1902, two years before he bought the cottage next door. The property was altered in the twentieth century.

On leaving Moor Lane, Francis turned towards the three cottages on the corner facing the Square, at the heart of the village. These were tied cottages belonging to Grove Manor Farm Estate and had stood there for centuries. Fifty years after his visit they would be immortalised in a painting by Helen Allingham, but this did not save them from demolition some years later. The pair of thatched cottages next door also suffered the same fate in the 1950s.

Francis was feeling weary now, but at least he didn't have far to walk to collect the census returns from the houses clustered round the Square. He stopped briefly to pick up the returns from the agricultural labourers living in the two tied cottages belonging to York Farm. The first, built in the late seventeenth or early eighteenth century, is now known as The Square. Next door was a cottage known as Ardlui in 1919, but now called York Farm Cottage. The labourer who lived there had not yet returned from the fields so Francis decided to call back later, on his way home.

Before moving on, Francis stood in the Square for a moment, remembering what his father had told him about the village stocks which had once been a feature there. A shiver went down his spine at the thought of suffering such an indignity and he briskly walked across the Square to the house now known as Woodleys, which then served as both a bakery and a shop. Our enumerator was not the only

Three cottages on the corner of the Square, painted by Helen Allingham around 1900. The painting is reproduced on the cover of this book. The cottages fell into disrepair and were demolished in the late 1930s or early 1940s. The cottages on the left survived until the late 1950s

One of the tenants of the cottages on the corner of the Square was Bert Dawson, standing at the door in this photograph, with his son Bertie in 1932

Photograph of Ardlui, later known as York Farm Cottage, taken in 1910. The end of the thatched cob wall which ran between Ardlui and the house now known as The Square can be glimpsed on the right of the cottage. The neat thatched barn to the left of Ardlui no longer exists

© CROSSLEY

A view of some of the houses which front on to the Square, home to the village stocks in the eighteenth century. The house on the right is now known as The Square. During recent modernisation a bread oven and well have been rediscovered. Woodleys stands on the left of the photograph, which was taken early in the twentieth century

baker in the village. The other two were John Jefferies and John Woodley. This may seem a large number for such a small village but in earlier centuries bakeries did more than bake bread, as they often provided cooking facilities as well. Most cooking was done in pots on open fires until coal-fired ranges were introduced. Few houses, apart from the manors and farmsteads had their own ovens, but for a few pence a villager could take a prepared dish to be cooked in the baker's oven.

Woodleys took its name from the Woodley family who lived there for several decades. When Francis called, it was occupied by the baker John Woodley and his wife Sarah who kept the shop. When Francis stepped inside he glanced up at the central beam where '1688' was carved on one of the central supports. This has always been accepted as the date the house was built. On leaving Woodleys, Francis turned down the High Street, passing the great double doors of the barn. These were big enough to drive a cart through so that the grain could be unloaded directly into the loft through a trap door in the roof. Francis continued along Woodley's garden which stretched to the end of the High Street.

Finally, Francis headed towards his last stop on the census trail. He had planned his route carefully so that he ended his day at the Horse and Harrow public house, but first he slipped across to the little toll house at Scotlands Ash Corner where the widower George Bryant was the toll collector. After exchanging a few words with his old friend George and giving him a bit of help with his census form, he thankfully settled into his usual corner at the pub with his pint to fill in his own census return and review his day's work.

Francis didn't know the publican and farmer William Buckle or his wife Mary,

A very early photograph of the Horse and Harrow inn and a few locals enjoying the novelty of having their photograph taken. The old sign announces the 'Horse Harrow', suggesting that this may have been its original name

as they had only just arrived at the Horse and Harrow following the recent retirement of George Napper, the previous landlord. George had called himself an annuitant on his census return, which Francis had just picked up from the house next door where George lived with his family. Francis thought it would be hard to get used to a new publican after George Napper, who had been the landlord for so many years. He remembered the excitement at the inn nine years ago when Daniel Lousley held a public meeting there before drawing up the Inclosure Award. Francis was pleased to see the familiar face of his neighbour, Harriet Dearlove, behind the bar. She was a servant at the Horse and Harrow, but this evening she was helping out behind the bar, as quite a few travellers were staying the night on their way to the Abingdon fair.

As Francis started reading through the returns he had collected, he felt a bit concerned that he had got everyone's names down properly. Many of the people he had seen that day were unable to read or write and he had trouble spelling some of their names. However, many of the family names, such as Bullock, Woodley, Lousley, Dearlove, Powell, Napper and Broad were all familiar to him as they had lived in West Hagbourne for generations. When Francis did his final count, he found that the total number of people in the village on the night of the census was 209 (119 males and 90 females). Only one of those, the sawyer, Henry Saunders, was a visitor. Many people were originally from nearby Berkshire villages and towns, but a few came from as far away as London and Suffolk. Most of the children under the age of 14 years (50 boys and 34 girls) had been born in the village and Francis had known many of them all their lives. Some of them had occupations. One of these, Amos Fiddler, aged ten, was a shepherd boy and Francis hoped that one day he would become a master shepherd like Daniel Dearlove.

The thing which worried Francis the most was the paupers living in the village. There were four families, registered as eight people, on the census return, and several were over 80 years old. Most of them had been agricultural labourers on low wages with no opportunity to save for their old age. He hoped that William Tyrrell Charity or one of the other Hagbourne charities would help them.

Although he had recorded all the names, Francis knew that he still had a lot to do to complete the forms. He calculated that it would be a week before he could sign off the return and send it to the registrar in London. However, he had had enough for today and it was time to put away his papers and enjoy a drink with his friend George who had just arrived from the toll house.

Emigration from West Hagbourne in the Nineteenth Century

Although the names of many families appeared decade after decade on the West Hagbourne census returns, there were some who decided to try and make a better life for themselves on the other side of the world. Two such families were the Woodleys and the Powells. There had been Woodleys living in the Hagbournes since at least 1672, when Anne and Anthony Woodley were married. Some of their descendants emigrated to New Zealand in 1874.

According to the passenger list for the clipper 'Crusader' which set sail from Plymouth on the 25th of September 1874, John and Martha Woodley, their four children, John's brother Caleb and his wife Mary and their three children, as well as his younger brother Charles, aged 16, were all on board. Neighbours William and Elizabeth Powell and their seven children travelled out with them. The story of their journey, passed down by their New Zealand descendants, suggests that John Woodley decided to uproot his family when he was sacked from his job as an agricultural labourer in West Hagbourne for picking up a windfall apple.

The long journey to New Zealand was full of discomfort and danger. Charles related his memories of the voyage, still vivid many years later, to Mary Woodley, wife of his son Horace. This is the story of his journey, exactly as she recorded it:

> My two brothers, John & Caleb, with their wives and families and myself came from Berkshire in 1874 on the ship Crusader which made the voyage from Plymouth in 93 days.
>
> The married people with their families occupied the centre part of the ship. The single men were in the forepart and the unmarried women and girls had their quarters aft. In the Bay of Biscay we ran into a storm. All passengers were sent below and the hatches battened down. The ship heaved frightfully and almost everyone was sick, no one expected to come out of it alive. In one corner of the single men's quarters, where I was, was a group of men praying frantically to God for deliverance. In another corner was another group, blaspheming in terror, and some, too terrified for either simply clung together and howled. It was Bedlam. I climbed into my bunk (it was a top one) thinking I might as well die in comfort if I could. Almost by a miracle I slept and when I woke the storm was passed. The hatches were opened and though the waves were still high it was possible to get some fresh air.
>
> The ship had sprung a leak and the crew worked at the pumps in shifts, a gang of single men from among the passengers assisting. It seemed a hopeless task. Their utmost efforts could scarcely keep the water at one level till suddenly, the inflow of water ceased. (The cause of this was discovered only at the end of the voyage when the ship was laid up for overhaul. A fish had become wedged in the hole and thus proved our salvation). The Captain was afraid to put into any ports as he was afraid of the fevers that were then prevalent and there was no chance of obtaining fresh stores of food and water. Several young children died. The weather at the last was very favourable. On a bright clear night in December, with a following wind we made 300 miles and sighted Lyttelton next morning.
>
> From here we took passage in a timber skow [sic] to Akaroa and Timaru. A coach took the women and children to Temuka. The men followed by dray. Here I soon made friends with a Chinaman. He knew no English so we had to make each other understood by signs. The railway was then under construction and we got employment there, my previous experience with horses standing me in good stead.

After this I took a job driving a delivery cart regularly taking stores to the settlers as far as the McKenzie Country. My beard was then beginning to grow and on occasions the cold was so severe that my breath would freeze upon my whiskers and how welcome were the lights and fire of the small hotel which had been opened there by an enterprising Scotsman.

My next move was to commence farming at Ashburton. My mate and I put up a tent to live in and our first concern was to build a stable. For this we used poles from the bush. It was a windy season and one night our tent collapsed on top of us. It was of no use to try and do anything in the dark in that gale and rain so we just had to lie and wait as best we might until morning.

It was at this place that I met Miss Mary Ann Margetts and made her my wife. We had little of this world's goods but were devoted to each other and youth and strength were in our favour.

The family later moved to the North Island, finally settling in Palmerston. Charles married twice, fathered 16 children and lived to celebrate his 80th birthday. By 1992, there were 250 descendants of the original three Woodley brothers, bearing the name of Woodley in New Zealand. Several of them have made visits to West Hagbourne to see for themselves the village their ancestors left behind.

Sources – The Census

John Cannon (ed.), *The Oxford Companion to British History*, Oxford University Press, 1977, p183.
John Richardson, *The Local Historian's Encyclopedia*, Historical Publications Ltd, reprinted 1977, p72.
Census of England and Wales, Returns for 1841–1891 inclusive.
District of South Oxfordshire, *List of Buildings of Special Architectural or Historic Interest*, Department of the Environment, 1987.
Sale of land at corner of Pond Road and Town Piece Road: *Abstract of Title Deeds*, Slade Son & Taylor, various dates.
Dating of Ivy Farm Cottage: Brian Lingham (compiler), *Around Didcot and the Hagbournes in Old Photographs*, Alan Sutton, 1990, p123.
Dating of Enard Cottage: C R J Currie, 'Larger Medieval Houses in the Vale of White Horse', *Oxoniensia Journal*, Vol LVII, 1992, p132.
Sale notice for Woodleys, 1958.
Thatch Cottage fire insurance: Sun Insurance Registers, 1774, Guildhall Library. MS 11936/229.

Sources – Emigration

Passenger list of the Clipper Ship 'Crusader', Immigration Department, Wellington, New Zealand, 6 March 1926.

Chapter Nine

A Farming Village

West Hagbourne has always been a farming community. There are five farms within a mile of each other, so it is not surprising that agriculture has always been a way of life. Over the centuries, the community has had to respond to many changes, including famines, droughts, war, new developments in agricultural practices, and most importantly, to the major redistribution of land which took place in the nineteenth century. This chapter will describe these farming developments and the way that political forces and national events taking place beyond the boundaries of this tiny village, have affected the close-knit community of West Hagbourne. It will also follow the history of all the farms, including some which no longer exist, and tell the stories of those who have worked the land down the ages. 'A Farming Village' has been compiled from the reminiscences of a number of different people, many of them passing on the recollections of their own parents and grandparents.

Farming in Medieval Times

In medieval times, West Hagbourne's farm workers were tied to the two manors. Most were tenant farmers, paying rent to the lord of the manor. Farming in the village was a cooperative affair, particularly during ploughing time when villeins clubbed together to make up the team of eight oxen which were needed to pull the heavy wooden plough through the soil. This communal effort focused on the three-fields method of farming. Each year one field grew winter-sown wheat and another spring wheat. The third was left fallow to recover its fertility after two consecutive years of growing crops and providing grazing for the animals.

The arable land in West Hagbourne was divided into three common fields called the City, the Lower and the Down Fields (see the Craven Estate map of 1775, p80). The fields were divided into furlongs (a furlong being one eighth of a mile or about 200 metres). Each furlong was subdivided into strips which were separated, one from the other, by a raised baulk of unploughed land. There were also pieces of unploughed land called headland at the end of each furlong to allow access and to provide a space for the plough to turn.

Both freemen and villeins, depending on their status, held a number of these strips from the lord of the manor. Each individual's strips were scattered about the fields rather than being together, which made cultivation very intensive. All the strips in a single field were planted with the same crop so that the only place a villager could grow crops of his own choice was a small piece of land, called a close, by his dwelling.

Further from the centre of the village were the commons – not to be confused with the three common fields – where the villagers grazed their livestock. This privilege, known as the Rights of Common, was conferred according to the number of strips held by a villager and was jealously guarded. We know from a 1754 map of the village (see p82), that the commons of West Hagbourne consisted of the Cow and Sheep Downs near Down Farm and the Wet and Dry Moors in Moor Lane. The commons merged into wastelands and these, at the outer limits of the manor, into woodlands.

Hay played an important part in the economy of the village as it provided winter food for the livestock. The meadows were therefore out-of-bounds and enclosed between Christmas and late summer while the crop was growing. Anyone who let his animals wander on the meadows was fined. The hay was cut at the end of summer and divided between the villagers. The meadows were then opened for grazing until the following Christmas when the ploughing started. The person responsible for the meadows, pastures and haymaking was called a hayward.

Access to the commons and the surrounding woods and wastelands was central to village life. Grazing rights and fodder for livestock were vitally important, especially in the winter, as oxen were essential for the ploughing. The woodlands provided material for house building, household utensils, fencing and fuel, whilst gravel, turf, bracken and berries could be obtained from the wastelands.

Farming Beyond the Middle Ages

Farming continued in much the same way well beyond the Middle Ages, though foreign wars, changing agricultural methods, and new trading opportunities were to have their effect on the agricultural life of West Hagbourne. In Elizabethan times corn became an important trading commodity throughout Berkshire, as did wool and cloth. Most farms developed a mixed economy, encompassing both arable farming and sheep rearing. In the eighteenth century, the enclosure acts, inventions such as Jethro Tull's seed drill, the introduction of new crops and ideas about crop rotation, and advances in animal breeding radically changed farming methods.

Throughout the nineteenth century, the land continued to provide more employment than almost any other industry in Berkshire. The Industrial Revolution also had repercussions for rural England. There was agitation for free trade and the abolition of the protectionist corn laws of 1815. This was particularly true of the manufacturing towns eager to find foreign markets for their products, and wishing to keep food prices and wages down. Local landowners formed the Berkshire Association for the Protection of Agriculture in response to the growing influence of the Anti-Corn Law League, but they, and others, were defeated and the corn laws were repealed in 1846.

A period of prosperity followed for landowners in the golden years between 1846 and the 1870s. The profits of agriculture increased by a fifth in the four years following 1853. However, three disastrously wet summers in succession, and the periods of inflation which marked the last quarter of the nineteenth century, together with the arrival of the first cheap imports of produce from abroad, all took their toll on agricultural workers. Arable and livestock farmers were the worst affected, but the dramatic fall in wool prices also touched the sheep farming areas around the Berkshire Downs. In order to survive, farmers were forced to change their farming methods. Those who could afford to, invested in dairy farming and bought new, more mechanised, machinery. Others lost their livelihoods and many farms stood vacant.

Farming in the Twentieth Century

At the beginning of the twentieth century, farming still involved the whole village and until mechanisation became commonplace, nearly everyone worked on the farms. Women joined the men at certain times of the year to help with harvesting, haymaking, threshing and fruit picking. As one old-timer put it, nobody gave a thought to the long hours and hard work any more than they did to the need to find somewhere suitable in the middle of a harvest field to satisfy the calls of nature. That was all in a day's work, but some hardships were harder to ignore: cold hands that had to milk the cows on frosty mornings and backs that ached when picking up potatoes, swedes, mangels, turnips, or when hand-picking a field of peas. Happier memories were of reaching up high to get a cherry at the top of the tree and popping it into one's mouth when the boss wasn't watching.

The twentieth century saw significant agricultural changes, in particular, increased mechanisation, the application of modern scientific methods for both dairy and arable farming and the use of pesticides and artificial fertilisers. Miles of hedgerows were grubbed out to increase the size of fields to accommodate the larger machinery. Even so, the decline which started towards the end of the nineteenth century continued in rural Berkshire. The 1930s are remembered as being particularly hard for farmers in West Hagbourne as cheap imports of corn from Canada, and wool and lamb from Australia and New Zealand, flooded the market. Some farmers were even forced to seek work abroad in places like Canada. Other concerns, such as the tithing system, which had always been a great burden, finally came to a head in the 1930s. Richard Allen remembers his father going to London to march in protest against the tithes. The Tithe Act of 1936 finally abolished them once and for all.

In the last century, two world wars, Britain's membership of the Common Market, new trading arrangements, directives imposed by European Union regulators and fluctuations in the exchange rate of the pound, all affected not only farming and English rural life but the heart of the countryside itself.

A Farming Year in West Hagbourne

Despite all the upheavals which have taken place over the centuries, the rhythm of nature remains the same. The farming year in West Hagbourne continues to be governed by the seasons, just as it was in the Middle Ages.

Ploughing

Ploughing started as soon as the harvest was over to prepare the ground for the winter corn. It usually went on until January, depending on the weather. The fields were used in rotation, leaving each one fallow for a year. This was the only way of controlling weeds before the advent of spraying in the 1950s. The fields were marked out by 'stepping' strides for 30 yards at both ends of the field, which was then ploughed round and round, finishing down the middle. Today fields are ploughed across from one side to the other with a one-way plough.

Ploughing was originally done by oxen and later by horses on most West

Two of the last horses used in West Hagbourne belonged to the Lays at Manor Farm. They were a chestnut called Boxer and this grey called Punch, ridden here by Colin Mason

Hagbourne farms, though steam ploughs were also contracted in from the Oxford Steam Ploughing Company. The ploughman's day revolved around the horses, starting at five o'clock when he arrived at the yard to 'bate' (feed) and groom the working horses. On some farms he then went home for breakfast around six o'clock, returning to the yard to harness the horses and walk them out to the fields ready to start ploughing by seven. Some ploughmen remember having breakfast in the field at half past nine. This meal usually consisted of bread and cheese, with bacon or onion, washed down with a bottle of cold tea.

At half past ten there was a break of ten minutes, then work would carry on until about three o'clock. The ploughman was allowed to ride the horse back to the farm instead of walking it. He then went home for his dinner, returning to the yard at four o'clock in the afternoon to feed and groom the horses. In the summer they would be put out to graze and the ploughman's day would finish at half past five.

The men worked a full six-day week, calling into work on Sundays to feed the horses. Later, when tractors were used for ploughing, they were able to finish at one o'clock on Saturdays. The men and horses walked an average of 12 miles per acre. It took a whole day for two horses with a single nine inch farrow to plough one acre if the going was good, that is, not too wet.

The first tractors appeared in West Hagbourne in 1918. Dennis Napper of Grove Manor Farm owned two Crawley tractors. The Crawley tractor was one of the earliest and looked more like a motorised plough, the 'driver' walking behind like a ploughman. Dennis Napper's first driver was Mr Cox. York Farm purchased its first tractor in 1931. This was the 'International', a three-furrow plough on steel wheels. Later in the 1930s, a second tractor was bought, this time with pneumatic tyres. By the 1940s all the farms were using tractors, the 1020 International being the most common. The new tractors enabled farmers to plough three to four acres a day, so that ploughing was finished before Christmas.

Cultivation

Once a field had been ploughed, cultivation could begin. Some winter corn was planted between October and November but most corn was planted in the spring. The fields were first raked down using a Martin Cultivator, originally pulled by horses and later by tractors.

It was important not to have the soil too fine as the large clods helped to protect the grain from the winter weather. Once the ground had been prepared, planting was done with a Gilbert drill, again, originally pulled by horses. A wagon full of sacks of feed corn would be waiting at the side of the field to be planted. One man could drill about 12 acres a day; nowadays a tractor can cover 80 acres in the same time. Around the middle of April the wheat was harrowed to clean and aerate the growing crop. It then went through a rolling process which was always associated with springtime and the saying: "Get the rollers rattling, the spring's here".

At one time, Fred Jones worked for Charles Allen at York Farm and he recalls that the corn was planted after the Abingdon Fair in October. He particularly remembers this as Charles liked the men to meet him for a drink in the Happy Dick pub (no longer there) during the fair. He also gave them each five shillings as well as the day off. Anyone foolish enough not to turn up to share the boss's hospitality got nothing, so although Fred didn't drink, he would always go along.

Threshing

Whilst the next season's corn was growing, last season's ricks had to be dismantled and the corn thrashed. Threshing, or 'sheening' as it was known locally, could take place at any time but was usually done during the winter when money was short. The threshing machine remained stationary, originally operated by a steam engine and later by a tractor.

Threshing needed a lot of labour. While three men stood on a rick throwing sheaves to one or two men standing on the machine cutting the bonds and feeding the sheaves into the thresher, someone else was taking away the filled sacks of corn. Two others worked on a baler, if there was one, whilst another stacked the bales. The dustiest, noisiest and dirtiest part of threshing was the 'chaff and caving'. This involved bagging up the husks and small heads of straw expelled by the threshing machine onto the ground. This was the least popular job as the chaff and cave-ins had to be kept clear at all costs. The bagged-up chaff was used for cattle feed. Some of the corn was 'dressed' for seed for the next year's planting. It took one day to thresh 20 bags of wheat corn, a bag weighing 2¼ cwt.

The gang of men who worked the machine were called a side. Threshing machines were contracted out, together with a side, to work at small local farms in the area. Lay's threshing machine and side were contracted to thresh many ricks at

Jack Dawson, carter, with (L to R): the black mare called Blossom, Prince, and Gilbert the chestnut, at York Farm, in the late 1920s

Frank Napper's side threshing a rick. Standing on the rick is 'Beef' Thornhill with Tommy Butler. Holding the scales is Joe Butler with Horace Butler on his left

Taken about 1914, this photo shows the steam engine owned by Charles Allen and Joseph Napper, with the threshing machine on the right. The group are standing in front of Ivy Cottage close to the pond which provided the water to operate the steam engine. There was a shop at Ivy Cottage at this time and the shop door can be seen on the left

other farms, including Lime Tree Farm in West Hagbourne. In the 1940s, Manor Farm's side included Tubby Shaw who did the caving; Ern Carter, the suitably named carter; Frank Austin and Mrs Fisher who worked up on top of the thresher, there being no automatic feeder; Noel Carter who looked after the tractor; Mervyn Roberts; Gerald Stovin ('Cheddar'); Phil Watson ('Whatie') and Frank Boulter. At the busiest time, strappers joined the side. These were casual workers and included 'Barber' Warner, Henry Powell, Wipsi (William Powell) who also had his own farm, and Ron Jubber.

The first threshing machine at York Farm was brought from Kingston Bagpuize (previously threshing was contracted out). Jack Dawson and a farm-hand set off with five horses early one morning to collect it. On the way back, Steventon Hill was almost too much for the tired horses, and for Jack too, when a passing labourer refused to help them get the machine up the hill. Jack eventually arrived back that evening to a hero's welcome, as an excited crowd gathered to catch a glimpse of the first threshing machine to arrive in West Hagbourne.

Haymaking

Haymaking began in June or July. The grass was cut for hay in West Hagbourne's orchards with a scythe until the 1950s. Later, horse mowers were used in the fields, the hay being swept to the rick by attaching a sweep between two horses. This was

Building wheat ricks thatched with wheat straw. In the 1940s the farmers had to organise a 'rick patrol' because ricks were being burnt down. The farmers took turns to watch the ricks during the night

before tractors took over from horses. Joe Napper remembers Ern Carter coming up to the pumping station next to the Horse and Harrow with the last two horses used to mow the fields.

In the 1940s the Lays at Manor Farm used an Armstrong-Siddeley car with sweep tines attached to the front. This was driven round the field and was considered "great fun" by the labourers. The hay was pushed towards the rick and pitched onto an elevator which took it to the top. When the rick was finished it was thatched with straw to keep it dry.

Harvesting

Harvesting took place in the summer when the corn was ripe. It was originally done by hand with a hook. Later a scythe and a cradle were used, the cradle gathering each swathe and lifting it, ready for bundling up. This saved ten hours of labour per acre compared with using only a hook.

A reaper, pulled by horses, was the next change, cutting the corn and leaving it untied in bundles called sheaves. Tying was done afterwards, usually by women. Later on, a binder was used to cut and tie the corn into sheaves. Before the binder could start, the edges of the fields needed to be cut by hand with a bagging hook to allow the binder to turn. The sheaves, which were left to dry in groups of six or eight, were known as stooks; this work was called 'stooking up' or 'shocking up'.

Noel Carter and his father, Ern, with a tractor and binder on Hagbourne Hill during harvesting in the 1950s before the days of combine harvesters. Ern Carter spent most of his working life as a carter for the Lays before machines replaced the farm horses

The carter worked the binder and the other men did the shocking up. When this was finished, the stooks were collected and built into ricks in a convenient place, and then thatched with wheat straw to keep them dry. At one time they were a common sight alongside the old turnpike (Harwell) road.

Harvesting was a busy time with an early start at five o'clock in the morning. Everyone stayed out in the fields all day with food and beer brought out to the labourers, whose overtime pay was 6d per hour. Horses were needed round the clock to keep everything moving. In the days before tractors, six horses were used in the harvest field, three resting while three worked.

Fruit growing

West Hagbourne is situated in a rich fruit-growing area and most of the local farms, large or small, once produced fruit of one kind or another. Damsons were grown round the village boundaries because they flowered early and attracted bees. Produce was sold locally, in Oxford and at the Covent Garden fruit and vegetable

A group of cherry pickers, consisting of villagers and their friends, about 1953. L to R:
Back row: Bob Blond, Jim Blond, Henry 'Barber' Warner, Wipsi Powell
Second row: Mabel Powell, Ruth Butler, Edna Woodley, Pat O'Donnell, Dee Butler
Third row: Win Warner, Freda Dawson, Annie Warr, Dick Powell
Front row: David Blond, Cyril 'Tid' Dawson (accordionist), Freddie Butler, Peter Dawson
Extreme right: Philip Blond

West Hagbourne's orchards, 1876.

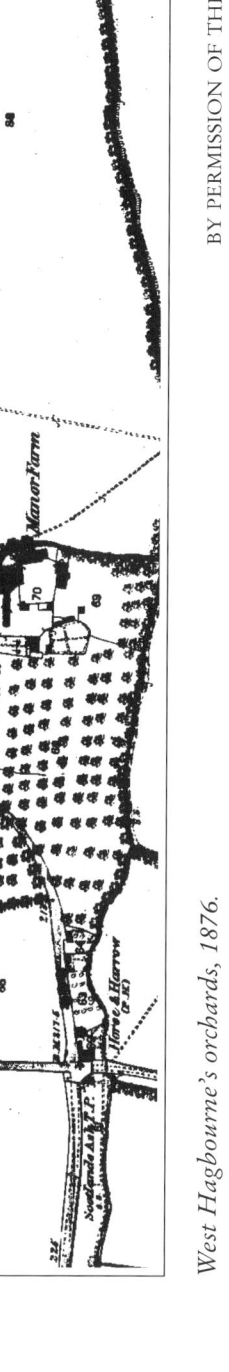

market in London. Both Down and York Farms had extensive orchards. In 1936 there were 428 apple trees, 230 plum trees, 74 cherry trees and 12 pear trees. Some of the old varieties of fruit are still around, such as Victoria and Pershore plums and Bramley, Cox's, Newton and Blenheim apples.

At Grove Manor Farm, Dennis Napper grew large white cherries, called Elton Hearts, in the 'New Orchard' which was not all that new, having been planted in the 1890s. Frank Napper also had fruit trees at Ivy Farm. At Ragged Farm, William Powell, always known as Wipsi, grew apples, pears, damsons, plums and cherries. He hired fruit pickers to pick not only his own fruit, but also the fruit of other growers. Most of the fruit was picked during the autumn when lots of villagers were employed on a casual basis. Some men even came over from Didcot, working in between their shifts on the railway. A lot of the fruit was sent to Durhams, or Hicks and Son, in Oxford. Cherries were often sold at the side of the road.

Cherry picking for Wipsi and his partner 'Barber' Warner was often a lively affair as most of the pickers were villagers with their families and friends. The cherry trees were big and high so Wipsi and Barber would set the heavy ladders against the trees for the women. As they were picked, the cherries were put into baskets hanging from hooks in the trees. After the cherries had been harvested there would often be a bit of a party and sing-song.

West Hagbourne's Farms, Past and Present

More is known about the history of the oldest farms in the village, particularly those with links to the original manors, because documents relating to the running of the estates such as court rolls, rent agreements, dowries, wills, and inventories have survived in official archives. Many landowners have also kept their own detailed records and accounts relating to the management of their farms. Some farms no longer exist and we are reliant on sale notices, photographs, maps and personal recollections to tell their stories.

Down Farm

Down Farm is situated to the north west of the village on the parish boundary adjacent to Harwell and Didcot, on what was once common land, known as Hagbourne Down. Like the rest of West Hagbourne, Down Farm was originally part of the manorial estate of Walter, son of Other, and founder of the Windsor dynasty. It was part of the land identified in the Domesday Book in 1086. The earliest known written document which refers to the Down is a grant by the lord of the manor, Thomas Wyndesor (Windsor), his wife Mary and their son Andrew, to William Dunche of Little Wytenham and James Braybroke of Sutton in Berkshire. It refers to: "Woods, pasture, &c., called West Haguebourne Downe". The deed was signed by Mary Wyndesor, née Beckingham, heiress of Watlingtons

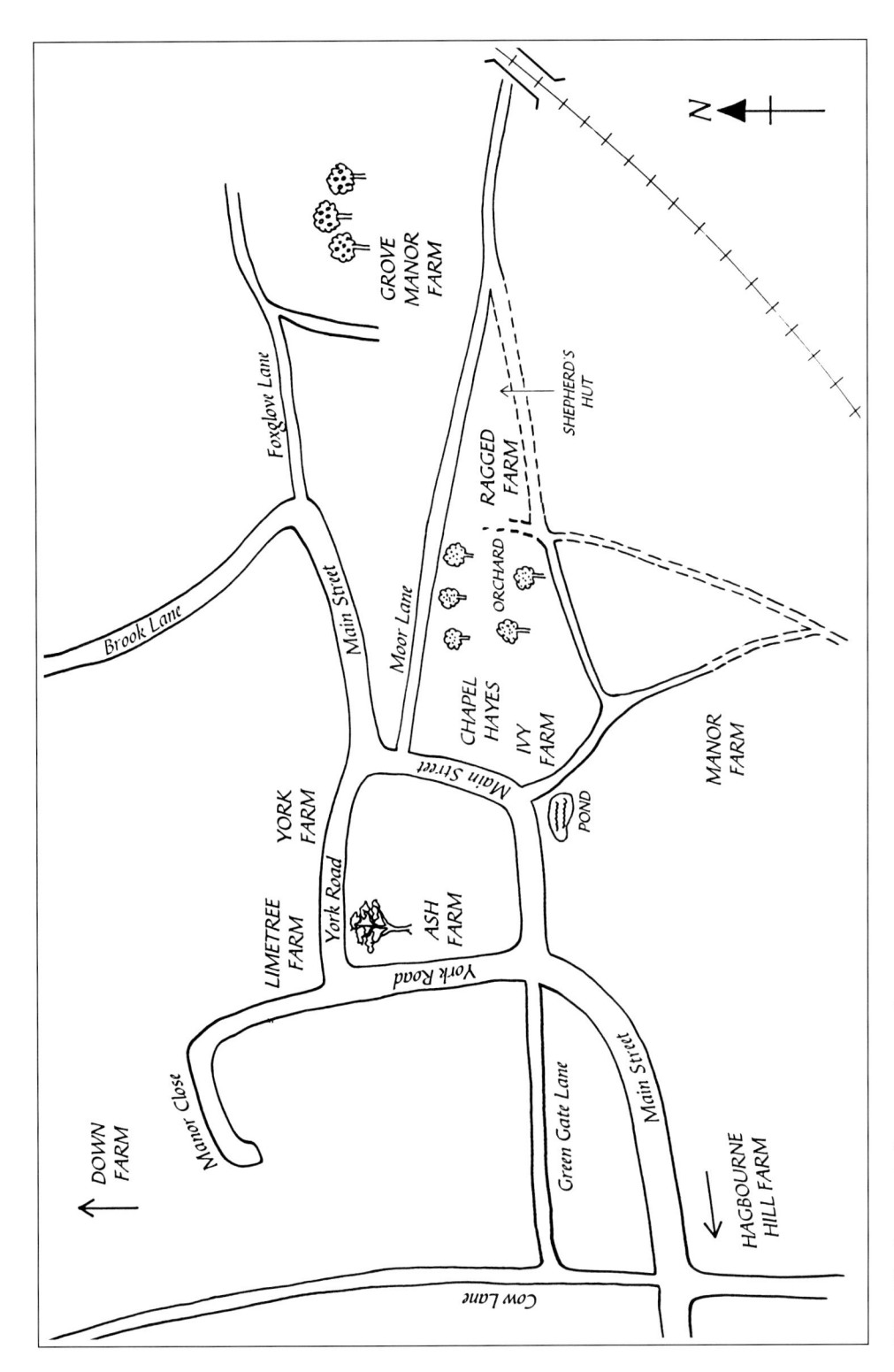

West Hagbourne's farms, past and present

and Windsor manors (see p25). The exact date of this deed is uncertain as the clerk omitted the year when he transcribed it, but wrote "20 Nov., 8 Nov", repeating Nov where he should have put the name of the reigning monarch. Mary Wyndesor died in 1574, during the reign of Elizabeth I, which points to 1565, the 8th year of Elizabeth's reign, as the date of this grant of land on the Down by the Windsors to Dunche and Braybroke.

The next reference to the Down is a document dated the 5th of March 1642, which appears to be an agreement to enclose the common land on the Down. This was one of the very earliest enclosures to take place in West Hagbourne. The agreement was between the lord of the manor, Richard Windsor, and Edmund Dunch of Little Wittenham on the one hand, and John Wise of Harwell, together with a number of other people, mostly from West Hagbourne, who were probably tenant farmers holding Rights of Common, on the other. These were: Henry Cussell (Cressell), Thomas Field, William Tirrold the younger, Robert Sawyers, Thomas Rosely (Bosley), Richard Coxhedd (Coxhead), Robert Tirrold, William Wellman, John Rose, Gregory Coxhedd, Thomas Hutchins, William Bewd, Richard Sawyer, William Tirrold the elder, Richard Cussell, Henry Smith, Geoffry Farmer, Jane Steere and Avery Reignolds. All parties mentioned in the document signed it.

This was a busy time for these men as they had only just met five days previously, on the 28th of February, to sign West Hagbourne's Protestation Return (see Chapter 4). The Return was signed by all those whose names appeared on the Downs enclosure agreement, with the exception of Jane Steere (no women signed the Return), William Bewd, Robert Sawyers, Henry Smith and Geoffrey Farmer. As was the case with the later enclosure of 1843, the signatories would have agreed to forgo their Rights of Common, which in this case would have been their right to graze their stock on West Hagbourne Down. They would have been compensated

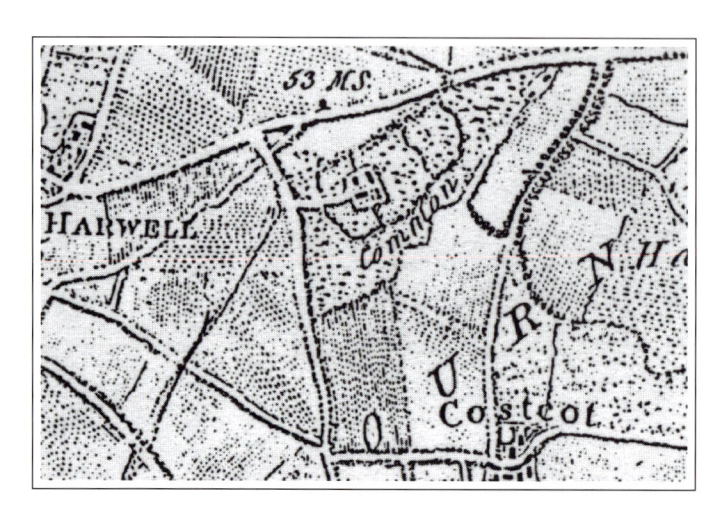

Detail of the Rocque Map of 1760 showing Down Farm surrounded by the Sheep and Cow Downs, much as it is today

by money or land elsewhere. The Down was then enclosed, apart from the Cow and Sheep Downs to which the villagers retained their "right of intercommonage". The enclosed land later became Hagbourne Down Farm, shortened to Down Farm around the 1930s.

Since 1642, the ownership of Down Farm has been mainly vested in three families: the Jennens who acquired it soon after the enclosure, the Haywards, and the Allens who still own it to this day. William Jennens described it in his will of 1708 as "all that wood, woody ground, downe pasture ground and land commonly called Hagborn Downe lying in West Hagborn".

Hagbourne Down Farm remained in the hands of the Jennens family until 1784, when their groom, John Hayward, became the new owner. The Hayward family were originally from Hagbourne but had recently settled in Long Wittenham. The Haywards held Down Farm for almost 100 years.

William Stephens Hayward was perhaps the most colourful character associated with Down Farm. His father had been of a reckless disposition and had gambled away his own inheritance. In 1857 at the age of 22, William was firmly following his example and whilst adventuring abroad had mortgaged his future inheritance in the shape of Down Farm Letters of concern were sent to his great aunt, Ann Hayward, but proved to be of no avail as the inheritance was sold in November of that year to Jacob Appleford of East Hagbourne. William Hayward returned from Italy in 1860 and spent the next seven years writing novels in order to support himself. In 1868, as a result of ill health, he wrote to the Royal Literary Fund seeking support. Describing himself as "the eldest son of a once wealthy family… not brought up to any profession", he further related how he had supported himself "as a gentleman entirely by my pen". He explained how investment in two magazines had left him in debt, and how he was "obliged to sell or pawn – it is an unpleasant word – books and anything of value I possessed". Fortunately for him, the fund was moved enough by his letter to grant him £30. He died in August 1870.

Jacob Appleford, having purchased William S Hayward`s inheritance in 1857, eventually succeeded to the property in 1874 upon Ann Hayward`s death at the age of 96. In financial difficulties from 1876, he was forced to sell the farm in March 1883. James Scott Smith of East Hagbourne became the new owner and it was rented out to Frank Betteridge of Harwell. Asher Lousley lived there as farm bailiff until he died in October 1892. His wife and daughter remained there until Scott Smith sold Down Farm to Asher Lousley's cousin, Charles William Allen of Coscote in 1896.

Charles William Allen married Mary Skuse, whom he met when she came to work as a governess and nurse at Grove Manor Farm. They had five daughters and one son. The Allen family moved "up to the Down" on the 15th of October 1896. Charles's youngest daughter Gertrude, aged just under five at the time, later recounted that whilst the furniture travelled by horse and wagon, the family followed along the field path. She was last and had to carry the coffee-pot!

Charles William Allen and his wife Mary with four of their daughters (L to R): Elsie, Alice, Sarah Elizabeth (Bessie) and Gertrude Annie (Gertie) taken in July 1922 at Down Farm

Photograph of young cattle being fed at Down Farm in the 1920s. The farmhouse has not changed much since it was built in the seventeenth century, after the partial enclosure of the common land on West Hagbourne Down in 1642. The remaining Sheep and Cow Downs were enclosed in 1843

Down Farm was once a half-timbered, wattle and daub dwelling. In the mid seventeenth century the wattle and daub was replaced with brick. The house has not altered that much since then, apart from some remodelling of the south face in the mid eighteenth century (probably in John Hayward's time). Larger windows were installed during the twentieth century. Some of the things found during the alterations included silver coins (circa Charles II), handmade children's shoes, carved clay pipes and a carved cow horn. The large barn, made of oak and elm with a Welsh slate roof, was erected in 1854. Its construction, however, suggests that it was built earlier than this and was originally on another site.

At the beginning of the nineteenth century, Charles Allen (CW, as his descendants remember him) made substantial improvements, including the installation of iron fencing and gates, some of which remain today. He changed the field layout, and built and renovated barns. He also planted many fruit trees. It was a mixed farm, producing fattened cattle and sheep and growing potatoes, wheat, some barley and other root crops for animal feed. There were no milking cows on the farm until CW's grandson Ronald took over the farm. Cart horses were used for ploughing and other heavy work. Farm workers walked from West Hagbourne and Harwell, often returning home for lunch.

Photograph taken at Down Farm in October or November, 1925. A heap of prize-winning mangel-wurzel are proudly displayed in front of a cut stack of hay. L to R: Standing: Albert Woodley, Jake Norris, Charles Allen and Amos Belcher. Seated: James McClean (son-in-law of CW)

Ernest W Allen in the uniform of the Queen's Own Oxfordshire Hussars, circa 1910

One of these Harwell men was Jake Norris. One day Charles caught Jake poaching. He asked him "Why aren't you at work?" Jake replied "I haven't got any work". So Charles told him he'd better start to work for him. Charles gave him a bicycle to ride back and forth from Harwell but he soon fell off and wouldn't ride the bike again. He said he had two good legs and he didn't need a bike. Jake Norris continued to work for the Allens for 40 years.

CW joined the Berkshire Yeomanry as a young man in the early 1870s. When it was the turn of his son Ernest to join, the annual exercise clashed with the hay harvest, and so instead he joined the Oxfordshire Yeomanry whose training occurred at a more convenient time from a farmer's point of view.

In June 1905, Charles Allen's daughter Elsie married George Napper. George served in the First World War, as did James McClean who was to marry Alice, another of Charles and Mary Allen's daughters. The youngest sister, Gertrude, became a member of the Voluntary Aid Detachment (VAD) based at Didcot and married Bernard Dearlove. In 1915, Ernest married Phoebe Susanna Townsend of Harwell. They moved to York Farm when Charles Allen bought it in 1919. Charles Allen served as chairman of the West Hagbourne parish meeting (forerunner of the parish council) for some years before he died in 1931.

These days land at Down Farm is mostly used for arable crops and grazing. The farm no longer has any dairy cows but continues to buy in calves to sell on for beef after a year. Charles Allen's grandson Ronald Henry Allen remains at Down Farm today.

York Farm, West Hagbourne's oldest house

The house at York Farm is by far the oldest in West Hagbourne. It is also one of the earliest, complete timber-framed houses to survive in England. According to the vernacular architect C R J Currie, in his article 'Larger Medieval Houses in the Vale of White Horse', the oldest part of the house dates back to 1264 or 1265. Currie describes the architectural features of York farmhouse in great detail. Despite modernisation in the seventeenth and eighteenth centuries, which destroyed many of the early features, much of the original timber framing remains. Tree-ring samples taken in 1992 suggest that both the hall and wing were built in the winter of 1284-85, or soon afterwards (halls were usually additions). Evidence of pre-1350 methods of construction are still discernible, particularly in the two-storey wing and the hall. Currie compares the overall design with that of Upton Court in Slough. He likens the carpentry features of the hall to those of Sutton Courtenay Abbey. However, York Farm is older and, in Currie's opinion, far more austere than either of these buildings.

The history of York Farm

The very early history of York Farm is uncertain but it was a freehold of the Windsor manor for several centuries. The property became known as York Place after the York family who held it in the latter part of the fourteenth century. John York married Clarice, the widow of Richard de Windsor, and held Windsor manor in his wife's name. He was responsible for building the present south aisle of St Andrew's Church in East Hagbourne and he and Clarice and their son are buried there (see Chapter 7).

The Yorks later acquired a freehold belonging to Watlingtons, the other West Hagbourne manor. However, they were absentee landowners. Two of their tenants were Thomas Aldworth and his son William, from Sutton in Berkshire. On the 26th of September 1475, an indenture was drawn up between William York and the Aldworths. The contract was for seven years and went into a lot of detail concerning the payment of the rent for each freehold, and even the management of the farm itself. The freehold for the larger piece of land belonging to the Windsor manor was valued at 5s, while the rent for the Watlingtons freehold was 12d. The Beckingham family owned Watlingtons at this time.

The terms of the lease included the maintenance and repair of all thatched property except where the manorial corn lay, and for everything to be kept in the state in which the Aldworths found it. Manure was considered to be a valuable asset in the days before fertilisers and the indenture was careful to rule that no dung was to be removed from "the place", except to be spread on the land.

York Farm remained in the possession of the York family well into the sixteenth century until it became part of the eminent Dunch family's extensive estates. The Dunches were sheriffs of Berkshire throughout the sixteenth and

LOT 2.
Coloured brown on plan.

The Capital Compact

FREEHOLD PROPERTY

KNOWN AS

YORK FARM,

comprising in all about

═══ 145a. 3r. 25p. ═══

of very rich

ARABLE, PASTURE & ORCHARD LAND,

together with the quaint

Old-Fashioned Farm House

half timbered and tiled, containing 2 Sitting Rooms, 3 Bedrooms, 2 Attics, Kitchen, Pantry, Cellar, &c. Adjoining is the

— HOMESTEAD —

of 2 Barns, Cart and Nag Stabling, Cart and Trap Sheds, Cattle Yard and Sheds, Pigstyes, Granary, Lean-to Motor Garage, and in the rear a Lambing Shed There is in addition a Cottage Residence known as "Ardlui," and another Cottage.

SCHEDULE.

No. on 1912 Ordnance Map.	Name.	State.	A.	R.	P.
58	Bullock's Orchard	Pasture	8	1	35
59	Coscote Field	Ditto	7	2	22
61	House and Homestead	Buildings	1	3	33
62	Brook Lane Field	Arable	15	0	31
66	Gooseberry	Ditto	10	1	22
69	Down Field	Ditto	80	1	7
72	By Down Farm	Pasture	5	3	6
73	Ditto	Ditto	7	0	3
77	Ditto	Arable	9	0	26
		A.	145	3	25

Apportioned Rectorial Tithe Rent charge, present value ... £57 : 10 : 0
" Vicarial " " " ... 11 : 10 : 0

York Farm sale notice, 1919

seventeenth centuries. Sir William Dunch married Mary, daughter of Sir Henry Cromwell and aunt to the Protector, Oliver Cromwell. Their son Edmund, who held Down Farm in 1642, was made Governor of Wallingford Castle by his cousin Oliver Cromwell.

From about 1684, York Farm was owned by the Loder family. The Loders were a very successful farming family in neighbouring Harwell and owned a large piece of land next to York Farm. Francis Loder sold his share of York farm in 1750. According to the village map of 1754 (see page 82) the farmhouse was then owned by Dr Cooper. He owned a lot of property in West Hagbourne through his wife Mary, the daughter and heiress of Edward Sherwood whose father John had bought Watlingtons manor around 1675. The Coopers lived in East Hendred and leased their properties in West Hagbourne to tenants.

Dr George Cooper graduated from Oxford University with a medical degree in 1729. He was known to be a collector of medical books and sounds like a rather irascible character. George Woodward, the parson at East Hendred, was a great correspondent and a bit of a village gossip. In a letter dated the 7th of February 1756, he wrote:

> *You have often heard me speak of Dr. Cooper of this parish, as an odd sort of a man, conceited of his own abilities and very over-bearing in his talk: he has lately had a quarrel with a substantial young farmer of this town, at his own house, which began with words and ended in blows...I hope it will make him a little more orderly for the future, for he is apt to take to great liberties with his tongue.*

York Farm, one of the oldest complete, timber-framed houses in England, 1999

George Cooper died in 1763 and his wife Mary in 1788. Sadly, Mary was declared insane and intestate. After her death, her property, including York Farm and Watlingtons, passed to her second cousin Sir John Pollen and was eventually sold to the Aldworth family sometime before 1843. All these properties owned by the Aldworth family, including York Farm, became part of Grove Manor Estate.

York Farm continued to be let to tenant farmers. John Bullock was named as the tenant on the census returns for 1841, 1851 and 1861. He was such a long-standing tenant that the farm became known locally as Bullock's Farm. His name lived on in Bullock's Orchard which appeared on the York Farm sale notice of 1919. When the Bullocks left, bailiffs ran the farm until the whole of Grove Manor Farm Estate was put up for auction. C W Allen & Son (Charles and Ernest Allen of Down Farm) bought York Farm, plus two cottages and 145 acres of land at the auction in 1919. The two cottages were York Farm Cottage (known as 'Ardlui' at the time) and the house next to it, now called The Square. Allens have continued to live at York Farm ever since. Charles Allen's grandson Richard, who married Mary Lay of Harwell, took over York Farm after the death of his father, Ernest.

The Allen family in West Hagbourne

The Allens were not new to the village. Charles Allen's great, great grandfather, Richard Allen, was farming in the village in 1778. We know this because he insured his two houses, his stables, stock, barns and stacks in West Hagbourne with the Sun Fire Insurance Company for £400. The threat of fire was never far away for the owners of thatched and timber-framed houses and the memory of the disastrous fire which destroyed East Hagbourne in 1659 must have lived on in the Hagbournes.

One of Richard Allen's houses was called Coopers. This house could well have been York Farm since it was once held by Dr Cooper, and Richard's son William and his wife Nanny (née Robinson) and their large family of 15 children are known to have lived at York Farm. The names of 15 Allens, including Nanny and two of her daughters, were engraved on one of the windows at York Farm in 1821, presumably when William Allen's family were living there. Unfortunately, the window no longer exists.

Richard's other house in West Hagbourne was rented by John Woodley. Richard Allen died in 1792 and the will of his widow, Ann, described the property as a messuage, barn, stable yard and orchard in 1796. Richard's grandson, Moses Allen, sold a house, garden and orchard in Moor Lane on the north side of Braid Piece to the Aldworths in 1861. This was most likely the same property rented by John Woodley in Moor Lane.

When the Allens bought York Farm in 1919, Charles and his family continued to live at Down Farm, whilst his son Ernest moved to York Farm with his wife Phoebe. They had five children: Tony, Ronald, Gladys, David and Richard. The last three were born at York Farm. The two farms tended to be regarded by locals as one, which they referred to as 'Allen's Farm'. In those days the farm spread over 320 acres and employed 20 men. The land extended up Park Road to the Georgetown roundabout and across Edmonds Park, which has always been a meadow, except during the Second World War, when two thirds were ploughed up. Ernest Allen followed his father's example in taking an active role in village affairs. He was made a trustee of the William Tyrrell Charity, together with Frank and Dennis Napper in 1950.

The Allens kept meticulous records of all that went on at York Farm. They recorded such things as the number and type of fruit trees on the farm; the use of ash bought from the Great Western Railway at Didcot for the upkeep of the farm roads; the payment of tithes; veterinary surgeons' bills; blacksmiths' fees; the breeding and selling of livestock and income from farm produce. An example of this record keeping is shown here in the account of the sheep rearing year of 1936:

<u>1936   Number of Ewes: 123</u>
January 02	1 ewe had 2 lambs, both died
January 26	1 lamb born dead
February 03	1 lamb died
February 05	1 ewe died, bad cold, chill
February 06	1 lamb died, bad cold, chill
February 20	Cut 139 lamb tails
February 25	2 lambs died, tail cut – inflammation
March 12	1 lamb died, chill, tail cut
March 19	1 lamb died, tail cut
April 14	Young ewe died, 2 inflammation
May 14	1 lamb tail cut – inflammation
May 19	1 lamb killed for ourselves
June 27	Sheared 121 ewes
July 20	Number of own lambs 99
August 18	Dipped 90 lambs
August 21	Turned 3 rams in with 114 ewes. They went very fast at first

Lambing took place in the winter months and the ewes and new-born lambs were kept in temporary shelters. Later, when weather conditions allowed and they were strong enough to join the main flock, they were taken to the arable fields to feed off roots such as turnips, and also to enrich the soil with their dung. In the days before artificial fertilisers, sheep droppings were important for the fertility of the land. The flock was 'penned' by hurdles and moved frequently to fresh grazing. The hurdles were made from willow and the stakes which supported them were usually hazel. Four hurdles were tied together and thatched with wheat straw to provide shelter from the elements and protection from foxes. Hurdle-making was an industry in its own right in sheep rearing areas.

A shepherd was a very important employee. Before the introduction of a lambing shed at York Farm, the shepherd lived with his sheep during the lambing

Lambs penned by hurdles at York Farm, late 1920s

Farm yard at York Farm. Wheat sheaves are stacked in the rear barn and the sheaves on the staddle-stones are ready for threshing, late 1920s

Tony Allen and Arthur Dawson (driver) delivering milk in 1939

season. A shepherd's hut was maintained in the fields where the sheep were feeding. It was made comfortable with a stove for heating and cooking. It housed all the shepherd's tools and equipment and was home to the shepherd and his dogs until all the lambs were safely born. The shepherd sometimes helped with the harvest for short spells. During Charles Allen's time, the shepherd was Will Butler and he lived at Ardlui (now York Farm Cottage) when he was not with his sheep.

Lambing was just one of the shepherd's duties. He had to cut the lambs' tails, and as the records above show, not all the lambs survived. Shearing took place in June and July and sheep dipping in August, before the ram was put with the ewes and the whole lambing cycle started again.

York Farm bought its first motorised vehicle in 1930. This was a small Ford lorry which was used for everything and proved to be a great improvement on the horse and cart. Before the introduction of tractors, all arable operations were carried out by the mighty cart horses under the care of the head carter, another important farm employee. Jack Dawson was the carter at York Farm for many years. The horses all had names, and were looked after to a very high standard, housed in winter and given the best grazing areas in the summer. They were shod regularly by the visiting blacksmith from the Fleur de Lys in East Hagbourne which also served as a farriers yard. Horses were also bred at York Farm to sell in London and to the army and the Great Western Railway at Didcot. The mares were normally serviced by a thoroughbred stallion which was taken from farm to farm by an independent horseman.

In the early 1930s, York Farm had a milking herd of 20 Guernsey-shorthorns which were noted for their good quality milk at a time when a high cream content was considered desirable. They were milked by hand until the first milking machine came into use at York Farm on the 31st of March 1952. Before mechanisation, the milk was strained through special filters. In those days there was no refrigeration so the milk was allowed to cool naturally before being sold in bottles sterilised on the premises. The milk always had to be fresh and any surplus was fed to the few pigs on the farm. The milk was sold in the surrounding villages until Tony Allen was called up in 1942. The milk was then sent to Job's Dairy in Didcot. A few cows were always kept at York Farm for milk for the house, some of which was made into butter and for rearing calves for beef.

York Farm once kept both White Leghorns and several hundred Rhode Island hens which were noted for their brown eggs. These were sold on the milk rounds and at the farmhouse door, together with butter, and occasionally cream, poultry and rabbits. The Allens have continued to concentrate on dairy farming to this day, and there is still a milking herd at York Farm.

Manor Farm

The manorial estate of West Hagbourne was first mentioned in the Domesday Book in 1086. The first manor house, described in the dowry of Clarice de

Wedding of John Lay and Eliza Napper, 1917. L to R: Standing (back): Richard Lay and Dennis Napper, junior (bride's brother) Standing: May Napper, Friend, Lilian Lay, Joseph Lay (bridegroom's uncle), Charles Lay (bridegroom's brother), Elsie Napper, Friend, Fred Napper (bride's brother), Mame Smallbone (bride's aunt), Charles Smallbone Seated: Kath Lay, Anna Lay, John Edwin Lay, Eliza Napper, Dennis Napper, senior (bride's father), Mary Napper (mother) Front: Betty Napper, Bob Lay, Ben Lay, Eileen Napper

Windsor (see Chapter 3), was in ruins by 1403. It was probably rebuilt, or at least repaired, by subsequent heirs to the Windsor estate. The oldest part of the present farmhouse at Manor Farm dates from the late seventeenth century. Richard Windsor sold the manor to Stephen Thompson of London for £600 in 1661. Shortly after this it was bought by the Pocock family, who leased it out to a variety of tenants over the next 200 years.

Sometime in the nineteenth century, the house was enlarged and in 1805 John Blagrave Pocock leased the property to Joseph Lousley. Joseph's son Job lived in the manor house, known at that time as West Hagbourne Farm, and ran the estate of about 200 acres from 1813 until his father's death in 1825. West Hagbourne Farm extended over about 200 acres in Job Lousley's time. Job took a particular interest in seeds and he compiled an alphabetic listing of all English wild herbs. This was published and held at one time by the Newbury Public Library. In 1825, the lease passed to Job's brother Daniel whose wife was Elizabeth Allen, daughter of William and Nanny Allen of York Farm. In turn Daniel passed the lease to Joseph Lousley, son of Joseph Lousley senior and Sarah Grimshaw.

Joseph married Hannah Norris of East Hagbourne in St Andrew's Church in 1833 and they lived in the manor with their 11 children. When Eliza Pocock married George Harrison, she inherited the lease. They were living at the manor house when the 1881 census was taken. Their son James Samuel Harrison sold the property to Eli and Leopold Caudwell in 1889. Eli bought out Leopold in 1892 and considerably extended the farm property. He built the house called the Laurels in York Road and in 1904 he built another house next door to it. After Eli Caudwell's death, Manor Farm was sold to Dennis Napper of Didcot.

Dennis Napper gave a farm to each of his three children, two of them being in West Hagbourne on the old manorial sites. He gave Grove Manor Farm to his son Dennis and he passed Manor Farm to his daughter Eliza (Tize). Eliza Napper married John Lay who had a wireless and electrical business called 'John E Lay'. After their marriage he continued with the business, but also ran the farm with his wife. At this time the arable land at Manor Farm extended to about 300 acres.

John Lay was very involved in village affairs and arranged garden parties in the grounds of Manor Farm to raise money to take villagers on outings, usually to the seaside. He was chairman of the parish council for 32 years, and after his death in 1957 the seat by the bus shelter was erected in his memory. In 1960 a plaque commemorating his years of service to the village was fixed to the seat. Unfortunately, the plaque has disappeared.

During John Lay's time, Manor Farm was mostly dedicated to arable farming and as many as seven horses were used to work the land. Cattle were reared for beef but there was never a dairy herd. There was a flock of free-range poultry and the farm sold eggs, pullets and cockerels. They also kept pigs and sheep.

John and Eliza had five children and in the early years the farm was actively worked by John's second son Charles who was later joined by Geoffrey, another son who lived at Harwell. Along with general farm work, Charles did contract threshing and baling to boost the farm's income and enable expansion. The farm also provided work for several local men. Charles and Geoffrey inherited the farm after the death of their parents and over the years expanded by tenanting, purchasing more acres and increasing stock. The other Lay brothers, Philip and John, took over their father's electrical business, which they ran in Didcot from 1935 until 1995.

The farming partnership grew when Geoffrey's two sons Dennis and Andrew from Harwell, and Charles's sons Christopher and Nicholas from West Hagbourne, joined their parents in the business. The farm, which included Hagbourne Hill Farm and the land at Harwell, expanded to 2400 acres with approximately 400 breeding ewes and 600 breeding sows.

In November 1996, the partnership was split. Charlie, Chris and Nick continued to run Manor Farm and Hagbourne Hill Farm, with a reduced acreage of about 1150 acres of arable land. The only commercial stock kept on the farm after 1996 were pigs. A new sow barn was built and a different breed of pig was introduced. The unit was running well until the severe drop in the pig market, which affected many pig farmers across Britain during the late 1990s, took its toll at Manor Farm. It was decided that diversification was the only solution for survival and the decision was made to close down the pig unit as it was no longer considered to be viable.

As part of diversification, Manor Farm is taking part in various conservation schemes, including Countryside Stewardship. This scheme involves the protection of wildlife by replanting woodlands and hedgerows and the introduction of conservation headlands. Field margins are left unsprayed to encourage small animals, birds and butterflies and the growth of wildflowers and various grasses. Other local farmers, such as Dick and Jeff Powell of Ash Farm, are also cooperating in this scheme.

Pigs at Manor Farm in 1982

Aerial photo of Manor Farm, circa 1940, with possible signs of a previous moat in the foreground

These recent changes at Manor Farm have brought about a reduction in the number of local employees. The Lay family now run the farm themselves with the help of one member of staff. The farm buildings now standing empty may be converted into business units. All these changes will inevitably affect the rural aspect of West Hagbourne where agriculture has been the life-blood of the village for so many centuries.

Grove Manor Farm

Grove Manor Farm stands on the site of Watlingtons, West Hagbourne's second manor. Its early history has been told in Chapter 3. No one knows exactly when the name was changed to Grove Manor Farm (Grove Farm, for short), but it may have come from a piece of land on the north side of the manor named 'The Grove' on the Inclosure Award. The oldest part of the present house dates from the middle of the seventeenth century when it was a timber framed, three-roomed house. It was altered in the early part of the eighteenth century when two wings, linked by a narrow corridor, were added to the north and the original house was enclosed in brick. Further minor internal and external alterations were made in the first half of the nineteenth century and it was divided into two dwellings in the twentieth. However, many early features, such as the wide dog-leg staircase, the wood panelling in the dining room, the bread oven and the fireplaces have remained untouched.

There was once a lodge at the entrance to the drive which had arched gothic windows and a veranda. Ezra Dearlove was the groom at Grove Manor Farm and he and his family were living in the lodge when the 1871 and 1881 census returns were made. The lodge was demolished in the 1960s to make way for a more modern dwelling. More recently one of the farm's barns has been converted into a house.

In the early nineteenth century the extensive estate belonged to the Aldworth family. John Aldworth was lord of the manor in 1843. His daughter, Martha Edith, who was married to her cousin Philip Aldworth, inherited the property on the death of her father. Her husband died in 1875 but she retained the estate until 1919 when she sold Grove Manor Estate at auction in seven lots. The sale included 480 acres of arable farm land, nearly 30 acres of orchards, 15 cottages and extensive farmsteads, including York Farm, which was purchased by Charles Allen of Down Farm.

Dennis Napper bought Grove Manor Farm, its cottages and 327 acres of land. He lived in Didcot and built up a successful business selling horses to the Great Western Railway (GWR) there. His horses were used to cart hay at the Didcot Provender Store, which was established in 1885 as the chief fodder store for the several thousand horses used by the GWR. In turn, the GWR became a major buyer of local grain. Dennis Napper passed Grove Manor Farm to his son Dennis and daughter-in-law May, who in turn passed it to their sons Dennis and Rex.

LOT 6.
Coloured blue on plan.

THE GRAND YOUNG

Cherry & Apple Orchards

CONTAINING ABOUT

—— 29A. 3R. 16P. ——

Apportioned Rectorial Tithe Rent charge, present value	...	£12 : 0 : 0
„ Vicarial „ „ „	...	2 : 7 : 6

LOT 7.
Coloured green on plan.

THE VERY DESIRABLE

FREEHOLD ESTATE

KNOWN AS

GROVE MANOR FARM,

COMPRISING

The fine old Manor House

Brick built and Tiled, standing well back in its own Grounds, approached by a Carriage Drive past the Entrance Lodge. It contains on the

GROUND FLOOR—Corridor, Entrance Hall with heating Stove, Back Hall, Panelled Dining Room 17ft. by 16ft. with Alcove and French Doors opening into the Gardens, Drawing Room 18ft. by 12ft. with Alcove and cupboard, Study 16ft. by 11ft., Kitchen with Kitchener and cupboards, Scullery, Larder, Pantry, etc. The accommodation on the

FIRST FLOOR which is approached by a fine wide open Staircase, with finely carved oak balisters, and also by a second Staircase is 5 large Bedrooms, Dressing Room, Bath Room and W.C.; on the

SECOND FLOOR, 2 Attic Bed-chambers, and up another Staircase an Apple Loft.

In the **BASEMENT**—Good Cellarage.

In the Court Yard is the Dairy, Wash-house, Wood-house, etc.

—— THE STABLING ——

is Brick built and Slated, and includes Stable with large loose box and 2 Stalls, large Motor Garage or Carriage House, Harness Room, etc., and Loft.

Sale notice for lots 6 and 7 of Grove Manor Estate, which included the orchards and manor house, 17 June 1919

The main cattle yard at Grove Manor Farm in 1904. On the left is the granary and on the right is the barn which was recently converted into a house. The horse was called Lady and the cattle trough stands against the wall behind her. The barn at the centre of the photograph no longer exists

Southern aspect of Grove Manor Farm, 1989

Dennis (Den) and Rex's main income was from their wheat and barley harvests, as well as cutting and making hay. Grove Manor Farm was well known for its cherries until the orchards surrounding it were dug up in 1952. Gooseberry bushes were prolific enough to give rise to the Gooseberry Orchard. Until 1980 the farm ran a herd of cattle which was bought in March and sold on in the autumn for beef.

Ironically, the railway which had helped Dennis Napper, senior build up his business, meant that the lovely view of the fields from the house was blocked by the railway embankment near to the house, when the Didcot to Newbury section of the Didcot, Newbury and Southampton Railway was built in 1882.

Many people including the Napper family, friends and villagers who worked there, have their own memories of life at the manor. Gert Bilby was the housekeeper in the days when Dennis and May Napper lived there with their family. She passed on her recollections of the ten bells in the servants' quarters connected to all the rooms in the house, including the bathroom. These were obviously a novelty at the time. Until the mid-1930s, a daily chore was to pump water from the outside well to the storage tank in the attic; 36 pumps were needed to supply the daily needs of the house. Electricity was installed in 1940. Irene Butler had fond memories of family parties at Grove Manor when she had been called in to help with preparations. She remembered watching people dancing to a wind-up gramophone in the panelled dining room from her vantage point on the main staircase. A pony and trap used to transport guests to and from the front door, down the carriage drive past the lodge at the entrance to the property.

Grove Manor Farm was a lively place during the 1970s when the farm was run by Den and Rex and their families. The two brothers were both sociable, out-going characters and Den's loud voice could often be heard shouting for Rupert, his friendly golden Labrador. Bantams, geese, ducks and guinea fowl were all allowed to roam freely around the farm. During the spring, lambs were always being bottle-fed in the kitchen, by the warmth of the Aga, which was often home to an egg keeping warm on the top until it was hatched. Den himself had a Jersey cow which he milked by hand, as well as a billy-goat which his son, Charlie, christened Sidney.

This menagerie drew many of the village children to Grove Manor Farm, and the hospitable natures of Rex and Den meant that they always had lots of visitors. Shooting parties were regularly organised from the farm and the participants would return to celebrate their success at these popular 'shoots'. At Christmas, the school carol singers would go back to the farm for mince pies and other seasonal refreshments after they had sung their carols around the village.

Young Charlie had lots of friends amongst the boys of the village and they enjoyed riding around the fields on the motorbikes and old cars which the family kept on the farm. Harvest time was always an opportunity for fun and games amongst the stubble, once the hard work was over. 'Scrumping' for the odd apple, pear or plum from the orchards around the village was always a popular pastime for the village teenagers, who were more closely involved with farming and the country way of life in the 1970s than they are today.

Rex Napper who died in 1999

However, along with the good times, the farm was also touched with sadness when Den's son, Charlie, died in 1992 at the age of 29, leaving behind a widow and son, also called Charlie. Rex and Den both ran the farm until Den became ill. Rex died in 1999, leaving a widow, Joan, who continues to live at Grove Manor Farm with her family. Dennis and his family no longer live in West Hagbourne.

Ragged Farm and the Powell family

Ragged Farm was a small holding of about a quarter of an acre situated in Moor Lane near a pond, which is now nothing more than a ditch. On the village map of 1754 (see page 82), it appeared as a plot of land called Eltam, with a cottage and its own well. By 1843, the cottage at Eltam had been replaced by gardens. A small piece of land fenced off at the lower end of the plot was known as Picket Piece. Eltam, together with Picket Piece, belonged to the Loders and became known as Ragged Farm (sometimes called Rugged Farm). This land changed hands several times in the nineteenth century until it was bought by Edwin George Bullock (Father Antony) in 1901.

Alice Maud, daughter of William and Alice Powell at Ragged Farm in the late 1920s. Alice married Henry Bishop and they lived for many years at Thatched Cottage. Their daughter Mary married Joe Napper, the son of Arch Napper, landlord of the Horse and Harrow for many years

The plot next to Eltam was known as Reynold's Land in 1754. It also had a cottage and its own well. The Reynolds family had been living in West Hagbourne since at least 1548. The Inclosure Award indicates that by 1843 the plot was called Reynold's Orchard and included a cottage and a garden. At that time it was owned by the Herbert family. In 1881 the cottage was lived in by a shepherd who was called Tim Belcher . A shepherd's hut still stands on the land, though rather the worse for wear. The last family to live in the cottage were the Butlers, Mrs Butler being the sister of Joseph Napper, the publican at the Horse and Harrow in the 1890s. The cottage at Reynold's Orchard was demolished sometime after the First World War.

William Powell bought Reynold's Orchard in 1915 and after the death of Father Antony, in 1923, he also bought Ragged Farm which he was probably renting at the time. This meant that William Powell then owned the two adjoining pieces of land in Moor Lane, thus enlarging the farm. He built a bungalow there and gave up his job on the railway to realise his ambition to become a fruit and vegetable farmer. Sadly he died in 1934, aged 54, leaving the property to his wife, who passed it on to their daughter Barbara Blond. Her brother William, known to everyone as Wipsi, managed the farm, whilst their mother, Alice Powell, lived at the bungalow until a few years before her death when she was over 90 years old. The bungalow then fell into disrepair and was finally pulled down, but the land is still managed by the Powell family, though it is no longer called Ragged Farm.

Generations of Powells have lived in West Hagbourne and are thought to have descended from John Poel who was born in 1796 in Lockinge and came to West Hagbourne to work on the land. Among other things, the Powells have worked as agricultural labourers, plough boys, house servants and land owning farmers in West Hagbourne. One branch of the family emigrated to New Zealand in 1874. The Powells are closely linked with many other old West Hagbourne families through marriage, including the Woodleys, Dearloves, Bishops, Dawsons and Nappers. A few of John Poel's descendants still live in West Hagbourne today.

Shepherd's hut which still stands on the plot once known as Reynold's land, though now rather worse for wear

Wedding photo of Alice Woodley and William Charles Powell, taken in Main Street, on the 4th of April 1904. Most of the families living in West Hagbourne at the beginning of the twentieth century are represented in this photograph, and their descendants are still associated with the village. Some of the young men are wearing the uniform of the Berkshire Regiment. Not all the names are known, but the following people have been identified: Numbered, L to R: Standing: 7) Sara Powell (groom's mother), 8) Jack Dawson (groom's brother-in-law), 9) William Powell (groom), 10) Alice Woodley (bride), 12) Mrs Woodley (bride's mother) Sitting: 1) Anne Aldridge (bride's sister) holding daughter Mary (later Mrs Moss), 3) Florence Dawson (groom's sister) holding daughter Alice (later Mrs Joe Butler), 4) Charles Powell (groom's father), 8) Louise Day, 9) Jane Nobes (bride's sister) holding her son Fred. Seated on ground: First left: Albert Powell (groom's brother). Florence Dawson's daughter Annie, aged five, is one of the little girls. She later became Annie Warr. The group is facing away from the village, towards Didcot

178

William Powell, always known as Wipsi

Ash Farm

William Powell's son Wipsi continued to acquire land in West Hagbourne. Most of the farmland was bought between 1930 and 1986 by the partnership known as W H Powell and Son, which consisted first of Wipsi and his son Richard, and following Wipsi's death in 1980, by Richard and his son Jeff. Wipsi bought the land in York Road known as the Ash from the Warners. The farmhouse was built by Henry and William Warner for Wipsi and his wife Mabel in 1955.

Compared with the other farms in the village, Ash Farm is relatively new. The farmland belonging to Ash Farm amounts to 300 acres, with much of the land situated in West Hagbourne and Harwell parishes. In 1989 a building plot next to Ash Farm house was used to build Little Ash, where Wipsi's grandson Jeff Powell and his family now live. Wipsi's widow Mabel still lives just across the farmyard at Ash Farm. Like York and the manor farms, Ash Farm remains very much a working farm and part of the village community.

Lime Tree Farm and the Dearlove Family

The story of West Hagbourne's farms would not be complete without mentioning Lime Tree Farm. It once stood at the end of York Road next to York Farm. Lime Tree Farm is most strongly associated with the Dearlove family who lived and

Ezra Dearlove and his horse, circa 1900

Lime Tree Farm, home to generations of Dearloves, before it was pulled down in 1971

farmed there from at least 1841 and probably earlier. Dearloves have lived in the Hagbournes for centuries and the family name appears time and again in the parish records. Many of the Dearlove men were shepherds.

The earliest known record of a Dearlove in Hagbourne is the register of the birth of Andrew Dearlove in the Bishop's Transcripts of St Andrew's Church, East Hagbourne in 1615. Avery, William and Matthew Dearlove all signed the Protestation Return in 1642. In 1715 the shepherd William Dearlove left an interesting will when he bequeathed over four acres of arable land, including two and a half acres in the common field, a cow and calf and all his household goods to his wife Mary upon the condition that "she keep herself a widow and unmarried".

Another William Dearlove, a yeoman who died in 1800, left "a dwelling house, barns, stables, outhouses, orchards, gardens, backside and all other the appurtenances together with all my arable land, meadow ground and commons both freehold and leasehold within the liberty and precinct of West Hagbourn". He left a wife Mary, who died in 1812, and eight children.

The property described in this will written in 1794 could well be Lime Tree Farm because William Dearlove's grandson Joseph was living there in 1841 with his wife Ann and their son Isaac, as tenants of Robert Hopkins. Joseph probably inherited the tenancy of Lime Tree Farm through his grandfather. Also, the contents of William Dearlove's will with its barns, stables, orchards, freehold and common land suggest a small tenant farm, rather than a simple family dwelling.

In the nineteenth century, Lime Tree Farm expanded from 45 acres in 1851 to 57 acres in 1881. By then, the farm was big enough to employ farm labourers and domestic servants. Successive generations of Dearloves continued to live at Lime Tree Farm well into the twentieth century.

One of the most prominent occupants was Ezra Dearlove, who lived at Lime Tree Farm with his wife Elizabeth. Ezra was born in the village in 1840, the son of Daniel, a master shepherd, and his wife Emma. Before inheriting Lime Tree Farm, he was a groom at Grove Manor Farm and lived in the lodge there in the 1870s. Ezra Dearlove took an active interest in village affairs and from 1899 until his death he was a member of the West Hagbourne parish meeting. He was also a churchwarden and overseer of the poor, and for many years he was the only trustee of the Tyrrell Charity representing West Hagbourne, the others being churchwardens from East Hagbourne.

When Ezra died in 1919, the contents of the house, the farm implements and machinery, all the livestock, hay and corn stacks were sold at auction. The livestock included 100 hens, 11 head of cattle, 3 cart horses named Captain, Jolly and Dumpling and a cob called Tom. The house was quite large with four bedrooms, two parlours, a kitchen and dairy. It is not clear why the contents of the farm had to be sold, but it may have been in order to raise money to pay death duties which was quite a common occurrence in those days.

Another Dearlove character was Jack, who lived in West Hagbourne in the 1930s. He was known for his dry sense of humour. One day, while working on his allotment digging up his potatoes, Dr Chitty, the doctor and vicar of Upton, passed by on his horse. The potatoes were all small as it had been a dry season. Dr Chitty pulled up his horse and called across to Jack "fine potatoes you have there Dearlove". Jack answered "much bloody finer and I shan't find 'em at all".

The next tenants of Lime Tree Farm after Ezra were his daughter Elizabeth and her husband Mark Pinnell. When Mark died in 1946, his son William (known as Bill) and his sister Mrs Hutt managed Lime Tree Farm as a dairy farm. Bill Pinnell had five or six shorthorn dairy cows which were milked by hand. He helped to supplement his income by selling milk door-to-door round the village and later to Didcot Dairy. Villagers remember tales of milk being taken round on a tricycle and measured from a churn into customers' jugs. The farm grew a small amount of grain to feed the cows and this was harvested with the help of casual labourers, including Bert Parsons and Jack Luckett, both teachers from East Hagbourne School. Another helper was Wipsi Powell.

Life was not easy at Lime Tree Farm as there were few modern amenities. In the winter the cow shed was lit by candlelight as there was no electricity in the yard. All the water was taken from an outside tap for both the house and the cow shed. When Bill left Lime Tree Farm to go into a rest home in 1971, the house was pulled down to make way for a housing development. Bill died in 1980.

The last Dearlove in the village was Ezra's son Bert, who lived at Rose Cottage. He died in 1972, more than 300 years after the first mention of the Dearlove name in West Hagbourne. Thus, the last Dearlove and Lime Tree Farm, the Dearlove home for so many generations, disappeared within a year of each other.

Ivy Farm and Chapel Hayes

Very little remains today of West Hagbourne's orchards. As fruit growing became less sustainable and land became more valuable for housing, particularly after the Second World War, the orchards made way for much-needed houses. The only orchards left in the village now are at Chapel Hayes, a small holding in the heart of the village owned by Fred and Edna Scott. The land bought by the Scotts in 1974 was once part of Ivy Farm.

Ivy Farm was a small holding of $2\frac{1}{2}$ acres with a farmhouse in the centre of the village, and about 28 acres situated off the road leading to Chilton, near the land belonging to the William Tyrrell Charity. Joseph and Hannah Lousley lived there after they moved from West Hagbourne Farm (Manor Farm) to Ivy Farm sometime before 1881. Joseph died in 1883 and after Hannah's death in 1895, it was bought by Thomas Keep. In 1915, Ivy Cottage, the barns, stables, garden, orchard and outbuildings were bought by Ernest Roland Napper. Four years later he sold it to his brother Frank, who in turn left it to his son Guy Napper. The remaining 26 acres of land, known as Hagbourne Land, were sold separately.

The property was split further in 1971 when the Sages bought Ivy Cottage and its outbuildings. Fred and Edna Scott purchased the rest of the land from Guy

Napper in 1974 and built their home, appropriately naming it Chapel Hayes. West Hagbourne's medieval chapel is believed to have stood somewhere on the land behind the house. In 1832 there was also a chapel at Enard Cottage on land adjoining Chapel Hayes (see Chapter 7).

Chapel Hayes is included in West Hagbourne's Conservation Area in recognition of its old orchards and rural aspect. The pears are the oldest trees but there are also a few ancient apple trees and some old plum trees which are popular with the woodpeckers. The fruit grows high on the old trees because Guy Napper used to put his calves in the orchard once a year and the trees were therefore pruned low down, to protect the fruit. Today, instead of calves, it is hens which roam free in the orchards. The Scotts keep a flock of about 130 Isa-brown hens and people come from miles around to buy their eggs.

The colourful birds strutting their way round the orchards would have been a familiar sight round the village to previous generations, and harks back to a time when all the farms sold their produce to the villagers, whether it was eggs, milk, butter, poultry or the odd rabbit, and when many West Hagbourne families kept their own animals, including pigs.

Farming has changed beyond recognition since the hamlet of West Hagbourne was first mentioned in the Domesday book and agriculture was a way of life for the whole village. Many aspects of rural life have disappeared for ever and village life is further threatened by the steady encroachment of the town. Changes in farming practices, mechanisation, the use of modern scientific farming methods and the move from animal to arable farming have made farming less labour intensive, with

Hens in the old orchard at Chapel Hayes, 2000

the result that farms employ fewer local people today than at any other time in the village's history. The uncertainties facing farmers at the dawn of the twenty-first century are forcing them to reconsider farming practices, including active conservation of the countryside itself, and re-employing farming methods used by their ancestors. Despite all the difficulties farmers have faced, West Hagbourne still has as many farms today as it did in the golden age of farming in the third quarter of the nineteenth century.

Sources – A Farming Village

P H Ditchfield and William Page (eds.), *The Victoria History of the Counties of England – Berkshire*, Vol 1, The St. Catherine Press, 1923, p302.
G M Young, *Victorian England*, The Folio Society, 1999, pp63, 64.
Corn laws: Judith Hunter, *A History of Berkshire*, Phillimore & Co. Ltd., p64.
Farming in the twentieth century: reminiscences of Arthur Butler of West Hagbourne.
Ordnance Survey Map, *East Hagbourne and Blewbury Parishes*, 1876, The British Library Board, 1986.

Sources – Down Farm

Windsor grant and enclosure agreement: *Antiquaries list of Berkshire deeds*, Berkshire Record Office, Reading. No 358 (1565) and No 359 (1642), Box 3.
Jeremy Gibson (ed.), *Oxfordshire and North Berkshire Protestation Returns and Tax Assessments 1641–42*, The Oxfordshire Record Society, Vol. 59, 1994.
West Hagbourn Inclosure Award, 27 July 1843, Berkshire Record Office, Reading. Q/RDC 39A.
William Jennen's will, 1708, Public Record Office, Kew.
William Stephens Hayward's application: *Royal Literary Fund*, 3 March, 1868, British Library.

Sources – York Farm

C R J Currie, 'Larger Medieval Houses in the Vale of White Horse', *Oxoniensia Journal*, Vol LVII, 1992, pp81–132.
Indenture between William York and Thomas and William Aldworth, 26 September 1475, Public Record Office, Kew. C146/10207.
Edmund Dunch: Enclosure agreement for Down Farm, 1642, *Antiquaries list of Berkshire deeds*, Box 3, No 359, Berkshire Record Office, Reading.
Donald Gibson (ed.), *A Parson in the Vale of White Horse – George Woodward's Letters from East Hendred, 1753–1761*, Alan Sutton Publishing, Ltd., 1982.
Census of England and Wales, Returns for 1841, 1851 and 1861.
Richard Allen's Insurance Policy No 379492/258, May 1778, *Fire Insurance Registers 1775–1787*, Sun Fire Insurance, Guildhall Library, London. MS 11936.

Will of Ann Allen, 16 April 1796, Wiltshire Record Office, Trowbridge.
York Farm records, 1936, by kind permission of the Allen family.
Reminiscences of Richard Allen, Joe Napper and Fred Jones, West Hagbourne, 1980s.

Sources – Manor Farm

The Victoria History – Berkshire, Vol 3, pp475–480.
Lessees of the Manor of West Hagbourne, 29 November, 1661, Berkshire Record Office, Reading. D/EM/T63.
Job Edward Lousley, 'Job Lousley (1790–1855) of Blewbury and Hampstead Norris', *Berkshire Archaeological Journal*, Vol 63, 1967–8, pp57–65.

Sources – Grove Manor Farm

West Hagbourn Inclosure Award, 1843.
Grove Farmhouse, *NMR Listings for the Parish of West Hagbourne*, RCHM England, 1998. 18/149.
Census of England and Wales, Returns for 1871 and 1881.

Sources – Ragged Farm and the Powell Family

Map of West Hagbourne, 1754, Berkshire Record Office, Reading.
A Plan of the Hamlet of West Hagbourn in the Parish of East Hagbourn and County of Berks. inclosed, 1843, Berkshire Record Office, Reading. Q/RDC 39B.
Sale of Ragged Farm and Reynold's Orchard from deeds.

Sources – Lime Tree Farm

Census of England and Wales, Returns for 1841, 1851, 1871 and 1881.
Bishop's Transcripts, *St Andrew's Parish Register*, 1615.
Gibson (ed.), Protestation Returns and Tax Assessments 1641–42, Vol. 59, 1994.
Will of William Dearlove, 25 April 1715, Berkshire Record Office, Reading. D/A1/64/69A.
Will of William Dearlove, 1794, Berkshire Record Office, Reading. D/A1/65/217.
Sale notice for auction of goods and chattels of Lime Tree Farm, 1919.

Sources – Ivy Farm and Chapel Hayes

Census of England and Wales, Return for 1881.
Deeds of Chapel Hayes, by kind permission of Fred and Edna Scott.

Chapter Ten

The Second World War Comes to West Hagbourne

The Second World War affected the rural community of West Hagbourne in many ways and changed some things for ever. The minutes of the meetings of the Parish Assembly (now Parish Council) held during the war, and the period leading up to it, give some insights into the concerns of the village at the time.

In August 1936 there were already thoughts of war. The Parish Assembly was advised by the Town Clerk of Wallingford to appoint a committee to control air raid precautions in the event of a war. By March 1938, two air raid wardens had been appointed; one of these was Mr Fletcher. These intimations of war, however, did not affect plans to celebrate the Coronation of King George VI in 1937.

In January 1939, the Minister of Health expressed concern about the emergency evacuation of civilians from the crowded areas of large towns. Members of West Hagbourne's Air Raid Precaution Committee were requested to carry out an urgent survey to ascertain the amount of suitable surplus accommodation in the village, on the basis of one person per habitable room, and whether there were householders willing to receive unaccompanied children or teachers.

In the event, the only evacuees anyone remembers being billeted in West Hagbourne were the Bulpit family, who were housed in the old lodge at Grove Manor Farm. Evacuee children attended East Hagbourne School but they did not live in West Hagbourne. As a precaution, however, the Parish Assembly had requested a supply of small and children-sized gas masks in 1939.

Like all agricultural communities throughout the country, West Hagbourne's farms were placed on a war footing. The ministry of food introduced rationing in January 1940 as a means of distributing food supplies more efficiently. The country had to become more self-sufficient, which meant more land had to be ploughed to grow wheat and other grains, sugar beet and potatoes. It was also recognised that cereals for human consumption had ten times the value of crops grown for animal feed. As a result, beef production was cut and fertilisers were used increasingly to promote cereal production. The numbers of poultry and pigs were reduced on all the farms and the sheep at York Farm were sold. Summer time was made to last all year round during the war and from 1941 double summer time was introduced in the summer months to enable farmers to achieve greater production rates.

As the war years dragged on and the labour shortage continued, the Women's Land Army was brought in to help the farms in the war effort. Towards the end of the war, prisoners of war from the camp at Churn were used at York Farm, mostly for gang labour during the harvesting of cereals and roots, and later threshing out the corn ricks and digging out and cleaning ditches. Some stayed on after the war and settled locally, and one who returned to Germany came back on a visit to the village some years ago.

Obviously, the war years were difficult for everyone, but there were humorous moments, and one villager has taken a light-hearted view in the following reminiscences of life in the Home Guard during the war.

The Home Guard defends West Hagbourne

It is a long held belief among older residents of the village that an important factor affecting Hitler's decision not to invade this country was the formation of the West Hagbourne Unit of the Local Defence Volunteers, subsequently renamed the

Some of the men who served in West Hagbourne's Home Guard, about 1942 or '43. L to R: Back row: A Butler, G Luker, L Cummings, F Dean, P Parsons, H Jones, C Dawson (Tid) Middle row, left to right: F Wootten, C Parsons, D Dean, P Robey, R Cox. Front row: C Jones, R Eustace, M Aldridge

Home Guard (and later still, affectionately known as Dad's Army). This Unit, under the command of Captain P Blond, consisted of those villagers who were old soldiers, those in reserved occupations and those young men waiting to be 'called up' into the armed forces. They were a combined unit with the East Hagbourne branch of the same service and many training sessions and drills took place as a shared responsibility.

However, the West Hagbourne arm of the service had a number of individual important amenities to guard and defend in its own area. These included the reservoir at the top of Hagbourne Hill, the local farms, the pub and the water pumping stations close to the village. The reservoir, in particular, was given special attention, to the extent that people got very wary of using the roads in the vicinity in case they were mistaken for invaders, or some enemy out to blow it to smithereens. Indeed, it was said that many of the RAF personnel returning to the aerodrome after a pint or two at the Horse and Harrow preferred to go back the long way round over 'Wipsi's Hill' and Harwell Village rather than face a fully armed Ronnie Dearlove, Wilf Butler or 'Nozzle' Carter on the top of Hagbourne Hill.

Be that as it may, however, among those who were around in those dark days of the war, who will ever forget the effort put in by those individuals – the shepherd's hut that served as a company HQ and guard post, the strategically dug slit trenches, or the stout tree trunks placed in such a position that they could quickly be swung across the roads to act as barriers? Hitler's paratroops ought to be grateful that they were not required to land in this area – they would certainly have had a hot reception.

We owe a lot to those men and women who served in the two world wars, especially those who did not come home. We must not forget, however, those who served on our own doorstep – the men of the Home Guard.

The men of West Hagbourne who were called to serve

Perhaps those most personally affected by the war were the men and women who were called to serve their country and the families of those who did not return. Among the names of those who did thankfully return were: Peter Bishop, Bob and Philip Blond, Ernest Coster, Percy Dearlove, Jim Gordon, Ron Jubber, Jack Napper, Les Pullen and Sid Townsend. One of the last to get back from Dunkirk was Philip Blond who was declared missing for a while, causing much consternation amongst the village community. However, much to everyone's relief, he turned up one day, coolly strolling through the village, and wondering what all the fuss was about.

One of those whose war story can be told was Percy Dearlove, son of Annie and Bert Dearlove of Rose Cottage. Percy enlisted in the Nottinghamshire Yeomanry, an armoured division known as the Sherwood Rangers, the first British troops to enter Germany. He became a tank driver and not only took part in the

Percy Dearlove   *Bob Blond whilst serving in India in 1942*

frightening first sweep of the D-Day landings at Normandy, but also in the fierce battles in the Western Desert at El Alamein. A very brave man, he was wounded in action and brought home, but as soon as he was sufficiently recovered, he returned to fight for his country. Percy was decorated for his campaigns, but modestly never showed his medals to anyone although he was very proud of his service in the army. So much so, that at the end of the war, he stayed on for a further three years, serving in the famous Tank Regiment stationed at Bovington.

Sadly, Percy's neighbour, Leslie Denning of Little Cottage, a sergeant with the Queen's Own Royal West Kent Regiment, was one of four West Hagbourne men not to return. He was buried in a war cemetery in Italy, not far from where he died in combat, aged 29, on the 6th of February 1944. His widow, Queenie, was the daughter of Mr and Mrs Roberts who also lived in West Hagbourne.

Fred and Hilda Butler's son, Frederick John, was only 21 when he died on the 16th of October 1945. Fred had been serving with the King's Own Scottish Borderers, when he died after the liberation of the city of Brussels, where he is buried. He left a young wife, Sylvia, daughter of Henry and Winifred Warner, who ran the village shop. Fred was killed before his second son was born. The family suffered a further tragedy, as Fred's sister, Irene, lost not only her brother, but also her husband, Kerry Ryan, a corporal in the Royal Army Ordnance Corps. He was killed in the Far East on the 22nd of December 1944 at the age of 25 and is buried in Hong Kong.

The fourth West Hagbourne son to die in the war was Anthony Allen from York Farm. The poignant letters exchanged between Tony and his mother during the war reflect the feelings of a young man from the quiet rural village of West Hagbourne, suddenly thrown into a war far from home. These letters which have been preserved by his family, also tell us a lot about what was happening on the farm during the war and also share with us his own deep love of village life and the countryside.

A West Hagbourne boy goes to war

Anthony Ernest Allen was born on the 15th of October 1915 to Ernest and Phoebe Allen of York Farm. Tony, and later his younger brothers and sister, went to school in East Hagbourne. On leaving school he worked on his father's farm. He was responsible for many initiatives at York Farm, including a milk round covering West Hagbourne and Upton. When the Second World War began, Tony was 22 years old, living at home and working to improve the farm. He had several girl friends and his other interest was bell-ringing.

On the 14th of February 1942, Tony attended a medical board at Reading and was declared fit for war service. He joined the army as a driver in the Royal Army

Anthony Allen

Service Corps and was sent to Boscombe Training Battalion in Hampshire on the 6th of April. Two days later, the postscript of his letter to his mother gives some indication of his first impression of life in the forces: "Tell dad he must keep Ron from the army, make a farm over to him, it will send him mad if he joins". On the 8th of May 1942, his mother wrote: "Ron came down every morning from Down Farm for milking. Do you wish you were back at the old job?… Dad seems to be settling down a bit better now but it did upset him, your having to go away, to say nothing of myself." Later, Tony wrote: "I am now a motor cyclist, it is a smashing job. I feel rather proud as I was the only one from our old squad picked for the job."

In June 1942, he was moved to his new unit near Bishop Auckland, Durham, "sleeping in a pallet four hundred miles from little West Hagbourne". On the 7th of July, Tony described his thoughts whilst on a route march that day: "I could see hay makers at work, what a pretty sight! Marching through farms and meadows brought back pleasant memories, little did I think that I should be in the forces this time last year. In fact it brought tears to my eyes thinking about it all. As I looked across the field there was one of the men going round thatching the rick and others were up around the rick. I imagined Jake to be thatching the rick and there I could see the master men in white shirtsleeves looking on, which would be Dad. Yes folk up here go on the same as we do".

On the 5th of July 1942, his mother wrote: "Dad has brought Dennis Napper's cherries. Ron has had his calling up Home Guard papers, Richard belongs to ATC and Home Guard. A lot of folk about here have had the papers for calling up. Have you been to the parks lately? Mind the girls. I guess you can always get one, cheeky lad." Tony replied: "Now I have to take over a lorry (a three ton Bedford Troop Carrier). What a difference driving one of those great things after our little lorry. I rather enjoy the job. On the 29th of July he wrote: "Something is going to happen shortly. Leave has been stopped and we have been asked to send home all personal belongings." However, nothing happened during August, and in September he had ten days harvest leave.

Tony returned to Bishop Auckland, setting off for London by train from Didcot. The journey from King's Cross took over eleven hours and he had to sleep in the corridor. He had forgotten to take sandwiches made for the journey and wrote: "Yes mother, how I missed those sandwiches but a kind gentleman gave me a sandwich and a tomato".

On the 1st of October 1942, his mother replied: "I received your looked for letter on Wednesday, yesterday morning. I just had to do a little weep when I saw the lovely sandwiches I took the trouble to cut, all left behind, but never mind I knew you would have been glad of them. They have finished picking up the barley." On the 3rd of October Tony wrote: "How is the root pulling going on? Ron and Richard are not to neglect jobs putting oil in and topping up batteries." Later, he wrote: "Now mother tell me about what has been happening at home. Firstly how are all the tractors, lorries and car running, also engines? I hope the boys are looking well round their implements keeping them well lubricated and batteries well topped up".

On the 10th, his mother wrote: "Just a few lines to wish you many Happy Returns of your Birthday. I am enclosing a little note for you to go out and have a little drink or some fish and chips. You are twenty-six aren't you? Do you feel as old? I guess you do on a cold night. Dad went to Abingdon today to buy some corn for planting. Jake and Richard have been to drill today and got on well. Dad and Henry are still bringing the apples in, goodness knows when they will finish.

Tony was back with his motor cycle unit and on the 29th of October, he wrote: "Now I am spinning round the Durham area and notice that it is not all coal mines, more South has real good farming land. I notice how the hedges are trimmed and everything else done for the good of the land. Yes Dad, it makes me think I am back home again." He had tried to get more agricultural leave but on the 2nd of November he wrote that his commanding officer had said: "Allen I am sorry I can't grant you any more leave as you have already had your agricultural leave this year". Tony continued: "I saw that nothing could be done and replied 'Well Sir, I never aught to have been in the army.' He never made a reply". Saturday the 7th of November he was writing by candlelight (the lamp glass was broken). "I am getting my dirty clothes ready for laundry and sewing about a dozen buttons on. What a game!"

Tony received more farming news on the 15th of November 1942, when his mother wrote to let him know that "Bert Dearlove came and measured the ricks yesterday. We haven't got the sugar beet up yet, but have lifted all the spuds". Later, on the 19th of November: "Dad sold 100 bushels of apples this week to Hicks of Oxford, Fruiterers, and two hundred bushels last week. Young Greenough from Upton (used to be at Mr Fletchers) has been reported killed in the Middle East."

Later Tony answered: "We soon made short work of the cake, you know mum I always like to share my goods with the boys. Please fill it [box] up with plenty of apples I often fancy some. We have a Choral Society (eight strong) the leader is from the Salvation Army Band. Can't he sing well! I am looking forward to some time off. I shall be home on Saturday 28th of November, six to seven pm. Please send the car. I will walk up the Haydon Road. Tell Ron to be on the look out for me."

Back at camp on the 3rd of December, Tony wrote: "If you receive no letters for a while it means that I have left the country. How I envy your pigmeat breakfast – tinned rashers are not so good. Tell Dad the whisky made me cock my tail and also warmed my heart." On the 15th of December he wrote that his posting was "imminent" and on the 18th of December, only a note: "Mother we are in a terrific muddle everywhere here and by the time you receive this we shall have left". They were on the move.

Late December: "Well dear mother as I look from my port hole I see miles of sea, yes it's sea everywhere. I look backwards to the horizon and think of the land

I loved – dear Old England. I always wanted to go abroad and now I am spending Christmas Day on the water, of course we all made the best of it… Look out for frosts Richard and Ron! Have you got all the sugar beet up yet?"

Tony arrived in North Africa with flu and wrote on the 7th of January 1943 that he was "sitting up in bed" and that "I spent the last night in the ship's hospital …. And next morning I was taken to hospital by ambulance. We are under canvas and as I look through the windows of the marquee I see the lovely still blue sea…"

The next letter from hospital was on the 19th of January. He reminisced "I hope Dad, Dick and Ron don't have too many ups and downs. I remember there used to be a few when we were all at home. Mother it must be very quiet at home these days with only little Dick at home, but I expect he will soon be bringing his girlfriend home so there certainly will be life then. As I lay in my bed at night I think how we used to sit with all our knees under the kitchen table but what a family we were! What a difference a war does make and do you remember our Sunday joint, what a difference it must be these days. Mother I thought for a moment before I turned over to go to sleep, surely I thought to myself there will be another day when we shall all meet again and sit round that old kitchen table and tell of our experiences. That'll be the day."

On the 31st of January his mother wrote: "I can't imagine you so far from home. I expect it seems very strange to you, being an invalid in a foreign land. We

Tony Allen's mother, Phoebe, at York Farm in 1940

should all like to come and see you. Today has been a windy day. Talk about wind, trees blown down electric poles snapped in two and here I am sitting by the light of two hurricane lanterns – no lights tonight. Rain, I have never seen anything like it for years. Mr. Stratford round the lane died last Friday. You knew the old lady there, well she died just a week before. Do take care of yourself as best you can, I think about you such a lot. Dad has just come in and said they had a very good side of ringers. But Jimmy Gordon broke a stay. You know like you did once. He thinks it is the first time he has rung in the tower."

In February, Tony compared notes on Christmas and said that although theirs was probably quiet, he had never felt so miserable in all his life. "It was tinned pork for dinner, which I couldn't tackle because there was no beer. I thought of Dad, Ern, Mr Brown and Claude sat in the little room drinking their Xmas ale. I don't suppose Archie was closed to his favourites."

On the 28th of February, Tony wrote that he was posted as a driver with HQ. They would think nothing of riding 50 miles on dark wet and slippery roads. He was: "glad to hear that you have sold the milk round. It must be a load off your mind. I often think of the old dairy. Thanks for the Parish Magazine. How steadily I read the dear Vicar's letter. I bet he's having a better time than myself, I know these officers." On the very same day in Hagbourne his mother was writing: "We have been threshing this last fortnight. The weather being perfect… Roll on when

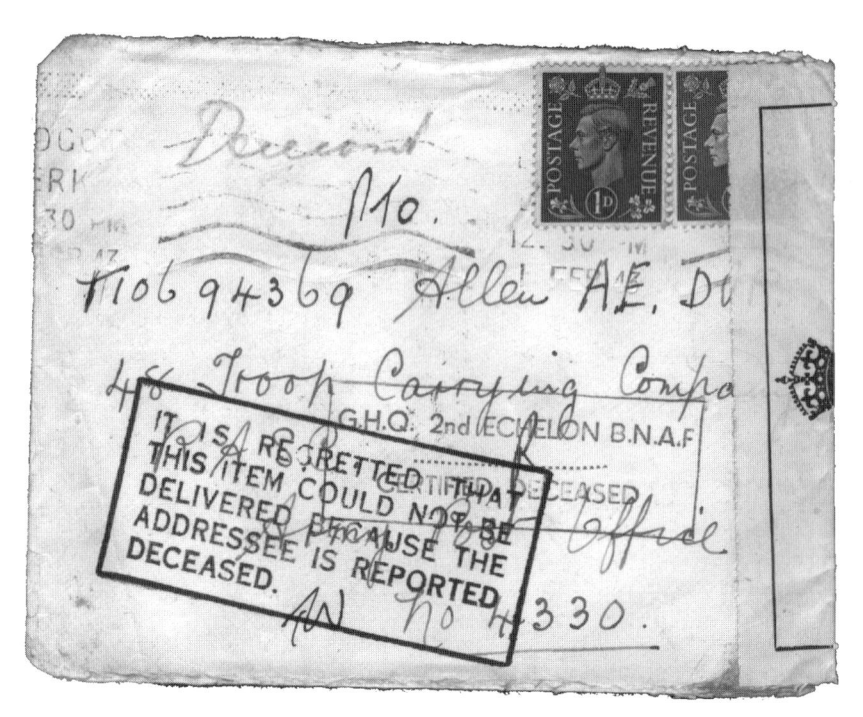

An undelivered letter returned to Tony's mother after his death

you all come home again. There are three more ricks left to thresh this week and that will leave ten. We have got to plough up the big meadow at Pill Pound and plant with oats, much against the gaffer's wish. But we must do it and help win this war eh!"

On the 17th of March she was able to write an aerogram and reported: "We are very much alive around here… We have been threshing for three weeks and not one wet day, which of course is very pleasing to man, and master too. Dicky and Ron work hard and only wish you were home to share a little of it… A great tank bashed into Ma Greenough's fence and smashed it to matchwood, also knocked the end of the barn in. I tell you talk about excitement." In Tony's next letter, he recommended that they numbered their letters: "Tell Ron to write soon. I liked his letter very much. Time passes much more pleasant if you have something to look forward to". On the 10th of March he wrote to Alf Webb [in charge of the ringers]. "How I am longing for the day when I can return to help ring those old tower bells".

Later that same day, the 10th of March 1943, Tony Allen was killed in a motor cycle accident after delivering a message to a nearby town. He was buried at Medjez-el-Bab Allied War Cemetery in Le Kef, Tunisia. He was 27 years old.

Many people were deeply affected by Tony's death. Official condolences and messages from those who knew him in the army were sent to his family at York Farm. On the day of Tony's death, Major P H Moreton wrote: "I cannot disclose any of the circumstances… all I can say is that he was on duty and that he suffered not one moment's pain. Your son was one of those men who are so invaluable, in that he did his work quietly, efficiently and without fuss, and his death was a very great loss".

Local people, some of whom had known Tony as a boy, were also shocked and moved by his untimely death. The vicar of St Andrew's, the Reverend Harold Smith-Masters, stationed in RAF Palestine wrote: "How well I remember our early days at West Hagbourne when your Tony and ours were small boys together. He is a great loss to the village and especially to the Church and ringers."

Elsie Smith, a teacher at East Hagbourne School, wrote: "Tony was a lad I never thought for one moment would pass the doctor for tough army life. Tony is the second of my nice lads I used to teach and love in school, who has given his life for his country." Hilda Pinnell, the wife of one of the local farmers also passed on her heart-felt views on the war: "They got no mercy for us poor mothers… one dreadful man has given us all this trouble. We said at the time they never ought to of taken the poor kid."

A memorial service for Tony Allen was held at St Andrew's Church, East Hagbourne, where he had worshipped as a boy and loved to ring the bells. During the service, members of the tower rang a plain course of Grandsire triples on the hand bells. Tony Allen left his own memorial in St Andrew's Church in the form of a shepherd's crook which he had presented to the church at the beginning of the war.

Victory and remembrance

For Britain, the war finally ended on VE-day (Victory in Europe) on the 8th of May 1945. Church bells were rung, floodlights replaced the blackout and there was dancing in the streets. Victory was celebrated jointly by East and West Hagbourne on the 8th of June 1946. Bonfire celebrations took place in the village, near the Horse and Harrow.

A public meeting was held at the school in East Hagbourne on the 13th of November 1947 to discuss the form the Hagbourne war memorial should take. As a result, a tablet was placed in St Andrew's Church, in memory of those who fell in both World Wars, Corporal William Smith being the only man from West Hagbourne killed in the first War. It was also agreed that the names of those who died in the Second World War should be added to the memorial at the Lower Cross in East Hagbourne. The names of Anthony Allen, Frederick Butler, Leslie Denning and Kerry Ryan, all from West Hagbourne, can be found on both memorials.

It was also proposed by the then chairman of the parish meeting, Mr John E Lay, that a bus shelter should be built in West Hagbourne, in memory of the four men. This was duly built, and a memorial plaque was dedicated on the 26th of June 1954 by the vicar of St Andrew's Church, the Reverend Harold Smith-Masters, accompanied by the church choir in full regalia, in a simple, but moving ceremony.

Dedication of the bus shelter as a war memorial to the four men from West Hagbourne who sacrificed their lives for their country in the Second World War. John E Lay is standing by the bus shelter, whilst the choir of St Andrew's Church stand on the right during the service on the 26th of June 1954

Sources – The Second World War comes to West Hagbourne

A J P Taylor, *England 1914–1945*, The Folio Society, 2000, p402.

Home Guard: Reminiscences of Arthur Butler (Sonny).

Details of Percy Dearlove's war service, written by Christine Jones, and read at his funeral in 1998.

Burial details of those who were killed in the war: Commonwealth War Graves Commission.

Anthony Allen's letters selected and edited by his niece, Jillian Hedges.

Drawing of bus shelter

Chapter Eleven

A Village Community

West Hagbourne has never had its own village hall or school and the last village shop closed in 1970. However, the lack of these amenities does not mean that the village has no vibrant community spirit. In earlier centuries, communal events and celebrations tended to be focused around religious festivals or the farming year, particularly at the end of the harvest or the fruit picking season. West Hagbourne once had a 'chapel of ease' but that disappeared at the time of the Reformation and the last of the little chapels which sprang up on private premises closed in the 1920s. Inevitably, as in most rural villages, the inn became the local meeting place, particularly for the men of the village. Women were generally tied more closely to the home looking after their large families.

For several centuries, West Hagbourne had two public houses, the Horse and Harrow Inn and the Wheatsheaf Inn (originally called Down House). However, the latter was a long way from the centre of the village and tended to cater for the people of the village of Didcot and those using the Wallingford – Didcot – Faringdon turnpike. The widow Jane Woodley was recorded as a publican on the 1841 census return and as she acquired over two acres of land, including Down House, when the village Inclosure Award was drawn up in 1843, she was probably the publican there. However, it was the Horse and Harrow, close to the village centre which became the focus for community activities.

The Horse & Harrow Inn

The Horse and Harrow situated at Scotlands Ash appears on a village map of 1754 but is probably older than that. No one knows how the pub got its name, but it may originally have been the 'Horse Harrow' as can be seen on an early photograph of the pub on page 139). It seems an appropriate name for an inn which has always been at the heart of a farming community.

Public houses, or pubs as we refer to them today, evolved from three quite distinct types of drinking establishments. Alehouses specialised in beer, taverns also sold wine and inns provided accommodation. A census of alehouses, taverns and inns compiled in 1577, revealed that in Berkshire there were 252 ale houses, 17 taverns and 63 inns at that time.

Malt is the basic ingredient of brewing and comes from barley which has been partially germinated and then dried. The alcohol is produced from the fermentation of the sugar contained in the malt. Brewing and malting processes were widespread in Britain by 2,000 BC and there is evidence of ale being brewed in almost every village by the Middle Ages. Ale was produced from the barley grown on the manorial estates and was drunk by everyone including children, and was probably safer than the water in Medieval times.

In earlier centuries there was a distinction between ale and beer, the latter originally being a beverage flavoured by hops. Beer was unknown in Britain before about 1400 when it was introduced from Flanders. It took a while before its bitter taste became acceptable to the English palate. Henry VIII would not allow his brewers to add hops to the ale of the royal household. However, it was probably its better keeping qualities which won the day over the traditional ale. Wild hops were probably used as herbs from a very early date but the first evidence of local domestic hop growing is the farm accounts of Robert Loder at Harwell between 1613 and 1620. Hops were grown in East Hagbourne where one oasthouse and the foundations of two others remain.

Brewing became an important trade in Berkshire and Oxfordshire where malting barley grew in plentiful supply. West Hagbourne is known to have had its own malt house and maltster in the nineteenth century. The Horse and Harrow Inn has had a long association with the brewing company Morland. The first known mention of a Morland in connection with beer-making is the yeoman John Morland who bought West Ilsley House "including the malthouse" in 1711. West Ilsley is a small village on the Berkshire Downs just five miles from West Hagbourne. John Morland's son Benjamin built a new brewhouse in 1726 and his grandson William continued in the trade, identifying himself as a brewer in local records. The West Ilsley brewery included a cooperage and was one of two breweries in the village.

William's grandson Edward Henry Morland inherited the brewery in West Ilsley in 1855 and purchased premises in Ock Street, Abingdon in 1861, resulting in the founding of the Eagle Brewery there. Five years later Edward acquired the Abbey Brewery, also in Ock Street, through Mary Spenlove, the daughter of his aunt Susanna Morland who had married into the Spenlove brewing family in Abingdon. The Morland brewing business became concentrated at the Eagle Brewery and brewing ceased at West Ilsley and the Abbey. Morland's became a registered company in October 1887.

The earliest known written document to link the Horse and Harrow Inn with Morland's is the Inclosure Award of 1843 which records that the Inn was owned by William Morland. But it is likely that Morlands owned it long before that, given the closeness of Benjamin Morland's brewery at West Ilsley which was established as early as 1726. It is possible that the Horse and Harrow was one of Morland Brewery's first tied estates.

There was a further connection with Morland's through the Harwell-Streatley turnpike which once ran past the Horse and Harrow. Thomas and William

A group of men congregating on the bank opposite the Horse and Harrow waiting for it to open. On this occasion they have just had a visit from the barber and his cloth is hanging on the fence

The Horse and Harrow Inn sometime in the early 1900s. The man in the centre is the publican Joseph Napper, possibly with two of his sons and the dogs which were then a feature of pub life

Morland were two of the turnpike trustees in 1845. The rights to the turnpike were sold to the then owner of the pub, Edward Morland, in 1870 by the trustees. A toll gate was positioned outside the pub and a small toll house stood on the opposite side where the toll keeper lived. The road would have been narrower then and the boundary stream ran across it, forming a ford. The stream was enclosed in 1934 after a child drowned in it.

A conveyance dated the 18th of February 1888 lists the premises which were transferred to Morland's when it became a limited company. The Horse and Harrow is second on the list after the George and Dragon public house at Upton. The Horse and Harrow appears to have been owned at that time by Edward Henry Morland. The Horse and Harrow premises are described as follows:

> *The Horse and Harrow public house with homestead, two orchards and arable land containing together about nine acres and two poles AND also a messuage formerly a toll house with garden known as Scotland's Ash Turnpike Gate but now forming part of the Horse and Harrow premises.*

It is not certain which homestead is referred to in this conveyance but it could well have been the "farm homestead" which once stood on the corner of Main Street and York Road where the house called Lizard Bank stands today. According to the Inclosure Award, this was owned by William Morland in 1843. He also owned two orchards to the east of the Horse and Harrow, one on each side of Main Street, as well as several acres of land to the east and the west of the pub amounting to about nine acres. In other words, the land described in the conveyance as the tied estate of the Horse and Harrow is almost certainly the same land owned by William Morland in 1843. This was a strip of land along Main Street stretching as far as York Road to the east and nearly five acres to the west of the pub. Some of the latter was later owned by Arch Napper and is now farmed by his grandson, Rowan Napper. The site of the old toll house is still owned by Morland's to this day.

No doubt the Horse and Harrow was a busy place in the days when the toll gate was operating as it would have brought trade to the pub. It would have been a natural stopping place for travellers seeking rest and refreshments, and possibly the assistance of a local blacksmith or wheelwright, trades with which local publicans seemed familiar. The turnpikes were gradually made redundant after 1835 when the county councils took over responsibility for public roads. The coming of the railway and the opening of Didcot Railway Station in 1844 sounded the final death-knell for the turnpikes. When the last toll gate keeper left, the toll house was used to store apples and the local men played cards there whilst waiting for the pub to open. It eventually fell into disrepair before finally disappearing soon after 1900.

At the turn of the twentieth century the Horse and Harrow was literally a spit and sawdust place. There were spittoons for the chewed tobacco and the floor was bedded with bean straw because it did not burn easily. The straw was replaced every Saturday morning. Game was frequently laid out by the fire where the dogs also lay. It does not take much imagination to envisage the atmosphere inside the pub on a Friday night when the straw was past its best and the game had been lying around for a while.

As well as being close to the turnpike road, the Horse and Harrow was situated opposite Cow Lane, one of West Hagbourne's oldest tracks, running north from the Horse and Harrow. This was convenient for the cowmen or 'foggers' who used Cow Lane as a driftway for taking their cattle to Abingdon market. Sometimes a little fun fair would be set up in the lane opposite the pub.

When the weather was fine, Cow Lane was also a convenient place for the men to wait for the Horse and Harrow to open at 12 o'clock sharp. On Sundays, an itinerant barber would sometimes call at the pub in the days when the only transport was horse and cart or bicycle and visiting a barber in town was almost impossible for farm labourers. Not surprisingly, women tended to keep their hair long before the First World War.

The Nappers – a family of publicans

Just as some of West Hagbourne's farms are associated with the families who have owned them for generations, so the Horse and Harrow was for a long time associated with the Napper family. The first written record of a Napper at the Horse and Harrow was the census return of 1841, when George Napper was the publican. His name appears again on the village Inclosure Award of 1843. As today, the only public place for people to get together in the village in those days was the Horse and Harrow Inn. On the 11th of August 1842, a public meeting was held to discuss the forthcoming enclosure of common land at the "House of George Napper called or known by the name or sign of the Horse and Harrow Inn at Scotlands Ash".

George was probably a descendant of Thomas and Sarah Napper who were married in 1630 in Sutton Courtenay. Their great, great grandson John married Sarah Bushnell in 1773 and they lived in Appleford with their eight children. Their four sons moved to the Hagbournes and were soon absorbed into the two communities. Two of the sons became publicans. One of them, George, was also a wheelwright, and he and his wife Mary held the tenancy of the Horse and Harrow. George's brother William, a blacksmith, ran the Fleur de Lys in East Hagbourne with his wife Ann. They also managed a smithy there. George Napper continued to live in West Hagbourne after Mary died but he retired from the Horse and Harrow on a pension and died in 1851.

George's nephew William Napper and his wife Charlotte took over the Horse and Harrow sometime in 1852. William was also a blacksmith, like his father at the Fleur de Lys. By 1871 he also owned 30 acres of land and had three men working for him. Like most people in those days, William and his wife Charlotte (née Pether) had a large family. One son, John Pether Napper, was the census

Rosa Watts who married the publican Joseph Napper and died in childbirth in 1896

enumerator for West Hagbourne in 1891. Another son, Joseph Pether Napper, kept the family tradition going by taking over the tenancy of the Horse and Harrow after his father's death in 1881. Before taking on the pub, Joseph had gone into business with Charles Allen of Down Farm. Around 1875 they bought a steam portable engine (pulled by horses) and for many years they contracted it out to local farms. A photograph of their steam engine outside Ivy Cottage can be seen on page 149.

Joseph met Rosa Watts when she was working at Grove Manor Farm. They married and had twelve children. Seven of their sons and a daughter called Annie survived but Rosa died giving birth to another daughter Daisy on the 20th of December 1896. The baby died the following day. Annie stayed on to help Joseph run the pub. She later married a local man, Bert Dearlove. They lived next door to the pub in Rose Cottage which Annie inherited from her father. Some of Rosa's younger children were sent to live with relatives after her death. One of Joseph's sons, William, married a local girl, Patient [sic] Allen, and bought the toll gate rights which turned out to be a quite a lucrative business. Frank, another son, married Daisy Pullen and lived at Ivy Farm which he had bought from his brother Ernest.

Joseph and Rosa's son Archibald – called Arch by everyone – grew up to be yet another Napper landlord of the Horse and Harrow. He was born there in 1889, became the publican in 1930 and died behind the bar in 1958.

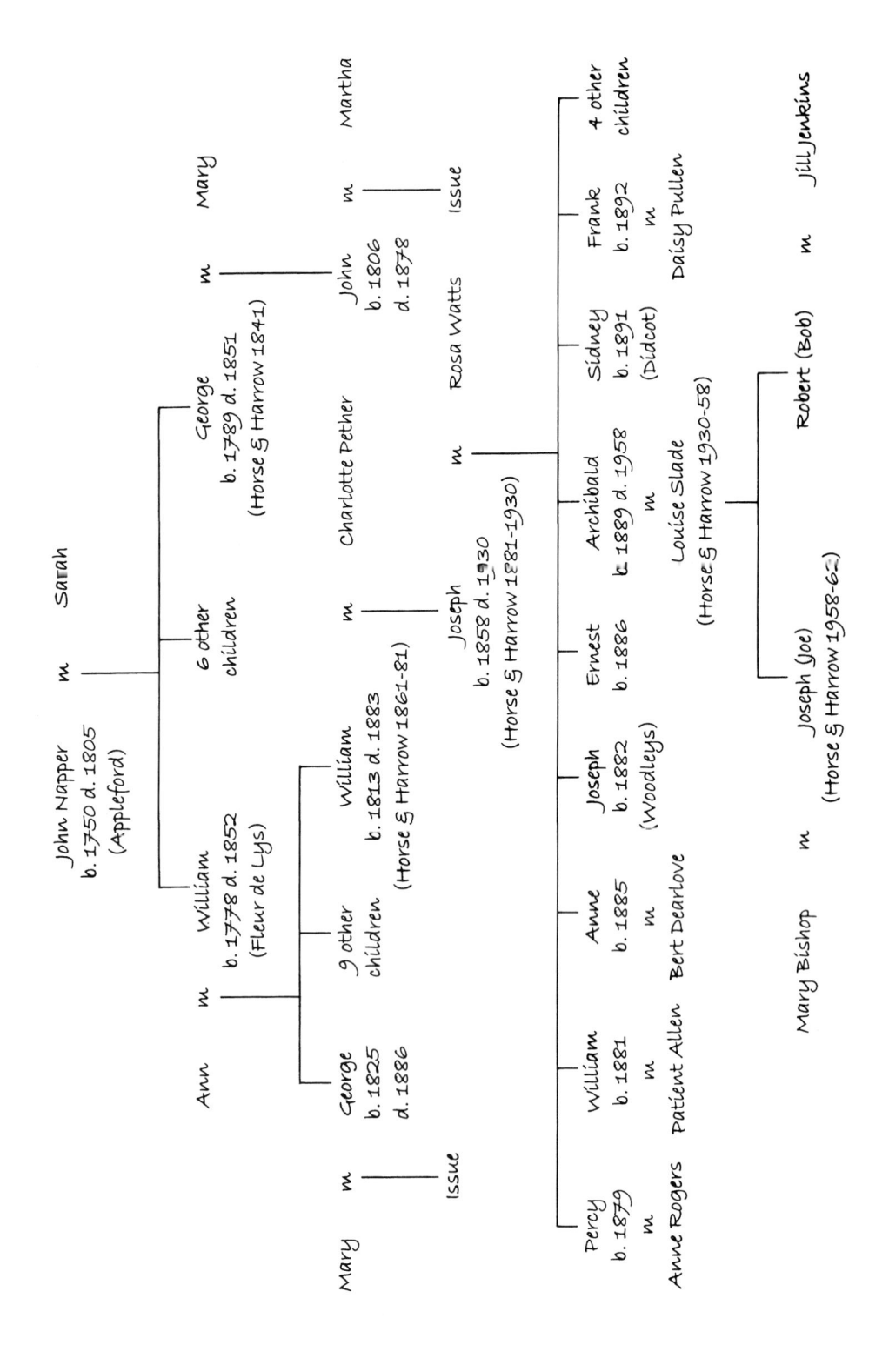

```
                          John Napper
                          b. 1750 d. 1805   m   Sarah
                          (Appleford)
                              │
        ┌─────────────────────┼─────────────────────────┐
        │                                               │
   William                                           George                 m   Mary   Martha
   b. 1778 d. 1852                                   b. 1789 d. 1851
   (Fleur de Lys)                                    (Horse & Harrow 1841)
        │                                               │
 ┌──────┼─────────────┐                    ┌────────────┴────────────┐
 │      │             │                    │                         │
Ann  George      9 other     William     6 other                   John           m   Mary
 m   b. 1825     children    b. 1813     children                  b. 1806
Mary d. 1886                 d. 1883                               d. 1878
     Issue                   (Horse & Harrow 1861-81)              Issue
                                    │
                                  Joseph              m        Charlotte Pether
                                  b. 1858 d. 1930
                                  (Horse & Harrow 1881-1930)
                                    │
    ┌────────┬──────────┬──────────┬─────────┬──────────┬──────────┬─────────┐
    │        │          │          │         │          │          │         │
  Percy   William     Anne      Joseph    Ernest    Archibald    Sidney    Frank      + other
  b. 1879 b. 1881    b. 1885   b. 1882   b. 1886   b. 1889      b. 1891   b. 1892    children
  m       m          m         (Woodleys)          d. 1958      (Didcot)  m
  Anne    Patient    Bert                          m                      Daisy Pullen
  Rogers  Allen      Dearlove                      Louise Slade
                                                   (Horse & Harrow 1930-58)
                                                        │
                                          ┌─────────────┴──────────────┐
                                       Joseph (Joe)                 Robert (Bob)   m   Jill Jenkins
                                       m  Mary Bishop
                                       (Horse & Harrow 1958-62)
```

Napper family tree

Annie, daughter of Joseph Napper. She married Bert Dearlove and they lived next door to the pub

Bert Dearlove at the gate of Rose Cottage which was once thatched. The land behind him is now farmed by Rowan Napper

Arch Napper behind the bar of the Horse and Harrow where he died in 1958 after serving as publican for 28 years

Arch was a country boy, born and bred, and for him West Hagbourne was enough. He hardly ever left the Horse and Harrow, never saw the sea and never felt the need to visit London. Arch kept pigs in the backyard between the pub and Rose Cottage. He and his wife Louise had two sons, Archibald Robert known as Bob, and Douglas Joseph known as Joe.

Arch was a well-known character and hospitable landlord. During the Second World War, soldiers and airmen stationed in the area used the Horse and Harrow as their local pub. Arch became a shooting agent and for some years he kept a record of the game that was bagged during his shoots:

	Partridge	Hares
1925	370	63
1926	281	60
1927	224	41
1928	631	60
1929	641	45
1930	671	77
1931	310	56
Total	3128	402

Arch Napper's personal tally from the shoots he organised between 1925 and 1931

A shooting party outside the Horse and Harrow shortly after the Second World War

Joseph Napper with three of his sons and Jim Lousley in the 1920s. L to R: Joseph Napper, Arch, Ernest (back), Frank and Jim Lousley

Micky Wirral, a famous shot around West Hagbourne

After Arch's death in 1958, his son Joe and his wife Mary (née Bishop) ran the Horse and Harrow for a few years, but left in 1962 before having a family. Thus ended the Napper's 120 year tradition as publicans at the Horse and Harrow, although Arch's granddaughter Robyn Napper worked there when the landlord, Clive Polley, was at the Horse and Harrow in the 1990s. She herself become the landlady of the Spread Eagle pub at East Hagbourne. Tragically, she died in a road accident in 1998. Joe and Mary had a greengrocer's shop in Park Road for a while but Joe's first love had always been farming. He had some land in West Hagbourne left to him by his father and he also continued another Napper tradition by renting part of the land belonging to the William Tyrrell Charity. This land has been rented by Nappers continually since 1832.

There is a local saying: "If you are not a Napper, you are a Napper's nipper" because descendants of those early Nappers who came to the Hagbournes in the late 1700s have spread not only locally, but as far away as Australia, Canada and South Africa. Several of the children of William Napper, the landlord at the Fleur de Lys in the nineteenth century, became publicans and others did well in trade and business. One son, George, born in 1825, was the father of Dennis Napper of Didcot who made his fortune selling horse fodder to the Great Western Railway. He brought a farm for each of his children, including Grove Manor Farm which he gave to his son Dennis, and Manor Farm which he gave to his daughter Eliza, who married John Lay. Many of the descendants of the first Nappers to come to West Hagbourne from Appleford still live in the village, whilst others are not far away in East Hagbourne, Didcot, Upton and Blewbury.

Horse and Harrow characters

Not surprisingly, there are many stories and a cast of characters associated with the Horse and Harrow and its publicans. One of these stories concerns a barn owned by Arch Napper which once stood on the corner of Main Road and York Road. Not only did this barn house a few cattle but it was also home to a few humans. It is a reflection of Arch Napper's wicked sense of humour that he christened this barn the 'Tin Hotel' and somehow the name stuck.

The 'Tin Hotel' was a timber-framed construction, clad with a mixture of wood and corrugated iron sheets. The floor was generally covered in straw or hay so it was easy to make up a bed, which the residents found congenial when returning from the Horse and Harrow late on a Saturday night and feeling a little worse for wear.

Three of the best known residents of the 'Tin Hotel' were veterans of the First World War. Two of them, Living Smith and Jack Strudwick, survived on a variety of casual jobs and stayed at the 'Tin Hotel' from time-to-time. Living Smith was known to strip off for a good wash in the cattle trough, much to the consternation of the two single ladies whose house was adjacent to the 'hotel'. However, the longest-serving resident was Jimmy Shaw who used the barn permanently during

Jimmy Shaw

The 'Tin Hotel' which once provided a home for a few of West Hagbourne's old soldiers

the latter years of his life. He worked at Lay's farm and was apparently invaluable at harvesting and threshing times despite being slightly handicapped with an old injury to his leg.

Jimmy Shaw was born in Upton and had relatives in West Hagbourne but they refused to have anything to do with him. Hilda Butler took pity on him, agreeing to feed him and do his washing, though he slept at the 'Tin Hotel'. This continued for many years and Jimmy Shaw became part of Hilda's growing family during the 1930s. He had a chair alongside the sink in the kitchen and a special mug for his tea. He used to sit in his chair reading the newspaper with the aid of a magnifying glass which he held against one eye, moving the paper from side to side.

Like many other men in the village, Jimmy used to join the Saturday night entertainment at the Horse and Harrow pub and it was common to hear him singing as he limped back to his free digs at the barn. There was a great deal of affection and respect for Jimmy on the part of the Butler children and this was reciprocated. Jimmy Shaw had few possessions but he did treasure his pocket watch and chain which he gave to Jack, the youngest son, before he died. It is believed that this watch is still in the possession of the Butler family.

Another well known village character and frequenter of the Horse and Harrow was Jack Dawson. Born in 1875, Jack came to live and work in West Hagbourne as a young man and married Florence Powell. They had nine children and many grandchildren and great grandchildren. To them he was always 'Grampy Jack'. He worked as the head carter at York Farm for many years and was responsible for bringing the first threshing machine to West Hagbourne from Kingston Bagpuize.

Jack continued to work long after retirement age and was active well into his eighties. He continued to be a regular customer at the Horse and Harrow, enjoying his favourite tipple of Mackesons until he died at the age of 91 on New Year's Day, 1967.

Until the end of the Second World War, the social life of most of the village men revolved around the village pub. For women, life was rather different as there were usually many children to care for, often on very little money and in very cramped and often unsanitary conditions. Cooking was done on a coal-fired range which had to be lit each morning. Water for washing, cooking and drinking came from a well in the back garden and baths were taken in a tin bath in front of the fire. Washing was done by hand and bed linen was boiled in a copper. A few people had septic tanks but for the majority, waste was disposed of in a trench dug across the garden.

Electricity did not come to West Hagbourne until 1936 and until then oil lamps and candles lit the way to bed. These candles and open fires used for cooking and heating were the cause of many accidents in the home and children were sometimes burned to death as a result. The saving grace of these hardships was that it was the same for everyone.

One mother whose devotion to her family has not been taken for granted is Hilda Butler who lived at 4 York Road. The following appreciation by her son

This caricature of Jack Dawson was drawn sometime in the early 1960s at Jack's favourite place, the Horse and Harrow, where he was a familiar figure. It is said to be an extremely good likeness

Arthur (always called Sonny) describes his mother's life but it can be read as the typical experience of most wives living in the village at that time.

> Hilda came from Ross-On-Wye to work for a family at Upton and it was there she met Fred. As often happened in those days, Hilda was soon in the family way and they married at St Michael's Church, Blewbury on 15 September 1915 and Rene came along in December 1915 and started the ball rolling. [There were five boys and five girls.]
>
> To say the least of it when we were young we had to rough it and we all owe a great deal to Hilda Mary for the way she coped and looked after us. There was never enough room in any of the houses we lived in and this was particularly so in the three-bed council house at West Hagbourne as we grew older.
>
> Hilda had learnt a good deal about cooking food during her years in domestic service. She could conjure up something out of nothing. She knew how to prepare and cook anything from chitterlings (stomach lining of pigs) to the choicest dishes – and although we never had any of the latter, the fact that she knew was reflected in the way she cooked turnip tops, swede and parsnip –

Hilda Warr and Sarah Powell outside the cottages which were opposite the post office until they were pulled down in the 1950s. Hilda died at the age of 12 when her night-dress caught fire on the 29th of February 1936, shortly after this photograph was taken

followed by 'skimmer lad' (flour, water and jam) or rhubarb batter for afters. She had a happy knack of making you feel you were having a banquet and more often than not it tasted like it. Her patience, understanding and most of all her love were outstanding features in our day-to-day lives and I'm sure none of us will ever forget it.

Although we were poor, in no way were we unhappy. I can see the house at Hagbourne now. Three bedrooms upstairs; two rooms down – a front room and a kitchen/scullery in which in one corner was a hand pump for pumping water up from a well in the garden and in another was a built-in copper in which a fire was lit to boil the washing. There was a small black lead grate with an oven over the top and this had two swing out hobs for keeping things boiling. There was a bathroom and a cupboard below the stairs that smelt of old socks and leather. This was "old digs" cupboard where you got put if you didn't behave!

The privy or lavatory was a small brick-built construction out in the garden – a seat with a bucket underneath and we, like everybody else, had to have a permanent trench dug across the garden for disposal purposes. The only difference with ours was it got filled up quicker. This outside lav was not the most popular place to visit on a cold winter's night, especially if the candle blew out on the way. Nor was it very cheerful if the bucket was full. Emptying it was

Photograph of Hilda and Fred Butler, probably taken during the First World War, not long after they were married

not the most popular of jobs! We would also not recommend four boys in a bed as being the most comfortable thing in the world, particularly when the bed got wet in the middle of the night!

But all in all, in spite of the fact that she had more to do than she should have had, she set a splendid example to us all. Her genuine belief in God and her love of the Church was reflected in all our lives. The whole family was baptised and confirmed and the boys encouraged (but not forced) to join the choir – as most of us did. She, with her neighbour Mrs Bishop, cleaned the church at East Hagbourne for many years.

We took her to her church as long as she was able to travel and we can only hope this gave her the comfort she deserved. If Jesus was a good shepherd and if anyone deserves to go to heaven, she does and we're all pretty sure she will.

In extreme old age Hilda lived at the Close Nursing Home at Burcot until she died just two days short of her 103rd birthday in December 1995, leaving behind five generations of descendants.

Hilda's husband Fred was another stalwart of the Horse and Harrow between the two World Wars when the economy of the country was shaky and thousands of men were out of work. Life was hard for both men and women in those days, especially with so many mouths to feed. However, Fred was not one to let things get him down as the following portrait of him, written by Sonny on behalf of his brothers and sisters, demonstrates.

As a young boy Fred went to Upton school but it is pretty certain that his attendance at this type of establishment was very limited indeed. His ability of the three 'Rs' was non-existent and as a pupil he must have been a holy terror to his teacher and this image stayed with him throughout his life. It would not be out of order to describe his character as a loveable rogue. We believe he lived for today and let tomorrow take care of itself. Some would say Dad not being able to read or write made him handicapped, but this was not so. The truth is, he made a success of his life and his obvious lack of academic ability in no way stopped him achieving what we all strive for but few achieve, an enjoyment of life.

Although we owe Hilda more than we can repay, we also owe Fred for some of the things we are today – in particular, we believe, a sense of humour and fun. Lady Luck played a big part, like his meeting and marrying Hilda. Fred and Hilda complimented each other and although they were as poor as church mice, they each had a personality that was able to overcome all their problems. The family was born between 1917 and 1935.

As a young man we believe he worked at Bucknell's Farm, Upton, with horses in particular. He was called up for army service in the 1914-18 war and was a driver (of horses) in the RASC. He never talked a lot about these days. After leaving the army he was employed at the Central Ordnance Depot, Didcot. As far as we know he was never out of work and this was quite something in the 1920s and 1930s when Britain was really in a slump.

There was obviously no easy transport to and from the village, only a horse and trap. Everyone had to walk to work or cycle if they had one. Cycles were precious and were kept maintained from spares found on dumps. More often than not, tyres were flat and there was never any money to buy a valve rubber. This is where Fred's ability to make do and mend came into its own. In fact, some of the miracles performed by Fred to keep cycles on the road had to be seen to be believed. Fred also mended our already third-hand shoes with material from old leather bicycle saddles and tin tacks.

The village shop and pub were the centres of social life. We believe all young men learned to drink hard from an early age but many, like Fred, became semi-addicted to the amber coloured liquid. For his sins, Fred had a reputation for wandering off the "straight and narrow" when it came to drink. There is no doubt he would have willingly spent his last 4d on a pint rather than buy a pair of socks. Although he occasionally washed his feet, he never had a bath in his adult life and no amount of cajoling could entice him to do so.

One of Fred's chief attributes was his desire and ability to work. Mind you, he had to with a wife and ten children to keep. Whatever else however, Fred did always bring home a weekly wage, right up to the age of 73 when he retired, being one of the last men employed at COD Didcot after its transfer to Bicester. He was never ill nor went to the doctor or hospital except for two occasions with his feet. He died in 1978 when he was 86 years old.

To sum up, Fred was a more than well-liked character in the village and we were perhaps lucky to be able to always call him our Dad.

The village shop

Although the social life of the men tended to revolve around the pub, the shop provided an opportunity for women to meet each other, especially in the days before freezers and fridges when food shopping was done on a daily basis. Early in the twentieth century, the village shop was an important part of everybody's lives and a place to exchange gossip and hear the latest news. For people living in rural villages like West Hagbourne it was the lifeblood of the community and many villagers still have memories of the last village shop which closed in 1970.

We know from early maps that in previous centuries West Hagbourne had several shops dotted around the village but little is known about them. The census return of 1881 identifies Kerzia Powell, a widow of 65 years as a small shopkeeper and John Woodley as a baker and grocer. He ran the grocery shop with the help of his wife Sarah, at the house in the Square called Woodleys where they lived. In 1891 John Woodley, by now a widower, was still in business at the age of 72, but by 1900 the bakery was closed, presumably after John Woodley's death. Bread was then delivered to the village from Upton and Didcot.

Ivy Farm Cottage next to the pond was a shop for some years and was advertised as such when the cottage was up for sale in 1919, complete with "counter and shelving". One can see the door of the shop on the photograph of Ivy Cottage on page 149.

The Randell family ran a sweet shop at Green Thatch on Main Street before moving to a wooden building close to the Square at the heart of the village. In the following extract Lillian Randell's shop is fondly remembered by Arthur Butler (Sonny):

> *Dear old Mrs Randell ran the village shop and 'open all hours' was the order of the day. She sold everything from paraffin to stale sweets on a hap-eny-tray [hap-eny was half an old penny] and this was brought into view from below the counter (providing you had a hap-eny) so that you could take your pick of sherbet dabs or your choice of chewing gum, bulls eyes, a bit of chocolate or a surprise packet which could be a chocolate drop or a sweet up to at least 10 years old.*

As well as sweets, the shop sold the usual groceries such as butter, flour, sugar and cheese. Tea was sold loose from a large wooden tea chest and scooped into a cone made from newspaper or brown paper. The paraffin mentioned by Sonny was important for the oil lamps in the days before the village had electricity.

Particulars.

IN THE PARISH OF WEST HAGBOURNE.

LOT 1.

THE COMPACT SMALL HOLDING,

CONSISTING OF AN

Old=fashioned Cottage and Shop

Known as "IVY COTTAGE,"

BUILT OF BRICK WITH TILED ROOF, and containing

On First Floor—Three Bedrooms.

On Ground Floor—Entrance Hall; Sitting Room; Kitchen with Range; Wash-house with Baker's Oven, Range, Copper, Dresser, Pump and Sink; Larder with Meat Safe and Shelving, Shop with Counter and Shelving; also Outhouse.

There is a GOOD GARDEN attached.

Adjoining is a YARD, approached through Double Gates from the Main Road, opening on to which is a

SET OF FARM BUILDINGS,

Mostly Timber-built with Thatched or Galvanised Roofs,

COMPRISING

Stabling for 3 Horses, Chaff-house and Loft, Barn, 2-bay Open Shed, Pig-Styes and Fowl House; also

A WELL-STOCKED ORCHARD

And Lean-to Cow-house with Tiled Roof.

SCHEDULE:

No. on Ord. Plan.	Description.	A.	R.	P.
27	House, Garden and Premises		1	18
28	Orchard	2	0	0
		A2	**1**	**18**

This Lot is in hand and vacant possession will be given on completion of the purchase.

OUTGOINGS:—The Property is subject to an unapportioned Tithe and Land Tax, with Lots 2 & 3, the payment for last year being as follows—Tithe Rent Charge, £8 15s. 6d.; Land Tax, £1 12s. 3d.

Sale notice for Ivy Cottage, 1919

Photograph of Mrs Randell and her son Alfie outside the village shop in the 1930s before it was rebuilt in brick

When Mrs Randell died during the Second World War, Jack and Alice Napper managed the shop and post office for the Randell family. Alice was remembered as a lovely, easy-going person who stayed very calm, even when the shop was full of children buying sweets. The Randells eventually sold the shop to Henry and Winifred Warner who rebuilt it in brick. The Warners also ran a wholesale grocery store from the sheds at the rear of the property, which they kept going after the shop was leased to Mr Greenough. Villagers considered him a very kind and helpful man, always prepared to bring back groceries on request from his trips to Didcot. He couldn't always afford to keep things in stock, probably due to debts run up by some villagers buying things 'on tick' (credit). Mr Greenough was the last person to run the shop until it closed in 1970 but the Warners continued to run the wholesale grocery business until the property was sold in 1973.

Villagers were never totally dependant on the village shop. Lots of trades people, such as grocers and butchers from neighbouring towns, took weekly orders which were delivered to the door. Bread came daily from Upton, whilst Tony Allen of York Farm ran an enterprising local milk round before the War. Bill Pinnell of Lime Tree Farm also sold milk from his own cows.

The village post office

On the 18th of July 1936, Mrs Randell's responsibilities were extended when, at the age of 67, she became West Hagbourne's first sub post mistress on an annual salary of £205 rising to £237. There were still some restrictions, as postal orders could be issued by Mrs Randell but not cashed. East Hagbourne was the nearest money order and telegraph office. At this point, in 1936, the sub post office was incorporated into the village shop.

Although the sub post office was not established until 1936, this does not mean that West Hagbourne had no postal service of any kind until that date. In 1854 John Woodley was operating an unofficial receiving house. This meant that he would have accepted letters from villagers and transported them for posting in Wallingford, West Hagbourne's nearest post office. He may have picked up others there for delivery back to the village if they were released by the Wallingford post office. This would have fitted in with his grocery business as he would have

In this photograph, Ernest White (left), the butcher from East Hagbourne has just made a delivery to the Horse and Harrow. Tom Woodley is sitting on his motorbike for a joke. The other two men are Ernest and Dennis Napper of Grove Manor Farm. White's was an old family butchers established towards the end of the nineteenth century by farmer Harry White. Ernest White took over the business in 1908 and the Horse and Harrow was a regular customer

travelled around buying stock for his shop. This arrangement was an entirely private one between Woodley and the villagers. Robert Appleford, the publican of the Greyhound Inn in East Hagbourne, ran a similar operation there. The free delivery of post based on a uniform postal charge was only granted in 1897 to mark Queen Victoria's Jubilee.

Sub post offices were established on the basis of the volume of post which went back and forth within a given area. This was monitored by the post office at Wallingford and by 1856 East Hagbourne had merited its own sub post office which is still in operation today. Things improved for West Hagbourne with the arrival of a letter box set in the cob wall near Ivy Cottage. This was there by at least 1876 as it is marked on a map of that date. By 1887 the post was coming to West Hagbourne via Didcot instead of Wallingford.

Although he was an unofficial postal worker, it is hoped that John Woodley was more trustworthy than Mr E Hearman, the Hagbourne messenger from the Wallingford post office. On the 5th of September 1857 he was taken before a magistrate for drunkenness whilst on duty and for the detention of letters entrusted to him for delivery. He was convicted by the magistrate who advised that he should be dismissed since his conduct in other aspects "has given cause for dissatisfaction to the inhabitants of the neighbourhood".

The establishment of West Hagbourne's sub post office and the appointment of Mrs Randell in 1936 came about following a special village meeting where it was agreed that the postal authorities should be approached with a view to establishing a post office in West Hagbourne. This was supported by what turned out to be a successful petition, signed by the villagers and sent to the head post master in Abingdon.

When the shop and sub post office closed in 1970, the post and telephone boxes were moved from their original positions outside the shop to a spot beside the bus shelter on the other side of the Square. When the shop was converted to a private dwelling, the house kept the name 'The Old Post Office', which is now all that is left to remind us that West Hagbourne once had a post office.

West Hagbourne's mystery man

Although much has been said about the social life revolving round the Horse and Harrow and the drinking habits of some of the men in the past, this does not mean that there is no spiritual dimension to life in West Hagbourne. Although there is no church in the village, West Hagbourne has always had important links with St Andrew's Church in East Hagbourne and these have been explained in Chapter 7. Despite having no church however, West Hagbourne may have had its very own priest in the shape of the Reverend Edwin George Bullock, better known as Father Antony.

Edwin George Bullock is something of a mystery as little is known of his life before he came to West Hagbourne. He was born in Garford on the 15th of

November 1859. His father was George Bullock, a farmer of some substance who had 379 aces of land and employed 16 men and 6 boys. Edwin's mother was Elizabeth, daughter of William Bullock of Appleton. It is not clear if his parents were related in any way but they may have been distant cousins. Edwin's known siblings were two younger brothers, Charles and Herbert.

The first mention of Edwin George Bullock living in West Hagbourne is the Kelly's Directory of 1899, by which time he would have been in his forties. His father George, brother Herbert and Miss Esther Bullock, his mother's sister, are also known to have lived in the village. There were Bullocks at York Farm at least between the years 1851 and 1861 but no connection has been proven between the two families. Whether the whole family moved at the same time, or whether Edwin's parents came to join his aunt and Edwin arrived later, is unclear. His brother Charles does not appear in any later documents or wills and may have died before his parents moved to West Hagbourne. His father died in West Hagbourne in 1900 and his mother died in Appleton twelve years later but the date of her return to Appleton is unknown. Edwin's aunt Esther and brother Herbert died in West Hagbourne in 1916 and 1918 respectively.

It is not known why the family came to live in West Hagbourne but George Bullock, Edwin's father, would have been well beyond retirement age. When he died, he left a considerable amount of money in stocks, the interest of which went to his wife and her sister. When he first came to West Hagbourne, Edwin rented Thatch Cottage at the corner of Moor Lane and subsequently bought it in 1904. In the meantime he bought Ragged Farm and the orchard further down Moor Lane in 1901, followed a year later by the purchase of the house next door to Thatch Cottage, known today as Enard Cottage. Presuming that Edwin George Bullock arrived in West Hagbourne a year or two before his entry in the Kelly's Directory of 1899, he had managed to buy up three adjoining properties and land in Moor Lane within five or six years of settling in the village.

The one thing which Enard Cottage and Thatch Cottage had in common when Edwin Bullock bought them was their chapels. There was an existing chapel in Thatch Cottage, and another exterior chapel adjoining Enard Cottage on the site of the present garage there. The chapel had been established by Moses Beavis in 1834 before Father Antony bought the cottage in 1902. These chapels are highly significant since Edwin's first entry in Kelly's Directory calls him Brother Antony. Later directories fluctuate between referring to him as Father and Brother Antony. He gave his address as St Francis d'Assisi Cottage (Thatch Cottage) and in the Kelly's Directory of 1903 it is claimed that he was the founder of the St Francis d'Assisi League of Mercy, though there is no known evidence of the existence of such an organisation. Father Antony did continue to hold services and celebrate Mass in both the chapels after he purchased the two houses, and it may have been these which attracted him to the properties in the first place. Older villagers recall that he ran some kind of Sunday School at the cottage. Others remember him as a piano tuner.

In his will he referred to himself as "The Reverend Edwin George Bullock, Catholic Priest of Hagbourne Berkshire (in religion Father Antony)" but there is no record to be found of his ordination in either the Roman Catholic or Church of England clerical directories. Churches of other denominations have no record of him either. He did not appear to officiate at baptisms, marriages or burials at St Andrew's Church.

His detailed will, written on the 25th of March 1923, provides some insight into the kind of man he was and his activities as a priest in West Hagbourne. Many of his bequests are to people outside the village but he also had friends close to home, such as the Russell and Uzzell families, Dr Harry Watts, William Hitchman the postman, and A E Rowland the baker at Upton. He was obviously a cultured and educated man who had a library and could play the piano and organ. He also enjoyed some of the finer things in life. Among his bequests were fine china and glass, paintings, jewellery and a wine cabinet.

Father Antony's will also provides some clues about his life before he came to West Hagbourne. It is known that he spent some time in the Manor Park area of London as choir boys from there gave him a silver key chain, a "memory of many happy days in Manor Park". He also had links with a Sister Rose Mary of the Order of St Benedict in Forest Gate, London, as he specified that the organ in the exterior chapel was to be returned to her after his death.

He left his property in Lincolnshire to "Doctor Barnado's Home" and named many people who were to receive gifts of money, furniture and other small

---

LOT 3.

A Brick, Plaster, Timber-built and Thatched

FREEHOLD COTTAGE,

With Garden, Orchard, Yard and Outbuildings,

Well-situate in the centre of the Village, at the junction of Moor Lane with the public Road.

It contains 2 rooms (one used as a Chapel), Wash-house, &c., and 3 Bedrooms, and is occupied by
VINCENT BEISLEY, a weekly tenant,

At a Rent amounting to £5 4s. per annum.

This Lot is bounded by property of Messrs. P. ALDWORTH and G. BEVIS and by the above-mentioned public way, and by the High Road.

The Timber thereon is valued at £13, and *is included in the purchase* ~~the Purchaser shall pay that amount for it in addition to his purchase money~~.

Sale notice for Thatch Cottage indicating that one of the rooms was being used as a chapel in 1895 when the property was put up for sale by the Lousley family

personal items, including his rosary. Father Antony possessed many of the trappings of the priesthood, for example, two chalices, as well as the vestments he wished to be buried in, described as "the alb cincture and girdle with the purple silk maniple stole and velvet chasuble". He expressed a wish to be buried in Garford, Berkshire where he was born, and named the Reverend Eric H Osmund Cooper of Exeter as the clergyman who was to officiate at his funeral in his own chapel in West Hagbourne.

He was clearly an animal lover and possibly a vegetarian since he left £100 to the National Canine Defence League in London and £25 to The Vegetarian Society in Manchester. He also refers to a painting of "Our Lord with the suffering dog" in his chapel. He had a dog named Kean, of whom he was very fond, and he asked Harry Uzzell, one of his executors, to take the following action as soon as possible after his death:

> *Put Kean to sleep in the leather box, about seven tea spoonfuls of spirit put on a piece of rag will be enough for the purpose a large bottle of this will be found on the chest of drawers by my bedside, do not close the holes until he is quite asleep, leave him in box all night and then will Harry make a nice coffin and line it with wool and put him in with all the reverence and bury him by the greenhouse putting something to mark the grave.*

In the event, he did not die in West Hagbourne but in Fleet Cottage Hospital in Hampshire on the 9th of July 1923, and was duly buried in the churchyard of All Saints' Church in Fleet. According to his death certificate, it seems he was staying in Pinegarth, Finchampstead before he went to hospital, but it is not clear why he was there. However, one gets the impression from his will that he travelled around quite a lot and had friends in various parts of the country, as well as in Scotland. He was particularly close to the Reverend Cooper of Exeter, whom he refers to as Father Cooper in his will. He was obviously prepared for the eventuality of dying away from his home as he states in his will: "If I 'pass on' when away from Hagbourne then I wish to be buried in the Church-yard of the parish in which I die."

On his burial record his address was given as St Francis d'Assisi Cottage, West Hagbourne, while the occupation registered on his death certificate was described as Roman Catholic Priest. There is no further record to show what happened to his dog Kean. After his death, most of his property was sold to Frank Napper by his executors.

Despite intensive research, there are many unanswered questions about the life of Father Antony, such as what he did before he came to West Hagbourne, what brought him here, how he came by his wealth and properties, his connections with Lincolnshire and whether he was ever acknowledged as an official priest by any church. Canon Frances Tony Starbuck, a previous incumbent of St Andrew's Church, has made some tentative suggestions:

My hunch is that he was not an ordained priest and perhaps never claimed to be. He may have thought of himself as a self-proclaimed 'monk' or 'hermit' while belonging to none of the recognised religious orders in either the Anglican or Roman Catholic Church. This would not have been all that unusual in the latter period of the 19th century or early part of the 20th when there were quite a number of 'pioneers' around – at least in the Anglican Church – seeking for a revival of the 'religious life'. This would also explain the (self-styled?) title of 'Brother' and even 'Father'. In the monastic tradition both titles can sometimes be used of a lay person. It is quite conceivable that 'Antony' served as a monkish lay pastor at West Hagbourne without celebrating mass or administering the Sacraments.

In any event it does seem that his 'ministry' had little or no official links with either the Anglican or Roman Catholic Churches, though whether he at any time sought recognition by either of the Churches is something that we may never know.

What we do know about Father Antony is that he appeared to have been a kind, good and helpful person who loved animals and was fondly remembered by the people of West Hagbourne where he lived and ministered for more than 20 years.

School days

West Hagbourne does not have a school in the village, but Hagbourne Church of England Primary School in East Hagbourne has always been considered to be the school of both villages. West Hagbourne children have attended the school for generations and have contributed to its development and continued success. People from West Hagbourne have always been active as school governors, members of the Parent-Teacher Association and as Friends of the school. Edna Scott of West Hagbourne was the school secretary for many years.

Before Hagbourne School opened in 1874, children were taught in two cottages which later became a barn. This 'school' was established in 1832 and parents paid 2d a week for their children to attend. When Hagbourne School was opened it was a four-class school with one master and Ernest Napper and Alice Childs acting as assistant teachers. Parents had to pay according to their occupation. For example, in 1880 a labourer paid 2d for the first child and 1d for any others. Tradesmen, engine drivers and policemen paid 3d for each child whilst a master tradesman or farmer was charged 6d per child. These fees were abolished in 1891.

A Sunday School was established as early as 1824 and had twice as many attendees as the weekly school in 1854. When the Hagbourne School opened it was made responsible for "the religious and moral instruction of all the scholars attending" and was also allowed to hold the Sunday School on the school's premises. Truancy and poor punctuality provided major headaches for the teachers. Mothers often kept the girls at home to look after the younger children whilst they worked in the fields, and farmers continued to employ children in contradiction of the Education Act.

By 1892 the numbers had grown to about 150 children. It was recorded that James Goodall was in charge and had "great difficulty in maintaining order through the school". In 1901 poor Mr Goodall died in the Radcliffe Infirmary of a perforated ulcer. During the First World War the school had four different head teachers, all women, while the head master, Mr Edward Packer, was away on military service.

The school became a true primary school in 1931 and the older pupils were transferred to Didcot Senior School. In 1970 the school was officially named Hagbourne Church of England Primary School. By 1978, Silver Jubilee Year, 127 pupils were on the roll. Corporal punishment was carried out until 1986 when it was abolished in line with the rest of the country. A punishment book was kept, recording each misdemeanour and the type of punishment meted out. This book still exists today.

Page from the East Hagbourne School punishment book featuring Nelly Woodley's name on the 14th of December 1911. She had molested a boy on the way to school

Nelly Woodley on a visit to the seaside

One West Hagbourne child to appear rather frequently in the punishment book was Nelly Woodley. Born in 1903, Nelly was christened Ellen Elizabeth. Her mother died a month after Nelly's birth, and she was looked after at the workhouse in Wallingford. Her father, Jabez, made sure that he visited her as often as possible, and when Nelly was five he remarried. Nelly returned to live in West Hagbourne with her father and stepmother Matilda in a small cottage in Moor Lane.

When Nelly grew up she moved to London but she kept in touch with her West Hagbourne relatives, particularly the family of her cousin Alice Powell. Nelly often turned up without any notice and she always caused a stir when she came to visit. She dressed in fur coats and very high heels and wore bright red lipstick. She also smoked cigarettes from a holder which was considered quite exotic by her country cousins. Some of her relatives visited Nelly and her son in London. Her niece, Mary Bishop, recorded the following entry in her diary on the 3rd of November 1947:

> ... *cycled down to Didcot Station with mum, arrived at Paddington Station and went in Taxi with Jimmy (Nel's son) to auntie Nel's basement. It was lovely and we had lunch in a café. Then went to Selfridges and had Tea in a big place where bands played to us.*

Nelly Woodley died on the 19th of July 1977 and is buried next to her relations in Hagbourne cemetery.

Despite vivid memories of being caned and made to stand on a form for a whole lesson, many ex-pupils have happier recollections of their school days. As there was no playing field at the school, rounders and hockey were played in a meadow down 'the moors' – the fields on either side of the school path between West and East Hagbourne. The moors were mostly meadows then, where violets and cowslips grew in profusion.

During the Second World War there were approximately 50 evacuee children attending the school, and it was about this time that school dinners were first served in the village hall. However, there were considerable problems with delivery of these meals. Sometimes the meals arrived late which meant that afternoon classes also started late. Until a kitchen was built in 1972 to provide school dinners on the premises, many children took sandwiches to school. They were allowed to leave the school grounds at lunch-time and they would often wander up to Cox's, a house just past the old village shop (no longer there), to buy fruit. Then they would stop to watch the village blacksmith, Curly Belcher, working at the Fleur de Lys where he had his smithy.

The school path

Many West Hagbourne villagers have vivid memories of the walk along the path to East Hagbourne as this was the only way of getting to school for many years. This is how it is remembered by someone who walked to school from West Hagbourne in the 1960s:

> Idealistically, the memories should be of hot summer days when the fields were full of corn and we dragged our cardigans along behind us, without any care for our mothers' wrath when we arrived home half an hour late with dusty clothes. But of course the most vivid memories are of winter days, when we had no feeling in our fingers or toes. Even after very heavy snowfalls, when we all prayed that the railway bridge would be impassable due to very high snowdrifts, we all made the trek to school. However, our hearts would lighten as we turned for home. It would then, of course, take another hour to get home as we were otherwise occupied with snowball fights and arguing over who had the largest footprint.
>
> On reflection, the school walk was an insight into the natural world that no 'town child' could ever envisage. I always remember the hedgerows on a white frosty morning, with huge white gleaming cobwebs and old birds' nests looking almost like little white baskets.
>
> Once or twice in spring we would be late for school because we had stopped to see a calf being born. The sight of this leggy little creature, covered in mucus and blood did not repulse us We always waited until the mother had licked it clean and then we were happy to continue on our way, knowing that we would have to creep into assembly, hopefully unnoticed!

I would imagine that we were quite a noisy bunch, as we never stopped chattering, and when the cuckoos were in full flow we actually believed that they were calling to us, and we answered accordingly.

The railway line was still operational – this was great fun. We could hear the train approaching us. The driver would always give us a huge wave and blow his whistle, and then we would run as fast as we could to try to be under the bridge when the train passed overhead. The noise was tremendous, and after the train had passed we would all scream and howl to get the full effect of the resounding echo that the bridge supplied.

Of course, we do have to come back to the 'hot sunny days' because it was absolute bliss to dawdle home, first stopping at Abbot's barn which exuded the unforgettable smell of apples, and if we were lucky we got a free sample – delicious – although slightly bruised. The next stop was the stream, where we raced our sticks, then removed our shoes and sat dangling our feet in the cool water. Then came the wheat fields, the best times were when the corn had been baled and we created a whole adventure playground by repositioning the bales. I don't quite know what the farmer thought of this, but as far as I know he never complained. Finally we would feed grass to the horses, have a chat to the cows, and make our way to our respective houses where I'm sure everyone would immediately ask for a long cold drink.

These memories may have been given a rosy glow by the passing of time, but to my mind they were truly 'halcyon days'.

Village traditions

There was more to school life than getting an education; there was also lots of fun. Some traditional celebrations which have since died out, though they are still remembered with nostalgia by some older villagers, have their origins in pagan times. One of these, the Hagbourne Feast, was a joint celebration enjoyed by the villagers of West and East Hagbourne and Northbourne. It was usually held during the week following the second Sunday after Whitsunday and lasted over several days. The actual Feast Day, or Festival of Dedication, was held on the Tuesday of that week and the children were given a day off from school. For many, the week of the Hagbourne Feast was the highlight of the year in the period between the two World Wars when most people's social life was confined to village activities.

The Hagbourne Feast took place in East Hagbourne and was a varied mixture of special church services, some outdoor hymn-singing in the orchards, wild flower competitions, sporting activities, country dancing and the famous afternoon tea. Sometimes there would be maypole dancing, once a feature of life in many English villages. Maypole dancing certainly originated in pagan times when the maypole was a symbol of fertility and merry making in Britain. The maypole was often a simple birch trunk decorated with garlands of May and other spring flowers. The plaiting of the maypole ribbons and the dancing that went with it were not introduced until the end of the nineteenth century. Until then, maypole dancing consisted of dancing round in a ring or country dances. Maypole dancing was forbidden by the Puritans during the Civil War but it was revived during the reign of Charles II and May Day celebrations and the crowning of the May Queen have survived in many parts of the country today. The maypole dancing at the Hagbourne Feast took place in the orchard, in a spot close to the headmaster's house so that the children could hear the musical accompaniment through his open window.

In the evening there was the much-anticipated fair with stalls and side-shows lining the village street. There were two roundabouts in competition: the one drawn by ponies and – according to the older children – the superior steam-driven version. The donkey rides, swing boats, confetti-throwing, water-squirting and coconut shies all provided an opportunity for everyone to let their hair down on this special occasion. The dance which followed in the village hall was worthy of Glen Miller himself, according to one veteran of the Hagbourne Feast days.

Although the Hagbourne Feast only remains today in people's memories, the Hagbourne Fête has carried on many of the traditions remembered from the Feast Day. There are modern versions of the rides, opportunities to win competitions

Photograph of maypole dancers, possibly taken at the Hagbourne Feast just before the First World War. At least two of the girls, Annie Dawson, far right and Jane Warner, third from right, were from West Hagbourne

based on harmless fun, side-shows and stalls. Just like the feast, the fête is focused on providing a memorable day for the children of both West and East Hagbourne, though the aim of raising funds to support the fabric of the parish church of the Hagbournes is more recent.

The May song

Another tradition rooted in pre-Christian times is the celebration of May Day. On the first of May each year, the children of West Hagbourne used to make flower garlands. Nobody knows when they first started to do this but we know it was practised in the early 1900s and the tradition continued into the 1940s. The children collected flowers such as cowslips and daisies from the meadows down Moor Lane, and made them into garlands the day before May Day itself. Originally they were made into hoops but later they made crosses. Early on the morning of May Day, the children went round the village and knocked on doors, holding up their garlands and singing the May song. For this they would receive a few pennies or possibly a telling-off. West Hagbourne was one of the last villages to keep this May Day tradition going locally, though it was discouraged by the school headmaster and eventually died out.

THE MAY SONG
(as sung by the children of West Hagbourne)

Good morning young ladies and gentlemen
I wish you a happy day
I've come to show you my garland
because it's the First of May,
Happy day, Joyful day,
Winter has gone and passed away.

The cuckoo comes in April,
He sings his song in May,
He sucks the little birdies' eggs*
Then flies away*
Cuckoo, Cuckoo, Cuckoo!

*These lines are a variation of the old May song:
In the middle of June he changes his tune, And then he flies away.

Nobody knows why the the children of West Hagbourne chose their version. Perhaps they thought that the old words were a bit tame and that by introducing a bit of sadness to the story they might bring tears to people's eyes and add a penny or two to the collection.

The origins of the old May song probably relate to the significance of the call of the cuckoo which was welcomed as a sign of good luck in most countries. It was the herald of spring and brought the promise of a new season of growing crops. The first note of the cuckoo's song was supposed to bring good luck and prosperity to those who heard it. The line sung by the children of West Hagbourne – "He sucks the little birdies' eggs" – probably refers to the cuckoo's habit of laying its egg in the nest of another bird. When it hatched, the cuckoo grew much bigger than the other fledglings and would oust them from the nest.

As well as Feast Days, May Days, sports days, Christmas parties and film shows at the school on Friday afternoons, the other big events to look forward to were the village outings. When a communal trip was organised, the favourite destination was the seaside which seemed so far away in the days before people had cars. The anticipation and planning of these trips turned into enjoyable events. A lot of effort went into raising money for these outings for the village children. John Lay organised village fêtes in his garden at Manor Farm. These were as pleasurable as the outings themselves and are still remembered as some of the happiest days of their childhood by quite a few long-standing villagers. After these West Hagbourne fêtes there would often be a village dance attended by villagers of all ages. The photograph on page 232 was taken after one of these dances.

Children enjoying activities during one of the fêtes held at Manor Farm in aid of a village outing to the seaside

It was not only the children who enjoyed the West Hagbourne outings to the seaside. One elderly lady who had quite a memorable experience on a trip to Brighton was Mrs Polly Sheard. She was always known as Granny Sheard although we don't know why because she didn't have any grandchildren. It was most likely a mark of affection by all those who knew her. Granny Sheard lived in a cottage miles from anywhere, right at the top of Hagbourne Hill. She was generous and gentle with a lovely smile but she was also tough and partial to a pinch or two of snuff.

She made few concessions to the changing seasons when it came to dress and was known to wear several black skirts, all at the same time. She always wore a wide brimmed hat which everyone believed was glued on because it never fell off, no matter how hard the wind blew. The pram she pushed on her regular visits to and from Didcot was known locally as her 'Austin Seven'. Locals swore that they had seen her sitting in the pram charging down a straight section of Hagbourne Hill with her skirts acting as a parachute cum brake. Whether this was true or not we don't know but what is certain is that she loved to join the other villagers on organised trips to the seaside.

There are a couple of incidents which some can still remember. The first

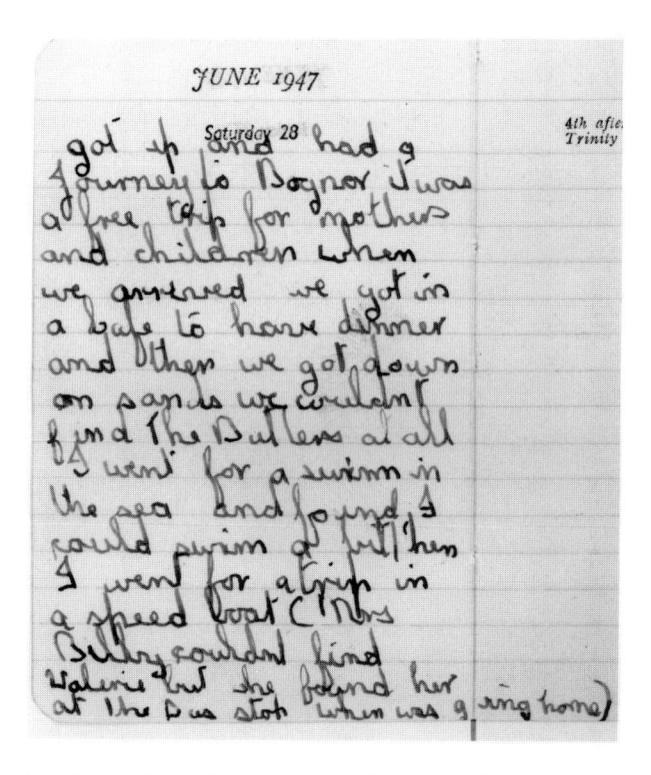

An extract from the diary of schoolgirl Mary Bishop, describing a trip to Bognor on Saturday the 28th of June 1947

Granny Sheard who lived on Hagbourne Hill

This photograph, taken at a village dance in the 1950s, includes representatives of most of the families living in West Hagbourne at the time. Back row, L to R: Maureen Webb, Robin Marshall, John Wernham, Alice Bishop, Pam Lay, Harry Bishop, Charlie Lay, next three unknown, Barber Warner, Wipsi Powell. Second row, L to R: Freda Dawson, Bert Dawson, Jack Butler, Mary Bishop behind Joy Dawson, Eileen Dawson, Sylvia Ingham, Alec Ingham, Margaret Butler. Front row, L to R: Elizabeth Buxey, unknown, Fred Warner, David Dawson, Hugh Ryan, behind unknown, Jack Spurret, Mervyn Goodenough

one was when she went for an involuntary swim with all her clothes on. She had intended to paddle but while standing still and looking down at the sand moving about her feet, she became dizzy and fell into the sea. Another time, on a day out at Brighton, she somehow got mixed up with the extras involved in making the film 'Brighton Rock'. No one knows if she got into the film but she certainly missed the bus home and spent the night in a police station, arriving home the next day courtesy of the police. She enjoyed it, she said!

Incidents like these never succeeded in removing the cheerful welcoming smile that was always on her face. This is one of the reasons why she will never be forgotten. She often said that in living on top of Hagbourne Hill she was "nearer to heaven" than the rest of us and there was perhaps more than a ring of truth in that.

Another ancient Hagbourne tradition which continues to this day is bellringing. The Hagbourne Bellringing Society is over 100 years old and has a chequered past. In 1897 the ringers were sacked by the vicar of St Andrew's Church, the Reverend William Baker, because of their inappropriate behaviour. Their misdemeanours remain their secret but such a thing would never happen today as Hagbourne ringers take their duties very seriously indeed. The modern society is one of the strongest in Oxfordshire and has always rung regularly for both Sunday morning and evening services at St Andrew's Church. Villagers get an extra treat on Tuesday evenings when the sound of the bells wafts across to West Hagbourne as the band of ringers hold their weekly practice session.

The Hagbourne ringers are just as skilled on the handbells. These are usually preferred for the annual Christmas concert in the church. The band have also rung the handbells in West Hagbourne at Christmas and they gave a special performance at the West Hagbourne Open Day in 1996. One of their most stalwart ringers for many years was the late Bob Blond who lived in West Hagbourne for most of his life.

Not all West Hagbourne's residents have been permanent or lived in conventional houses. Up until the 1950s gypsies lived in caravans in Moor Lane. They provided the fun fairs which travelled around the countryside during the summer months. One of these fairs was regularly held at Abbott's farm near the church. During their stay in West Hagbourne, the gypsies used to practice their ancient craft of peg-making. The pegs were made from willow which was shaped into two pieces, bound together by a piece of metal and fastened with a small pin. The willow grew in abundance in an area known as the 'withy beds' at the bottom of Moor Lane. The pegs were taken round the villages and sold door-to-door.

Whilst many village events were annual or seasonal, there were also lots of activities, clubs and organisations which continued on a more regular basis. One of these was the West Hagbourne cycle speedway team run by Mr Herbert. The team had the use of a track in Bill Pinnell's field behind the council houses in York Road.

It was a popular local sport in the early 1950s with village teams competing against each other.

Many women in West Hagbourne have been keen supporters of various organisations and clubs, and have been particularly involved in fund-raising and charity work. Two of the most well-known in recent years were Miranda Mayne and Isobell Walmsley who were close friends and neighbours. They were also very active in the Hagbourne branch of the Women's Institute (WI) during the 1950s and 1960s. Mrs Mayne was the president when the branch finally had to close owing to dwindling numbers as more women started going out to work. However, both women were able to join the Didcot branch and continue their membership of the WI. Mrs Mayne went on to serve a term as the Berkshire Chairman after being County Organiser for over 20 years.

Isobell Walmsley came to West Hagbourne in 1954 on the retirement of her husband Canon Walmsley. They lived at Blissetts together with their spaniel called The Flyer. They later built a modern house next to Blissetts when Canon Walmsley started to go blind. In 1971, soon after celebrating his ninetieth birthday, Canon Walmsley had a fall and died in hospital a few months later.

Photograph of the Hagbourne handbell ringers taken in 1912. A few faces have been identified but the rest are unknown. Standing, far right: Tom East. Seated, L to R: 1) Frank Napper, who lived in East Hagbourne 4) Dennis Napper, grandfather of Dennis and Rex Napper of Grove Manor Farm 6) Tom East, father of the boy behind him

One of the gypsies making pegs from willow in Moor Lane. It is believed that her name was Betsy Loveridge

West Hagbourne cycle speedway team photographed at Pinnell's orchard, West Hagbourne during the early 1950s. L to R: John Jubber, Pat Belcher, Mervyn Greenough, Victor Dawson, Melvin Herbert, Pat Dawson, Joe Napper, Dick Powell. Front: Mr Herbert

After a year of grieving, and of finding renewed strength, Mrs Walmsley launched into the fifteen-year period for which she is still so vividly remembered in West Hagbourne. She lived life to the full: mowing the lawn and, with the help and advice of Jack Napper, growing flowers and vegetables; driving the car and delivering meals-on-wheels; walking to church at Upton; making jams and marmalade for charity sales and, especially, re-making greetings cards for the Church of England Children's Society. A debilitating stroke in October 1986, when she was in her ninety second year, resulted in her having to spend her remaining years in a nursing home until she died in 1993.

Isobell Walmsley left £250 to the William Tyrrell Trust, a charity for the benefit of the poor of West Hagbourne. A prunus tree has been planted in the garden by the bus shelter and a plaque was erected there in her memory in 1994.

Another memorial to the many villagers who have contributed to village life in the past is the seat under the chestnut tree in the Square. The erection of this seat was prompted by the death of Ken Dawson in 1996. Ken was a keen gardener and champion vegetable grower. He is remembered with great affection by many people in the village.

Celebrations

Although most of West Hagbourne's entertainments and celebrations have been centred on the village, this does not mean that West Hagbourne has remained untouched by national events. West and East Hagbourne celebrated together the Coronation of Elizabeth II on the 2nd of June 1953, a year after she came to the throne.

In June 1977 the two villages celebrated her Silver Jubilee. The festivities lasted ten days, starting with a tea party for senior citizens and ending with a thanksgiving service in the church and community singing at Upper Cross. On Jubilee Day itself there was bellringing, a church service and a majestic procession and pageant which started from Manor Farm, West Hagbourne, wound through the village and finished up at the recreation ground in East Hagbourne where judging of the pageant took place. This was followed by sporting events and a barbecue.

A modern village

At the beginning of this chapter, the village pub was described as a spit and sawdust place at the start of the twentieth century. By the end of the century things were very different. The Horse and Harrow has been considerably enlarged, offers food and provides amenities for families as well as outdoor seating. The new licensing laws allow it to remain open all day, so that nobody needs to hang about in Cow Lane until 12 o'clock, as they did in the old days. Although Arch Napper would find a very different Horse and Harrow if he walked in today, it is still the focus for many community activities, in particular fund-raising for charity.

There are some keen gardeners in West Hagbourne and quite a few of them maintain impressive vegetable patches. There are always some prize-winning entries from West Hagbourne in the Hagbourne Produce Show, whilst the pumpkin club creates stiff competition for the largest pumpkin or marrow. Gardeners also vie for the Madge Trophy. This is a cup presented by Mrs Jean Madge in memory of her late husband Cliff, himself an enthusiastic gardener. The trophy is awarded annually for the 'best kept front garden' in the village.

West Hagbourne also had some success in the past in the 'Britain in Bloom' competition. The village came first in the small village section six times between 1982 and 1988. The trough of flowers by the pond, the garden next to the bus stop, the tubs under the chestnut tree at the heart of the village and the spring bulbs planted randomly all along the road in and out of the village, all contributed to these successes. However, in 1997, it was decided to withdraw from the competition when the judging criteria were changed.

Although there is no longer a Hagbourne branch of the Women's Institute, there are still plenty of clubs, societies and special interest groups in action, some of which are shared with East Hagbourne. One of these is the East and West Hagbourne Society, established in 1962 to promote and preserve the rural character

The Jubilee procession on its way from Manor Farm to East Hagbourne. Dennis Napper of Grove Manor Farm is driving the tractor

and integrity of the two villages when it seemed that Didcot was expanding into an area known as the Hagbourne Triangle. This did not eventuate but today there is a new threat posed by plans to further expand the town of Didcot by several thousand houses.

In 1991 a group of villagers got together to research the history of West Hagbourne. They called themselves the West Hagbourne Village History Group and this book is the result of their work over the past nine years. In the summer of 1996, the Group organised the first Village Open Day to raise funds for its publication. It was a great success, not just in terms of the money raised, but in the way it brought the village together. As one villager commented afterwards "Now I feel as though I am part of the village". Another said that the Open Day reminded him of the old days when John Lay held the village fête in his garden.

Not only was the Open Day a huge success but it also spawned a new village organisation called the West Hagbourne Village Association. This group was initially set up in 1997 to plan the next Open Day in 1998. Since then it has gone from strength to strength, organising popular village suppers and helping to stage the Millennium Pageant, together with East Hagbourne.

A new millennium

This story of West Hagbourne has looked back over a thousand years of history, with one step even further back into the Bronze Age. Now, at the beginning of a brand new millennium, the village looks towards the future. The threat of increased traffic through the village now seems a certainty. It remains to be seen how the increase in the number of houses in Didcot, on the northern boundary of the parish, will affect the rural nature of West Hagbourne. Farming is also in crisis as never before and although the village still holds on to its five farms, changes are already afoot as farmers struggle to respond to political and economic forces outside their control.

However, there are some positive aspects to some of these changes, not least the recent move by farmers to take an active role in the conservation of the countryside. The villagers of West Hagbourne are rightly proud and protective of their beautiful village and its historic houses and keep a sharp eye out for any threat to its environment. A whole section at the heart of the village has been declared a conservation area and this is carefully monitored by the Parish Council.

Also, after many years of lobbying on the part of the village children and their parents, a West Hagbourne playing field is finally in prospect. This will be especially welcome in view of the further impending increase in through traffic on roads which were once meandering village lanes.

The countryside has been at the heart of this story of West Hagbourne but the best way to learn about it is to experience it. One way to do this is to take one of the nature walks compiled by one of the villagers. These walks follow the public pathways and tracks which weave their way round the village and through the

Nature Walks
in and around West Hagbourne

Researched and compiled by Dee Smith

WALK 1
A short circular walk of about 1 mile starting from the Horse and Harrow and lasting approximately ½–1 hour.

Butterflies
Brimstone, Brown argus, Common blue, Fritillary, Gate keeper, Large skipper, Large tortoiseshell, Large white, Small tortoiseshell, Meadow brown, Orange tip, Peacock, Red admiral, Ringlet, Small skipper, Small white, Speckled Wood, Wall brown

Wild Flowers
How many of these wildflowers can you identify?

Winter/Spring
Colt's-foot

Spring
Bird's-foot trefoil, Black bryony, Bugle, Charlock, Common field speedwell, Common fumitory, Common poppy, Common sorrel, Common vetch, Cow parsley, Creeping buttercup, Daisy, Dandelion, Field forget-me-nots, Field pansy, Field penny cress, Goatsbeard, Greater plantain, Ground elder, Herb Robert, Lords-and-ladies, Mayweed, Meadow buttercup, Oxford ragwort, Red clover, Ribwort plantain, White dead nettle

Summer
Agrimony, Bittersweet, Bladder campion, Broad-leaved dock, Cleavers (Goosegrass), Common fleabane, Common mallow, Common nettle, Deadly nightshade, Dog rose, Field scabious, Great mullein, Hawkweed, Hedge bindweed Hemlock, Hogweed, Knapweed, Meadow cranesbill, Meadowsweet, Pineapple weed, Red campion, Scarlet pimpernel, Silverweed, Sneezewort, Spear thistle, Sweetheart, Tufted vetch, Vervain, White clover

Autumn
Field mushrooms

All year round
Common chickweed, Groundsel, Shepherd's purse, Various types of grass

Always follow the country code:
- Guard against all risk of fire
- Fasten all gates
- Keep dogs under proper control
- Keep to paths across farmland
- Avoid damaging hedges, fences and walls
- Leave no litter
- Safeguard water supplies
- Protect wildlife, wild plants and trees
- Go carefully on country roads
- Respect the life of the countryside

Further details of wildlife to be found in and around West Hagbourne are included on a separate Wildlife Information Sheet available from Mary Wiley, Silva Felix, York Road, Tel: 850451.

Illustrations by Anne Lawton

Sold in aid of the West Hagbourne History Group

WALK 1

❶ Starting from the Horse and Harrow on Main Street, cross the road and follow the cart track up as far as the ash tree.
❷ Turn right and head for the silage clamp.
❸ Turn right again and walk down the by-way to York Road. Continue straight on almost to the end.
❹ Turn right along the track between Lizardbank and The Laurels and follow track to the junction.
❺ Turn left to return to the Horse and Harrow.

Watch out for the following birds and butterflies which you should see on your way

Birds
Blackbird, Black-headed gull, Blue tit, Chaffinch, Chiffchaff, Collared dove, Common gull, Corn bunting, Crow, Cuckoo, Dunnock (hedge sparrow), Fieldfare, Golden plover, Goldfinch, Greater spotted woodpecker, Great tit, Greenfinch, Green woodpecker, Heron, Herring gull, Hobby (occasionally), House martin, House sparrow, Jackdaw, Jay, Kestrel, Lesser whitethroat, Linnet, Little owl, Long-tailed tit, Magpie, Mallard, Mistle thrush, Moorhen, Partridge, Peewit (Lapwing), Pheasant, Pied wagtail, Redwing, Robin, Rook, Serin, Skylark, Song thrush, Sparrowhawk, Starling, Swallow, Swift, Woodpigeon, Wren, Yellowhammer

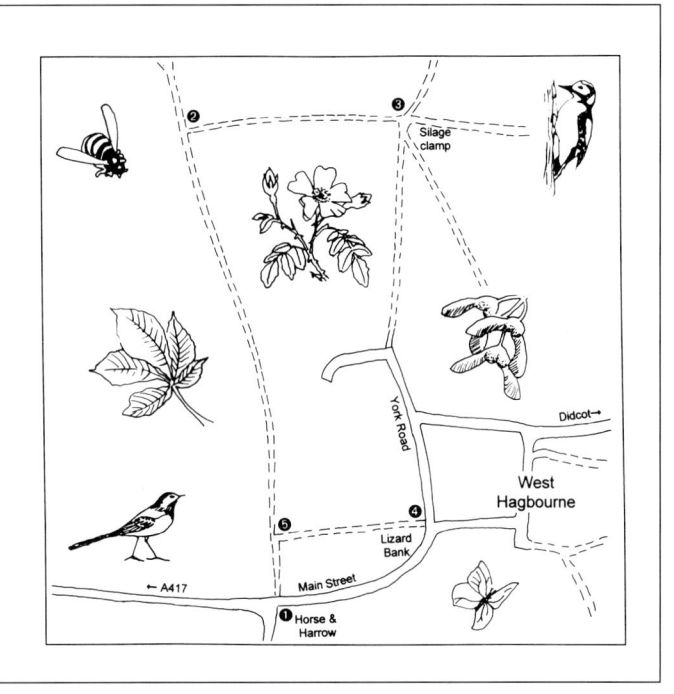

One of four nature walks in and around West Hagbourne, compiled by Dee Smith for the Village History Group

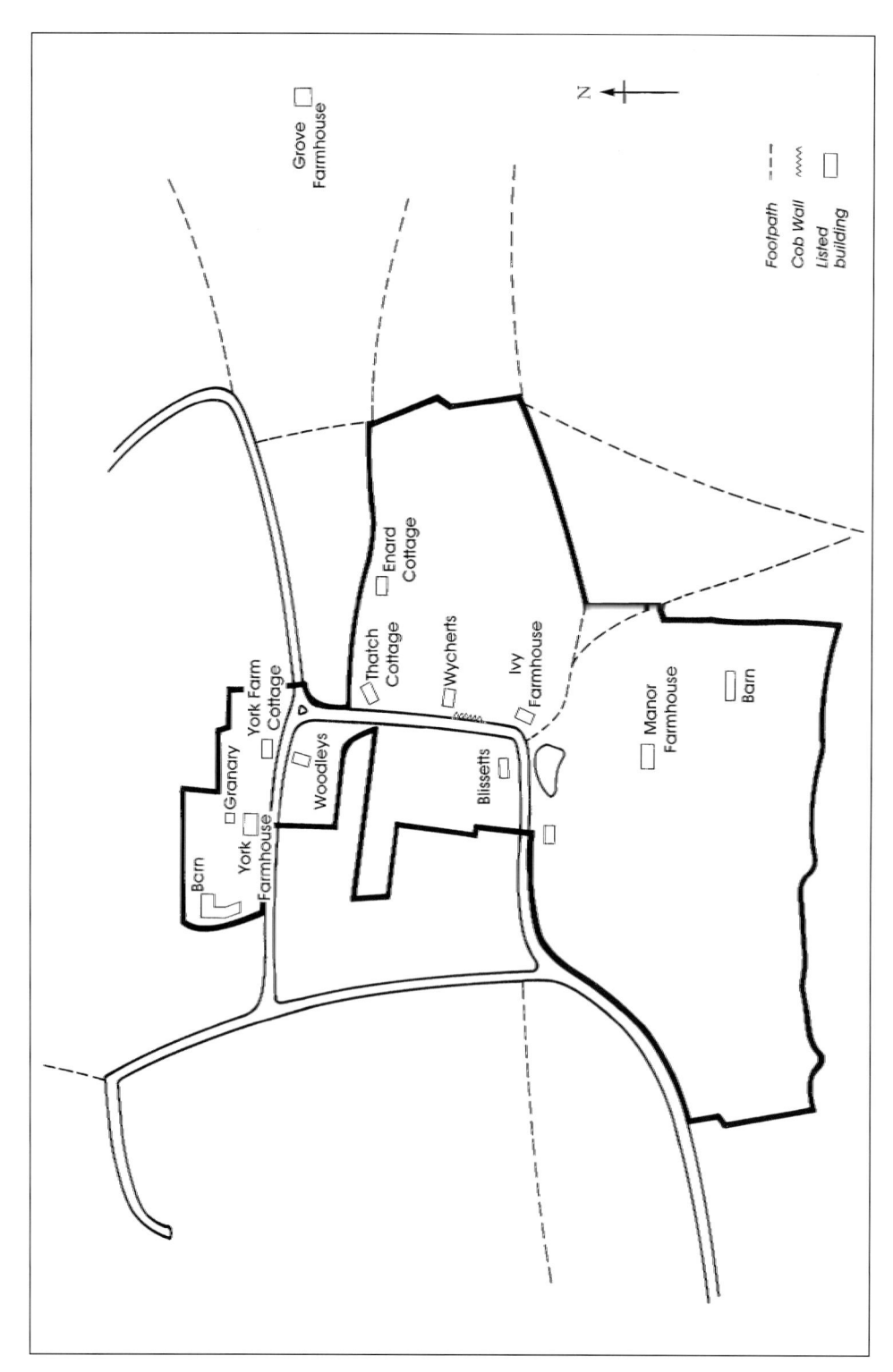

Map of West Hagbourne indicating the designated area of conservation

fields. The walks point out the local flora and fauna which one may see on the walk at different times of the year.

It is tempting to imagine Clarice de Windsor and John York strolling hand in hand across the fields along these ancient West Hagbourne tracks, perhaps stopping along the way to admire the ducks on the pond. Although this is a very romanticised idea, it is hoped that this story of West Hagbourne has brought to life the many people who have lived in this village over the last one thousand years.

Sources – Horse and Harrow

Map of West Hagbourne, 1754, Berkshire Record Office, Reading.
Census of 1577 quoted from: H A Monckton, *A History of English Ale and Beer*, 1966.
Norman Barber, *A Century of British Brewers*, 1890–1900, The Brewery History Society, 1996.
James Bond and John Rhodes, *The Oxfordshire Brewer*, Oxfordshire Museum Services, 1985.
West Hagbourn Inclosure Award, 27 July 1843, Berkshire Record Office, Reading. Q/RDC 39A.
Extract from the Company Trust Deed, Morland Co., Ltd, 27 November 1897. Morland Archive.
Story of the 'Tin Hotel' and Jimmy Shaw related by Sonny Butler.

Sources – The village shop

Reminiscences of Sonny Butler, Barbara Blond and the late Rene Pinkney.
Census of England and Wales, Returns for 1841–1891.

Sources – The village post office

Kelly's Directories 1887, 1903 and 1936.
Unofficial receiving house: *Wallingford Post Office Minute Book*, 1 January 1847.
History of Wallingford Post Office: letter from Reverend Ray Smith, quoting his, as yet, unpublished history of Wallingford Post Office, 10 April 1999.
Letter box: Ordnance Survey Map, *East Hagbourne and Blewbury Parishes*, 1876, The British Library Board, 1986.
Misconduct of E Herman: *Wallingford Post Office Minute Book*, Vol 184, 1857, p196.
The minutes of the annual assembly of the West Hagbourne parish meeting, 4 May 1936. Held by the Parish Clerk, West Hagbourne.

Sources – West Hagbourne's mystery man

Certificate of Marriage, George and Elizabeth Bullock, 2 June 1858, Abingdon Registration District.

Certificate of Birth, Edwin George Bullock, 15 November 1859, Abingdon Registration District.
Certificate of Death, George Bullock, 29 August 1900, Wallingford Registration District.
Certificate of Death, Herbert Bullock, 10 November 1916, Wallingford Registration District.
Certificate of Death, Esther Bullock, 20 April 1918, Wallingford Registration District.
Last Will and Testament, George Bullock, 16 July 1900, Oxford Registration District.
Kelly's Directory 1863, 1868, 1876, 1887, 1899, 1903, 1920.
Census of England and Wales, Returns for 1881, 1891.
Purchase of Ragged Farm: *Indenture of Conveyance*, 14 February 1901.
Purchase of Enard Cottage: *Abstract of Title Deeds*, 20 March 1902.
Purchase of Thatch Cottage: *Abstract of Title Deeds*, 29 September 1904.
Evidence of chapel: Sale notice for Thatch Cottage, 1895.
Last Will and Testament of the Reverend Edwin George Bullock, 25 March 1923.
Certificate of Death, Edwin Bullock, 12 July 1923, Southampton Registration District.
Letter from Canon F Tony Starbuck, The Anglican Church in Te Puke, New Zealand, 15 January 1994.

Other avenues of research:
All Saints with SS Philip & James and Ancell's Farm, Fleet, Hants.
Barnardos, Ilford, Essex.
Capuchin Provincial Curia, Franciscan Friary, Erith, Kent.
Catholic Church of Our Lady, Fleet, Hants.
The Catholic Family History Society, Ealing, London.
Diocesan Archivist, St Joseph's, Diocese of Portsmouth, Hants.
The Honourable Georgina Stonor, Henley-on-Thames, Oxon.
Little Ilford Rectory, Manor Park, London.
Manor Park Catholic Parish, St Stephen and St Nicholas, Manor Park, London.
Parish of the Sacred Heart, Exeter, Devon.
Probate Registry, Postal Services and Copies Department, York.
Provincial Curia of the Order of Friars Manor, Franciscan Friary, Forest Gate, London.
The Society of Saint Francis, The Friary, Dorchester, Dorset.
St Francis of Assisi Church, Stratford, London.
St Mary's Priory, Faringdon, Oxon.
Westminster Diocesan Archives, Kensington, London.

Sources – School days

Hagbourne Church of England Primary School: Information from Monica Lawson of East Hagbourne.
Hagbourne School 1874–1974, an informal history of Hagbourne School written to commemorate the school's centenary.
Reminiscences of Irene Butler, Barbara Blond and Jan Marriott.

Sources – Village traditions

Hagbourne Feast: information from Jill Churchman, Sonny Butler and Sue Robinson.
Maypole dancing and the May song: Jean Harrowven, *Origins of Rhymes, Songs and Sayings*, Pryor Publications, 1998.
Memories of Mrs Sheard from Sonny Butler.
Memories of Mrs Walmsley from her daughter Ann Farquhar.

Acknowledgements

The West Hagbourne Village History Group would like to express its gratitude to all those who have helped to make this book possible. Thanks go to Malcolm Brownsword, Joan Durbin, Ann Lawton and Andrea Mitchell for maps and drawings; to Jillian Hedges and Ted Kendrick for research assistance; to Robin Sanders and Susan Stewart for their assistance with translation and to Jo Cormier for deciphering manuscripts and editorial advice. We are indebted to John Baile, Janet Cockburn, Elizabeth Gill, Mary Jackson, Marion Judd, Rose Millett and Sue Totterdell for their invaluable proof reading and to Melanie Hill who has typed so untiringly for us. Thanks also to Judy and Stuart Dewey for their advice.

We would also like to acknowledge the help we have received from the Romano-British Department of the British Museum, Susan Lisk of Oxfordshire County Archaeological Services, the British Library, the Public Record Office, the Record Offices of Berkshire, Oxfordshire and Wiltshire and last, but by no means least, the staff of Didcot Library who have dealt so patiently and efficiently with our many requests.

Our thanks also go to all those who have given us donations, including the Lloyd Charitable Trust, the SODC (Millennium Project), UKAEA Harwell, the West Hagbourne Parish Council, individual villagers and all those who have supported our fund-raising efforts.

Finally, thanks must go to Arthur (Sonny) Butler for all his reminiscences as well as all those, too numerous to mention individually, who have lent us photos, deeds, account books and shared their memories with us.

The Village History Group: Eleanor Bowey, Diane Garland, Josie Hill, Jan Marriott, Mary Ann le May, Bernard Mead, Sheila Taylor, Linda Thompson, Val Walton and Mary Wiley (Chairman).

Time Chart

NATIONAL EVENTS

871	Alfred the Great becomes king
1042	Edward the Confessor becomes king
1066	Battle of Hastings William I becomes king
1086	Domesday Book completed
1100	Death of William II Henry I becomes king
1139	Civil War between Stephen and Matilda
1154	Henry II becomes king
1170	Murder of Thomas à Becket
1199	John becomes king
1215	Magna Carta signed
1265	First House of Commons
1266	Henry III becomes king
1270	Edward I becomes king
1284	Edward I erected Conway Castle
1327	Edward II deposed and murdered at Berkeley Castle Edward III becomes king
1348	Black Death – almost half the population died

WEST HAGBOURNE EVENTS

891	King Alfred's charter Hagbournes exchanged for other land
1042	Alwin holds West Hagbourne
1086	Domesday Book records mill in West Hagbourne; Walter fitz Other holds West Hagbourne, becomes constable of Windsor Castle and founder of the Windsor dynasty
1100	William fitz Walter becomes constable of Windsor Castle
1133	Henry I grants tithes of East and West Hagbourne to Cirencester Abbey

12th Century
   St Andrew's Church enlarged

1284	Oldest part of York Farm built
1355	Edmund de Cheldrey owns Watlingtons Manor

		1357	Approximate date of the marriage of Clarice de Drokensford to Richard de Windsor
		1367	Richard de Windsor dies
		1368	Survey of West Hagbourne manor recorded
		1372/1373	Clarice marries John York
1376	Alice Perrers impeached	1376	Alice Perrers; wife of William de Windsor and mistress of Edward III
1381	Peasants' Revolt		
1399	Henry III becomes king		
		Early 15th Century	York family rebuild and extend the south aisle and chapel
		1403	Clarice York dies. Windsor manor in ruins
		1410/1411	Rental of the manor of West Hagbourne mentions a High Cross in village
1413	Henry V becomes king	1413	John York dies
1415	Henry V defeats French at Agincourt		
		1445	John (son) and Joan York die
1455	The Wars of the Roses begin; end of feudalism		
1485	Henry VII; end of the Wars of the Roses		
1487	Court of Star Chamber established		
1509	Henry VIII becomes king		
1533	Henry VIII divorces Catherine of Aragon	1533	Sir Andrew, Baron de Windsor created
1539	Dissolution of monasteries	1539	Chapel disappears
		1545	Alice Aldworth buried at St Andrew's; Robert Tyrrold dies
		1549	Thomas Windsor marries Mary Beckingham, uniting the two Hagbourne manors
1555	Highways Act	*Mid 16th Century*	Both manors owned by the Windsor family
1558	Elizabeth I becomes queen		
		1565	Land at the Downe sold to Dunche and Braybrooke
1588	The Armada		

Late 16th Century
    Attempts made at colonisation
1597 Poor Law
1601 Poor Law
1641 Protestation drawn up   1641 Henry Fluddier's will
1642 Civil War begins   1642 Down enclosed; Protestation signed by villagers; Thomas de Windsor fights on the king's side

1644 Charles I summoned Parliament in Oxford; Second Battle of Newbury – Royalists' victory   1644 Royalist & Parliamentary forces billeted in the area

1648 Scots try to help king; Cromwell defeats them Charles I beheaded   1648 Trade tokens issued in East Hagbourne

1649 Commonwealth begins
1652 Total eclipse of the sun recorded by Ashmole

                                               1656 Timothy Tyrrell left legacy for poor and for a sermon

1660 Restoration of the monarchy Charles II becomes king   1660/1661 Manors sold
                                               1662 William Tyrrell Charity

1665 Plague   1665/1666 Elias Ashmole visits St Andrew's Church and notes Clarice's effigy
1666 Fire of London

1675 Foundation stone of new St Paul's Cathedral laid   1675 Cresswell Charity
                                             1678 Sherwood family owns Watlingtons manor
1685 Judge Jeffreys becomes Lord Chancellor   1687 Martha Tyrrell's Bill of Complaint before Judge Jeffreys

1688 James II flees England   1688 Woodleys built

1689 William and Mary become king and queen
1694 Bank of England established
1702 Anne becomes queen
1710 St Paul's Cathedral completed   1710 Wood near Didcot Hospital sold
1714 George I becomes king
                                             1716 Thomas Hearne visits St Andrew's Church
                                             1718 Mary Smith Charity
                                             1719 Eleanor Keate Charity

1721	George II becomes king		
1727	Death of George I		
		1728	Moses Hawkins Charity
		1734	Mary Harwood Charity
		1738	John Harwood's will
		1748	Timothy Tyrrell left legacy for the education of children
1752	Gregorian Calendar adopted; 11 days dropped	1752	Wallingford–Faringdon Turnpike Road Trust
		1754	First known village map
1760	George III becomes king		
1761	Rocque map of Berkshire		
		1772	Eaton Charity
1775	American War of Independence begins		
1783	Britain recognises American Independence	1783	Population: 171 Houses: 36
1789	French Revolution		
1803	Poaching in England made a capital offence	1803	Hagbourne Hoard discovered on Hagbourne Hill
1807	Abolition of the slave trade		
1825	Stephenson constructs The Rocket steam locomotive	1825	The Turnpike Road Act Harwell–Streatley turnpike
1834	New Poor Law		
1836	Commutation of Tithes Act		
1837	Accession of Queen Victoria		
1841	First detailed census	1841	John Woodley baker
		1843	Tyrrell Charity land allocated on road to Chilton Inclosure Award
		1844	Didcot Station opens
1850	Corn Laws	1850	John Armstrong Charity
		1854	Hagbourne Friendly Society
		1861	Hagbourne Hoard presented to British Museum
1874	Disraeli becomes Prime Minister	1874	John and Martha Woodley sail for New Zealand. C of E School built in East Hagbourne for 190 children
		1876	Letter box in village
1882	Preliminary work on Channel Tunnel; Didcot–Newbury–Southampton Railway Line opened	1882	Upton Station opens

1890	Elementary education is made free	1890	Toll cottage sold to Morlands for £35
1893	Parish Councils established	1893	Socketed bronze axe found on Hagbourne Hill
1894	Queen Victoria's Diamond Jubilee	1894	Parish meeting established
1900	Labour Party established	1900	Sunday School in village begins; Village bakery closed
1901	Death of Victoria; Coronation of Edward VII		
1910	Coronation of George V		
1914	First World War begins		
1918	End of First World War		
1919	First transatlantic flight by Alcock & Brown	1919	Grove Manor Estate sold by auction; contents of Lime Tree Farm sold; first tractor in the village
1926	General Strike		
1928	Women given same voting rights as men	1928	Council houses built in York Road; Rubbish collection started
1930	Depression in farming	1930	Reservoir built on Hagbourne Hill; Iron Age brooch found
		1934	Street lighting considered; Permission given for new school in East Hagbourne
1935	George V & Queen Mary's Silver Jubilee		
1936	George V dies; Accession and Abdication of Edward VIII; George VI becomes king; Tithe Act	1936	Electricity comes to the village; one socket per household; Oak tree planted for Silver Jubilee; Post Office opened
1937	Marriage of Edward & Mrs Simpson		
		1938	Chestnut tree planted to replace dead oak tree; Air raid wardens appointed
1939	Second World War begins	1939	17 council houses built; No church bells to be rung for the duration of the War; Romano–British pottery found on Hagbourne Hill; Re-dedication of Lady Chapel in St Andrew's Church; York brasses moved back to the south aisle
1940	Food rationing		

1945	VE Day (May)		
		1946	8th June, Victory celebrations
1948	National Health Service		
1952	Death of George VI Accession of Elizabeth II		
1953	Everest climbed; Coronation of Queen Elizabeth II		
1954	End of food rationing	1954	Bus shelter dedicated as a War Memorial
		1959	Seat next to bus shelter purchased
1960	Farthing ceased to be legal tender	1960	Plaque for seat engraved in memory of Mr J Lay who served on the Parish Meeting for 32 years
		1962	East & West Hagbourne Society formed
1964	Census in Britain: Population: 51,295,000	1964	Parish Council established Didcot–Southampton railway line axed
1969	Neil Armstrong lands on the moon		
1971	Decimal currency		
1972	Miners' strike; 3-day week		
		1973	Lime Tree farmhouse pulled down; new houses built on land
1974	End of 3-day week County boundaries changed	1974	Village now part of Oxfordshire
1977	Elizabeth II Silver Jubilee	1977	Silver Jubilee celebrations
1981	Prince Charles marries Lady Diana Spencer	1981	Public Holiday, pig roast at York Farm
1982	Falklands War	1982	Winner, Britain in Bloom
		1983	Roman coin found
		1984	Winner, Britain in Bloom
		1985	Winner, Britain in Bloom
		1986	Winner, Britain in Bloom
		1987	Winner, Britain in Bloom
		1988	Winner, Britain in Bloom; village entered for National Competition
1989	Britain's warmest year since 1659, country hit by storms	1989	Madge Trophy presented to village
1990	Violent storms lash southern counties of Britain	1990	Village suffers storm damage
		1991	Village History Group established

1999	Total eclipse of the sun	1996	First Village Open Day; funds go to Village History Group
		1997	West Hagbourne Village Association established
		1998	Second Village Open Day
2000	Millennium Dome and London Eye opened	1999	Iron Age pottery sherds found on Hagbourne Hill
		2000	Joint East and West Hagbourne village celebrations Pageant in East Hagbourne Third Village Open Day 'Windsor Hakeborne – The Story of West Hagbourne' published by the Village History Group

Index

Aldworth, Alice, will of 1545, 51; bells, 117, 118
Aldworth, William, 70
Alfred, King, charter of 895AD, 3
Allen family, 164-167
Allen, Anthony, 118, *166*, *190*, 190-196
Allen, Charles William (C W), *158*, 159, 160
Allen, Ernest, son of C W, *160*, 164, 190-196
Allen, Nanny née Robinson, 164
Allen, Phoebe, m. Ernest, 164, 190-196, *193*
Allen, Richard, farmer, d. 1792, 164
Allen, William, York Farm 1821, 164
Allingham, Helen, artist c.1900, front cover
Allotment to the Poor, 103
Alwin, freeman, 20, 28
archaeological finds on Hagbourne Hill, recent, 15-17
Ardlui *see* York Farm Cottage
Ash Farm, 179
Ashmole, Elias, herald, 113, 114
Aunt Soph *see* Sophia Broad

bakery, W H, 139
Beavis, George, son of Moses, 220
Beavis, Moses, chapel, 120, 134, 135, 220
Beckingham, Mary, heiress, 26
bellringers, 233, *234*
Bilby, Gert, housekeeper, 175
Bill of Complaint, Martha Tyrrell 1687, 61
Blissetts, *131*
Blond, Bob, *189*
Bloody Assize, 47, 61
Bradenham manor, Windsor seat after 1541, 31
Britain in Bloom, 237
British Museum, Hagbourne Hoard, 8, 11
Broad, Sophia, *133*
Bronze Age finds, Hagbourne Hill, 12
bronze axe, drawing, 10
bronze foundry, Dorset, 13
bronze spearheads, drawings, 10
Broomsticks, *133*

Bullock, Edwin George, aka Father Antony, 120, 219-223
Bullock, George, father of Edwin, 220
bus shelter, *196*; drawing, 197
Butler, Arthur (Sonny), 211
Butler, Frederick (Fred), m. Hilda, 214, 215, *213*
Butler, Frederick, 118, 189, 196
Butler, Hilda, 210-213, *213*

Cauldwell, Eli, 169
Cauldwell, Leopold, 169
Census, W H, 124-140
Chapel Hayes, 182-184, *183*
chapel of ease, 110-111
chapels, of W H, 71, 120, 134, 220
Charles I, 47
Chelrey, Edmund de, 26
Chitty, Dr, 182
Chitty, Lily F, 10, 11
Christopher Elderfield's Charity, 94
Cirencester Abbey, Augustinian, 109; tithes of W H, 111
Civil War, battles near W H, 43, 47, 50
cob walls, 1, 132
coins, Roman, 15
conservation map, *240*
Cooper, Dr George, 163, 164
Court Rolls, 60
Cow Down, 130, 144
Cow Lane, 74, 130
Craven Estate map 1775, *80*
Craven, Lord, East Hagbourne 1760, 60; W H tithing rights, 60, 81
Creswell's Charity, 91
cross, medieval, W H, 40-43
cultivation, 147, 148

Dawson, Bert, 137
Dawson, Jack, *148*, 210, 211
Dawson, Ken, 236

Dearlove family, 179-182
Dearlove, Bert, 203, *205*
Dearlove, Ezra, Lime Tree Farm, *180*, 181
Dearlove, Jack, 181, *182*
Dearlove, Percy, *189*
Denning, Leslie, 118, 189, 196
Dillon, Viscountess Margaret, 114
Domesday Book, W H entry, 19, 20
Down Farm, 154-160, *158*
Down House *see* Wheatsheaf Inn
Downs, The, 71
Drawings: bell-cote, *121*; bronze axe, *10*; bronze spearheads, *10*; bus shelter, *197*; coats of arms, *28*, *35*, *38*; Hagbourne Hoard, *9*; Hakka, *xiv*; Jack Dawson, *211*; medieval cross (remains) *41*; milestone, *86*; shepherd's hut, *177*; village pond, *24*
Drokensford, Clarice *see* Windsor
Drokensford, coat of arms, 35, *115*, *117*
Drokensford, John de, father of Clarice, 36
Drokensford, John, Bishop of Bath and Wells, 35
Drokensford, Margaret *see* Tany, Margaret de

East Hagbourne, fire, 2
Eaton's Charity, 93
Edward III, 39
Eleanor Keate's Charity, 92
Elizabeth I, 31, 47
emigration to New Zealand, 140-142
Enard Cottage, *135*; chapel, 220
Enclosure Award *see* Inclosure Award

family trees *see* Napper, Tyrrell
farming *see also* cultivation, fruit growing, harvesting, haymaking, ploughing, threshing
farming, beyond Middle Ages, 144, 145; farming year, 146-154; Medieval times, 143; strip, 143, 144; twentieth century, 145, 146
farms *see* Ash; Chapel Hayes; Down; Grove Manor; Ivy; Lime Tree; Manor; Ragged; York
Father Antony *see* Edwin George Bullock
Fluddier, Henry, will of, 52; inventory of, 53, 54, 59; house of, 55
fruit growing, 152-154

Green Thatch, *131*
Grove Manor Estate, sale notice, 173
Grove Manor Farm *see also* Watlingtons manor
Grove Manor Farm, 172-176, *174*; sale notice 1919, *173*
gypsies, 233, *235*

Hacca *see* Hakka
Hagbourne Benefit Society, 95, 96
Hagbourne charities, 89-96
Hagbourne Feast, 227
Hagbourne Hill, 6-17, *16*
Hagbourne Hoard, 6-12; drawing, *9*
Hagbourne School, 223-226
Hakebourne, Abbot John, of Cirencester Abbey 1508, 111
Hakebourne, John, priest, 111
Hakka, 3; drawing, *xiv*
harvesting, 151, 152
Harwood, John, will of, 56, 57; inventory of, 57, 58; house of, 59
Harwood's Charity, 93
Hawkins's Charity, 92
haymaking, 150, 151
Hayward, William Stephens, Down Farm, 157
Hearne, Thomas, 1678-1735, 113
Henry VIII, 31
Home Guard, 187, 188
Horse & Harrow Inn, *139*, 198-202, *200*, *206*
Houses *see* Blissetts; Broomsticks; Enard Cottage; Moggs; Rose Cottage; Thatch Cottage; The Square; Woodleys

Inclosure Award maps (redrawn), *72*, *73*
Inclosure Award, W H, 67-74
inventories *see* Henry Fluddier, John Harwood
Iron Age finds, Hagbourne Hill, 13
Ivy Farm, *128*, *149*, 182
Ivy Farm Cottage, sale notice 1919, *216*

Jeffreys, Judge, of Bloody Assize, 47; Lord High Chancellor, 61; judge in case of Tyrrell versus Sherwood, 61
John Armstrong's Charity, 94
King, Ebenezer, FSA 1808, 6
King, Jesse, find of skeleton, 8

lambing, York Farm, 165, *166*
Lay, John, Manor Farm, 168, 169
Leget, Helmingus, attorney, 33
letter box, 219
Lime Tree Farm, 179, *180*, 182
Lousley, Jim, *207*
Lousley, Job, farmer, 119, 169
Lousley, Joseph, father of Job, 169

Madge Trophy, 237
malt house, 133
Manor Farm *see also* Windsor manor

256

Manor Farm, 167-172, *171*; fêtes at, 230; pigs at, *170*
manorial courts, Watlingtons and Windsor manors, 60, 62, 63
manors *see* Watlingtons, Windsor
Maps: ancient routes, *4*; Berkshire, *xi*; conservation map, *240*; Craven Estate map, *80*; farms, *155*; field names 2000, *85*; Inclosure Award map 1843, *front endpaper*, *72*; old inclosures 1843, *73*; orchards 1876, *153*; Rocque map, *68*, *156*; route of the enumerator, *126*; site of Hagbourne Hoard, *7*; village map 1990, *back endpaper*; W H 1754 (redrawn), *82*
Mary Smith's Charity, 92
Mason, Colin, *146*
May song, 229
Mayne, Miranda, 233, 234
maypole dancing, *228*
milestone, *86*
Moggs, *132*
Moor Lane, 71, 79, 134
Morland brewery, 199, 201
Morland, Thomas, 201
Morland, William, 199, 201

Napper family tree, *204*
Napper, Annie, 203, *205*
Napper, Archibald (Arch), Horse & Harrow 1930-58, 76, 201, 203, 205-208, *205*, *207*
Napper, Dennis, brother of Rex, 175, 176
Napper, Dennis, father of Dennis and Rex, 168, 172, *218*
Napper, Dennis, Grove Manor Farm 1919, 26, 169, 172
Napper, Eliza (Tize), m. John Lay, *168*, 169
Napper, Ernest, son of Joseph, *207*, *218*
Napper, Frank, Ivy Farm, 203, *207*
Napper, George, Horse & Harrow 1841, 76, 202; Tyrrell Charity land, 103
Napper, Joseph, publican Horse & Harrow 1881-1930, *200*, *207*
Napper, Rex, 172, 175, *176*
Napper, Rosa, d. 1896, *203*
Napper, William, Horse & Harrow 1861-1881, 76
nature walk, *239*
Newton, Ann, 26
Norris Lane *see* Moor Lane
Nut Tree Orchard, 133

Oath of Protestation, 48-50

Oliver Cromwell, 47
orchards, 152-154
Other, Walter fitz *see* Walter de Windsor

parish church of St Andrew's *see* St Andrew's Church
Parry, Philip, 61
Perrers, Alice, mistress of Edward III, 39
Pevsner, Nikolaus, 114
Pinnell, Bill, dairy farmer, 182, 217
Pinnell, Mark, Lime Tree Farm, 182
place names, 78-86
ploughing, 146, 147
Pocock, John Blagrave, 169
post office, W H, 217-219
Powell family, 176, 177
Powell, Alice, *129*; Ragged Farm, 177
Powell, Kerzia, 215
Powell, Sarah, 133, *212*
Powell, William (Wipsi), *129*, *179*; farmer, 152, 177, 179
Powell, William Charles, wedding 1904, *178*
Protestation Return, 48-50
public houses *see* Horse & Harrow Inn, Wheatsheaf Inn

Ragged Farm, 176, 177
railway, 77, 78, 172, 175
Randell, Lillian, shop, *217*, 215-217; sub post mistress, 217-219
Reynolds's Charity, 91
Rocque map 1761, 68, 156
Romano-British cemetery, Hagbourne Hill, 12
Romano-British finds, coins 14; pottery, 14
Rose Cottage, 203
Ryan, Kerry, 118, 189, 190, 196

school path, 226-227
Scoolt, John, curate 1783, 118, 119
Scotlands Ash, 23, 202
Shaw, Jimmy, 208-210, *209*
Sheard, Polly, 230-233, *232*
Sheep Down, 144
Shepherd, Francis, enumerator, 127-140
shepherd's crook, 118
shepherd's hut, 177
Sherwood, Edward, case of Tyrrell versus Sherwood, 61-65
Sherwood, Mary, 26
shooting parties, *206*, *207*
shop, W H, 215-217, *217*; Ivy Farm Cottage, 215
Silver Jubilee, 236

skeleton, Hagbourne Hill, 8
Square, The, 136, *138*
St Andrew's Church, bell-cote, 121; font, *115*; south aisle and chapel, 111-116; window, south chapel, *116*; window, west, *116*
St Francis d'Assisi Cottage *see* Thatch Cottage
stocks, the Square, 136
stone pit, Hagbourne Hill, 63
Stotland, Thomas, 79

Tany, Margaret de, mother of Clarice, 36
Thatch Cottage, *134*, 220; sale notice, 221
Thompson, Stephen, 61
threshing, 148-150
Tin Hotel, 208-210, *209*
Tirrold *see* Tyrrell
tithes, of Lord Craven, 60
toll gate, 75, 76, 201, 203
toll house, 201
toll road *see* turnpike roads
turnpike roads, 76, 77, 199
Tyrrell Charity *see* William Tyrrell Charity
Tyrrell Family History Society, logo of, 100
Tyrrell family tree 1545-1748, 98
Tyrrell family, 96-100; coat of arms, 106
Tyrrell, Brook, son of Martha, 61-65
Tyrrell, Martha, widow, Tyrrell versus Sherwood, 61-65
Tyrrell, Robert, d. 1716, tombstone of, 99
Tyrrell, Timothy, d. 1656, will of, 97
Tyrrell, Timothy, d. 1748, will of, 99
Tyrrell, William, founder William Tyrrell Charity, will, 101
Tyrrell, William, son of Martha, 61-65
Tyrrell, William, Watlingtons manor, 61-65
Tyrrell, Avery, d. 1584, 97
Tyrrold *see* Tyrrell

Walker, Dr J W, East Hagbourne fire, 2
Walmsley Isobell, 234, 236
war memorial *see* bus shelter
Warr, Hilda, *212*
Watlingtons manor, descent of, 25; history of, 24-28; manorial courts, 61-65
Watts, Rosa *see* Rosa Napper
West Hagbourne Farm *see* Manor Farm
Wet and Dry Moors, 144, 79
Wheatsheaf Inn, 71, 75
Whitchurch, James, 61
William Keate's Charity, 91

William Tyrrell Charity, 100-107
William Tyrrell Trust *see* William Tyrrell Charity
wills *see* Alice Aldworth; John Harwood; Henry Fluddier; Timothy Tyrrell, d. 1656; Timothy Tyrrell, d. 1748
Windsor dynasty, 28-32
Windsor manor, history of, 21-24; descent of 1086-1279, *30*; descent of 1326-1403, *34*
Windsor, Clarice de: brass, *112*, 113; dowry, 22-24, 33, 79; lady of the manor, 32-40; pedigree, 37
Windsor, coat of arms, 28, *115*
Windsor, Miles de, heir, 39
Windsor, Richard de, m. Clarice, 32
Windsor, Richard de, sold Windsor manor, 26, 62-65
Windsor, Sir Andrew de, Baron, 31
Windsor, Thomas, m. Mary Beckingham, 26
Windsor, Walter de, founder Windsor dynasty, 28-32; constable Windsor Castle, 28
Windsor, William de, m. Alice Perrers, 39
Windsor, William de, m. Margaret de Drokensford, 35
Wipsi *see* William Powell
Wirral, Micky, 207
Woodley, Alice, wedding, 178
Woodley, Jane, publican, 198
Woodley, John, baker, 139, 215
Woodley, Nelly, *224*
Woodleys, house, 133, *138*, 139
workhouse, 90
World War One, veterans, 208; Fred Butler, 214; teachers, 224
World War Two, 186-197; W H men killed in, 189-196
Wycherts *see* Moggs
Wyndesor *see* Windsor

York Farm Cottage, *137*
York Farm, oldest house, *129*, 161, *163*; history of, 161-164; lambing at, 165, 166; sale notice 1919, *162*
York Place *see* York Farm
York, Clarice *see* Windsor, Clarice de
York, coat of arms, 38, *115*, *117*
York, Joan, m. John, brass, *112*
York, John of Twickenham, 38
York, John, m. Clarice, 38-40; brass, *112*
York, John, son of Clarice, brass, *112*

Wycherts
JOHN HILLMAN

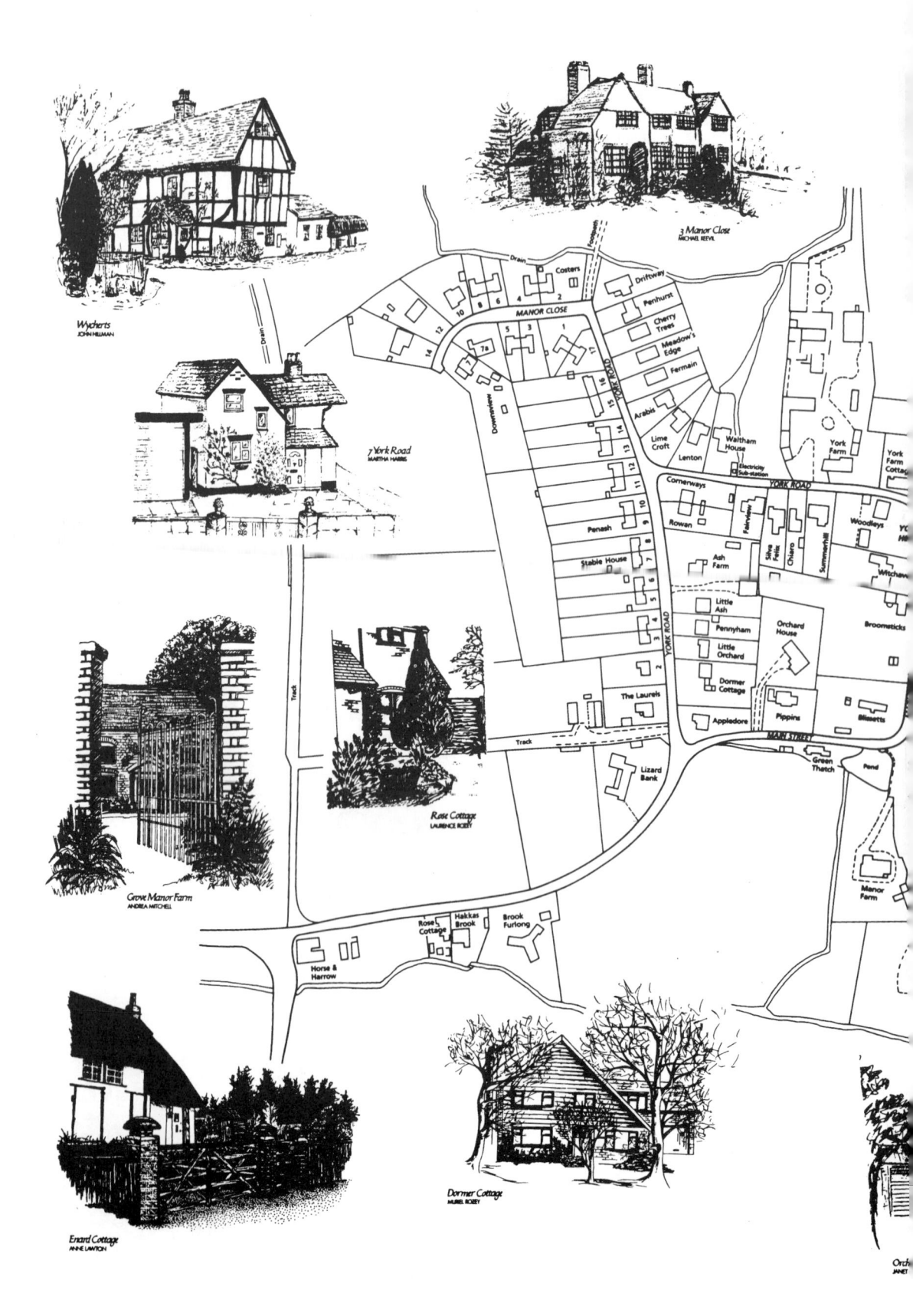

3 Manor Close
MICHAEL REEVIL

7 York Road
MARTHA HARRIS

Grove Manor Farm
ANDREA MITCHELL

Rose Cottage
LAURENCE ROSEY

Encard Cottage
ANNE LAWTON

Dormer Cottage
MURIEL ROSEY

Orch...
JANET